D1180095

New Studies in Berkeley's Philosophy

THE CONTRIBUTORS

HARRY M. BRACKEN
Professor of Philosophy, Arizona State University, Tempe, Arizona

D. M. DATTA
Professor of Philosophy, retired, Patna University, India

WAHEED ALI FAROOQI
Professor of Philosophy, University of Sind, Hyderabad, W. Pakistan

AUGUSTO GUZZO
Professor of Philosophy, University of Turin, Italy

T. E. JESSOP
Ferens Professor of Philosophy in the University College of Hull, England

ANDRÉ-LOUIS LEROY
Ancien chargé de cours à la Faculté des Lettres de Paris, France

A. A. LUCE
Berkeley Professor of Metaphysics in the University of Dublin, Ireland

F. W. MCCONNELL
Professor of Philosophy, Moravian College, Bethlehem, Pennsylvania

IAN T. RAMSEY
Nolloth Professor of the Philosophy of the Christian Religion, Oxford University, England

WARREN E. STEINKRAUS
Professor of Philosophy, State University College, Oswego, New York

I. C. TIPTON
Lecturer in Philosophy, The University, Keele, Staffordshire, England

COLIN M. TURBAYNE
Professor of Philosophy, University of Rochester, New York

W. H. WERKMEISTER
Director of the School of Philosophy, University of Southern California, Los Angeles, California

New Studies in Berkeley's Philosophy

Edited by

WARREN E. STEINKRAUS
State University College
Oswego, New York

HOLT, RINEHART AND WINSTON, INC.
New York • Chicago • San Francisco • Toronto • London

Thomas Nelson & Sons, Ltd., of London, England, is to be thanked for kindly granting permission to reprint so liberally from The Works of George Berkeley, *which they have published in nine volumes.*

The Open Court Publishing Co., of LaSalle, Illinois, is to be thanked for kindly granting permission to reprint D. M. Datta's article "The Objective Idealism of Berkeley" (from Vol. 43 of The Monist*), which comprises the first four sections of his chapter in this volume.*

The portrait on the cover is by A. R. Hinson.

Library of Congress Catalog Card Number: 66–13081

28135-0116

Printed in the United States of America

Foreword

Brand Blanshard

Why another book on Berkeley?

For one thing, because he is so curiously modern. He was one of the pioneers of the empiricism and nominalism so popular today. He discussed with great clearness many of the issues with which present-day philosophers are concerned—the status of sense-data, the nature of causation, the relation of primary to secondary qualities, the problem of universals, the importance of language, the existence of other selves, and how we communicate with them. Some empiricists of our time have been worried about the implications of their position for religious belief; for example, can an empiricist meaningfully talk of God? More than one of the essays that follow show that Berkeley was clearly aware of these difficulties and wrestled with them ably. He was interested in mathematics and its application to concrete things; he discussed the correspondence and causal theories of perception; he dealt shrewdly and suggestively with the problems raised by our strange power to abstract and generalize. Compared with many thinkers who are nearer to us in time, he seems singularly contemporary.

Secondly, it is only in the last decade that we have had Berkeley's full work before us. All students of philosophy knew the *Principles;* many knew the *Dialogues;* but this is about as far as anyone's knowledge extended, except that of the specialist. There has been no separate editor of *Alciphron* since 1803, of *The Analyst* since 1754, of *Siris* since 1747. It is true that these writings were included in the valuable four-volume edition of A. C. Fraser that appeared at the beginning of this century, but if I am not mistaken, it has long been out of print. The full range of Berkeley's writing, competently edited, has been available only since 1957, when the row of nine magisterial volumes edited by Professors Luce and Jessop was completed. It is pleasant to note that both these editors, to whom Berkeley students owe so much, are among the contributors to this volume.

A third reason for returning to Berkeley lies in the character of his philosophizing. If he is in line with present-day thought in the issues he discussed and the acuteness with which he discussed them, he is in other respects at odds with it, and could well serve as a corrective of it. One wonders what Berkeley would say if he could emerge again from Ireland or heaven and repeat his celebrated visits to England and America. Set him down in a corner with *Mind* or the *Philosophical Review,* or let him for an hour or two turn the pages of the latest treatise on existentialism, and how would he respond? I suspect that he would feel so depressed that he would call for a glass of tar-water to revive his spirits. He had no objection to "minute philosophy," if that meant the handling of technical questions with patience, exactitude, and clarity. He did object to it strongly if it meant devotion to such questions without regard to their importance, without asking whether their solution would in any way help us forward in understanding the world, or our place and business in it. "His thought," as Professor Steinkraus remarks, "raises the kind of perennial problems that are the life-blood of philosophy." Subtlety exercised for the sake of the exercise, the grinding of knives with which to cut nothing, the harnessing of a first-class intellectual engine to the breaking of a grain of sand, would have seemed to him a distressing waste. Berkeley's brain was itself such an engine, but it was operated by a rare and sane human being. For him a philosopher was a person who, if he dealt with minor problems, did so because they bore on major problems. He never lost the wood among the trees, and he had a sure sense of the paths that would bring him out on clearings or hilltops. "Philosophy," said Michelet, "is the art of losing oneself methodically." It was not so for Berkeley. His thought was governed at every step by a compass pointing to a humanly important goal.

There is another and fourth reason why students of our day may return to Berkeley with profit. He knew how to write. He stands as a permanent gentle rebuke to those—and they are many—who think that the appropriate language of philosophy consists of squadrons of Latin abstractions marching with the leaden tread of dehumanized pedantry. Berkeley avoided such language by an instinct blended of art, tact, and good sense. If expert testimony is needed, here is George Saintsbury on Berkeley:

> It may seem to some, after reading philosophers of all ages, from Plato to Schopenhauer, and from Erigena to Descartes, that there are only three styles perfectly suited to philosophy, that they are those of Plato himself, of Malebranche, and of Berkeley. In all philosophical writing there is a certain antinomy. By so much as it is popular, figurative, literary, imaginative, it seems to lack philosophical precision; by so much as it is technical, austere, unliterary, and what has been called "jargonish," it loses humanity and general appeal. If the golden mean was ever hit between these extremes, it seems to have been hit in the style of Berkeley. (Sir Henry Craik, *English Prose Selections,* Vol. IV, 27)

It is part of the price of clarity that its practitioner is more easily found out. Though the writers of the present volume are for the most part sympathetic to Berkeley, they have no difficulty in showing that on some issues he came down firmly on both sides of the fence, so that no such thing as *the* Berkeleian doctrine about them is to be found. Unhappily among these issues were some of great importance.

One of them was the nature of the self. It is a standard criticism of Berkeley that having shown that material substance was a fiction to which nothing corresponded, he went on to argue that there really were spiritual substances, for example the soul of George Berkeley, though the latter kind of substance was just as objectionable to a thorough empiricist as the former. Now there is no doubt that he did subscribe to the spiritual-substance theory; he says in so many words that the soul is "an active, simple, uncompounded substance." At the same time, under obvious pressure from his empiricist prepossessions, he denied this, declaring that the mind is "a congeries of perceptions," that it *consists of* its experiences, that "will and understanding constitute in the strictest sense a mind or spirit."

He held similarly conflicting views about "notional knowledge." In the first edition of the *Principles* he did not recognize such knowledge at all; it made its embarrassed appearance only in the second edition. The appearance is embarrassed because in the meantime Berkeley had come to see that with his earlier simple empiricism he had no right even to speak of God, of whose existence the whole treatise was supposed to be a proof. But clearly the term was not meaningless; we plainly have thoughts that do not derive from the senses; we must have "notional" knowledge. But what precisely do notions disclose to us? Here again Berkeley wavered. Sometimes, as we have seen, he declared that they revealed to us spiritual substances. But in the present book it is forcibly argued by Professor Ramsey and Mr. Tipton that this was not his dominant view, that the true object of notional knowledge was our own *activities* of mind, our processes of judging, willing, and feeling. Berkeley was clearly right that empiricism requires such an amendment. One may perhaps add that the most important question faced by the empiricism of our time is not whether such knowledge is to be admitted, but once admitted, how far it is to go.

The essays that follow bring to light many more evidences that Berkeley hesitated, vacillated, and fell at times into downright error. Nothing about the master is sacrosanct to these writers. But there is no mistaking their underlying consensus about him. He was a remarkably lucid, courageous, and original mind, whom the passage of more than two centuries has done surprisingly little to antiquate. The editor, in his own essay, maintains that the chief arguments by which modern critics have disposed of Berkeley were either anticipated and answered by him, or fail to survive present scrutiny. Contributors from India and Islam find unexpected parallels to his thinking in the philosophy of the Near and Far East. That he was a philosopher of historic importance we knew. Probably no reader of these essays will question that he is also worth hearing on the methods and issues that divide philosophers today.

Preface

Philosophy since the time of Berkeley has taken many different turns and undergone fluctuations in emphasis, but interest in Berkeley's thought persists and it is widespread—indeed, international, as this volume illustrates. No contemporary philosopher in any land can afford to bypass him, and many feel compelled to refute him or offer contrasting alternatives if they do not accept certain fundamentals of his view.

The reasons for his continued significance are indicated by the issues considered in the essays in this volume. These are all new studies, written (with the exception of a portion of Chapter IX) expressly for this volume, but they are not novelties. Nor do they cater to any so-called contemporaneous "needs." Rather, they point to what contemporary philosophy needs—rigorous but sympathetic appraisal and treatment of key themes of historical thinkers, grounded in a diligent study of primary sources. This book has many quotations from Berkeley. And it may well raise more problems than it solves.

Chief among the minor vices of learning, said Bacon, are the two extremes "admiration of antiquity and love of novelty." The contributors to this volume are united by a common conviction that the major thrusts of Berkeley's philosophy are in some sense eminently worthwhile, and some regard them as eminently sound. But there is no uncritical devotion to the eighteenth century any more than there is undue acquiescence in the concerns of the twentieth. The guiding principle of the writers was that they deal with pivotal problems in Berkeley's thought. Accordingly, the essays are concerned with logical, linguistic, epistemological, metaphysical, and philosophico-theological problems, because these are the issues that concerned Berkeley. There are other fine essays elsewhere dealing with his ethical, economic, political, medical, and religious doctrines. (See Bibliography.)

These collected essays have no inner logic binding them together, but the topics move from methodological and general exploratory treatments (Chapters I–IV) to specific notable problems (V–VIII) and then to questions of comparison, criticism, and interpretation (IX–XIII). The select bibliography should prove helpful for beginning students, and more mature scholars should find the indexes valuable.

All of the essayists have written on Berkeley before; some are bona fide Berkeleians; several will be immediately recognized as internationally distinguished Berkeley scholars. And all have cooperated in this joint effort in a spirit reminiscent of Berkeley himself, with suggestions, advice, and beneficial criticism. Writers from seven different nations are represented here (France, Great Britain, India, Ireland, Italy, Pakistan, and the United States), but in the course of preparation, expressions of interest and suggestions have come from philosophers interested in Berkeley from four other lands, Argentina, Japan, Taiwan, and Yugoslavia.

Special acknowledgment is due Professor T. E. Jessop of the University of Hull, England, for his assistance in planning as well as executing the volume. Not only did he make valuable suggestions, but he made the approved translation of the article by his friend Professor Guzzo and provided the select bibliography at the end of the volume, which is based on his own exhaustive research. I must also single out Professors Brand Blanshard, B. A. Dar, D. M. Datta, C. J. Ducasse, A. A. Luce, and I. T. Ramsey for their helpful recommendations. Certain of the contributors themselves have indicated their indebtedness to other scholars on their title pages.

I wish to thank also my colleague, Professor A. S. Cua, for his helpful suggestions, and the administration of the State University College of New York at Oswego for granting me a reduced teaching load while the book was in its final stages.

W.E.S.

Oswego, New York
December 1965

Note on Abbreviations

All the contributors have used the nine volume definitive edition of *The Works of George Berkeley,* edited by Professors Luce and Jessop and published by Thomas Nelson and Sons (1948–1957). Numerical indications refer variously to section, page, and entry numbers.

Those works referred to by section numbers are; *The Principles of Human Knowledge* (abbreviated PHK); *Essay Towards a New Theory of Vision* (NTV); *The Theory of Vision or Visual Language . . . Vindicated and Explained* (TVV); *Siris* (SIR); *First Draft of the Introduction to the Principles* (Draft); *DeMotu; The Analyst.*

The *Three Dialogues Between Hylas and Philonous* (abbreviated DHP) will be referred to by page numbers in Volume II of the *Works* and *Alciphron* (ALC), though divided into seven dialogues (I–VII) which are individually sectioned, will more conveniently be referred to by page numbers in Volume III of the *Works.*

References to the *Philosophical Commentaries* (PC), (called *The Commonplace Book* by A. C. Fraser) will employ the entry numbers established by Professor Luce. Berkeley's spelling, punctuation, and emphasis will be adhered to in all quotations.

Contents

New Studies in Berkeley's Philosophy

I

Berkeley's New Principle Completed

A. A. LUCE

The Discovery

Berkeley's New Principle, *esse* is *percipi,* to be is to be perceived, states the meaning of the term *exist* (as he saw it), when it is applied to sensible things. There are other things that are said to exist, and in regard to them the New Principle in its first formulation is incomplete. Berkeley completed the formula of the Principle (as he usually called it), or sketched its completion, in the two notebooks known as the *Philosophical Commentaries.* In these notebooks Berkeley in the years 1707–1708 did the bulk of the spadework for the *Principles,* drastically revising his earlier immaterialism and laying down the main lines of his published philosophy. This article, therefore, deals, however inadequately, with the heart of that philosophy in its climacteric period. I propose to offer here a study of the completing process, taken from the notebooks and confirmed, where possible, from the published *Principles,* and then to discuss the bearing of the Principle, so completed, on Berkeleian exegesis.[1]

The *new* Principle must be seen against the background of the *old.* Berkeley's old principle was the subjectivity of the sensible qualities, some or all. He tried it out for two years or so (c. 1704–1706) in his "first arguings."

[1] The entry numbers are those assigned in my (1944) edition of the *Commentaries,* repeated in Vol. I of the *Works* (Luce and Jessop).

Matter was to be pared or flaked away piecemeal to nothing. The constituent qualities of body—color, taste, smell, and so on—were to be shredded off one by one, and brought one by one into the mind till nothing remained outside the mind.

The old principle had only a limited success; it brought Berkeley a certain distance towards immaterialism, but it failed him at the pinch; it failed to provide a sure foundation for his "immaterial hypothesis." Berkeley refers to it in his published work, as well as in his notebooks. In §§ 14 and 15 of the *Principles* he speaks of modern philosophers (Malebranche and Locke) who "prove certain sensible qualities to have no existence in matter, or without the mind"; then, following Simon Foucher and Pierre Bayle, he proceeds to argue that, "the same thing may likewise be proved of all other sensible qualities whatsoever." He develops this line of argument, and illustrates it, and then puts the two principles, the old and the new, in sharp contrast in the following words:

> Though it must be confessed this method of arguing doth not so much prove that there is no extension or colour in an outward object, as that we do not know by sense which is the true extension or colour of the object. But the arguments foregoing [those turning on the *esse* is *percipi,* see especially §§ 3–6] plainly shew it to be impossible that any colour or extension at all, or other sensible quality whatsoever, should exist in an unthinking subject without the mind . . .

To get well inside this contrast and appreciate the major "breakthrough" represented by those words, we must turn to the earlier notebook, in which Berkeley wrote "ffrom Malbranch, Locke & my first arguings it cant be prov'd that extension is not in matter." (PC # 265) That looks like a sad confession for the young immaterialist to make; but it is not so sad as it looks. If it stood alone, it would spell a *nil* result to three years' research; but take it in its context, and we see that that sad-looking entry marks the end of his "first arguings" and a fresh start on a new scent. Turn a couple of leaves, and there is the New Principle, shining like a light at the far end of the long tunnel. "I wonder how men cannot see a truth so obvious, as that extension cannot exist without a thinking substance." (PC # 270) Even in these unemotional notebooks emotion will not be repressed. "I wonder not at my sagacity in discovering the obvious tho' amazing truth, I rather wonder at my stupid inadvertency in not finding it out before." (PC # 279) Like stout Cortez gazing at the Pacific, Berkeley is gazing in wonder, not now at color and spread or other particular quality of sense, but at the ocean of existence itself, where *esse,* he thinks, is *percipi.* The Principle is discovered.

Berkeley's "discovery" (the term is his) took place in the autumn of 1707, when he was two thirds of the way through the earlier notebook. It was a heartening and decisive discovery for him; it was heartening because it saved his "immaterial hypothesis" and salvaged much of his preliminary work on it (such as his *Theory of Vision*). It was decisive because it gave a new direction to his thought, heading him away from the panpsychist theosophy on which his "first arguings" depended and heading him towards the common-sense view, as he claimed, of the external world, set forth in his published *Principles*. Soon after the discovery a new capital letter "E" appeared in the margin of the second notebook. It stands for Existence, and the nature of existence, together with the meaning of the word, became for Berkeley the focus of attention.

The attack on abstract general ideas, which opens in entry # 318 (PC) was a collateral development, if not a direct consequence, of Berkeley's study of extension and existence. When he launched the attack in his *Essay on Vision,* he wrote:

> When men speak of extension as being an idea common to two senses, it is with a secret supposition that we can single out extension from all other tangible and visible qualities, and form thereof an abstract idea, which idea they will have common both to sight and touch. (NTV § 122)

There followed, also, a new approach to the problem of body (see especially entries # 282 and 293 in PC), and eventually (# 802) Berkeley found his way to a common-sense belief in the real existence of sensible things even when not actually perceived, "but still with relation to perception." I must mention also the great care bestowed on the Principle itself. Berkeley was determined to set it above criticism, if he could. If it was sound, it should be demonstrable, he thought; and he worked out the long and complex "demonstration" for it (# 378) which in fact he never used. Then having satisfied himself (## 379–380) that there are "other arguments innumerable . . . whereby to demonstrate the Principle . . . and not one argument . . . against it" with which he opened his second notebook, and gradually built up in it his revised system of immaterialism under the controlling influence of his new conception of "the meaning and definition of the word Existence."[2] (# 408)

The Completing

Such was the background. The actual completing of the Principle was carried out in two parts or stages, which no doubt interpenetrated, and which are both represented in the following entry (# 429, with the *addendum,* # 429a, on the facing page): "Existence is percipi or percipere (or velle, i.e. agere). The horse is in the stable, the Books are in the study as before." The first half of the entry speaks for itself and needs little comment. *Esse est percipi* expands naturally into *esse est percipi aut percipere*. To be is either to be perceived or to perceive. As soon as the rapture of discovery was over, and with it the relief and joy at finding a conclusive disproof of the existence

[2] For further details of the doctrinal development, here sketched, see my *The Dialectic of Immaterialism* (London: 1963).

of imperceptible matter, Berkeley began to consider the positive implications of the Principle. The first of these is the existence of the subject. There can be no object perceived without a subject perceiving. Implied in *percipi* is *percipere.* Both belong to the perceptual situation and are conditioned by it, and if the existence of the object is determined in relation to perception, so also must be the existence of the subject. If the *esse* of the object is *percipi,* the *esse* of the subject must be *percipere;* for the *esse* of both is determined by the perceptual situation in which both exist. I see the car; the car exists; its *esse* is *percipi.* I see the car; I exist; my *esse* is *percipere.*

Berkeley is not arguing that perceiving makes it so; he is discussing the meaning of the term *exist.* In the case of the subject, he says, existence is activity: I see the car; I exist. *Exist* means *am perceiving.* In the case of the object existence is passivity: I see the car; the car exists. *Exists* means *is perceived.* In both cases *exist* is said from within the perceptual situation, and has no meaning outside that situation, if Berkeley is right.

Prima facie he has a good case. In ordinary conversation it would sound rather silly to say, "I see the car, and it exists." "I see the car" is a sufficient statement, and the addition "and it exists" is a redundancy, which adds nothing and may mislead folk into thinking the car could be seen and *not* exist. The same holds of the subject. In ordinary life we would never dream of saying, "I see the car, and I exist." "I see the car" is a sufficient statement, and the addition "and I exist" is a redundancy, which adds nothing and may mislead folk into thinking that I could see and *not* exist. One can think up out-of-the-way cases in which the addition "and it exists" or "and I exist" has a semblance of meaning, but in all such cases it will be found, I think, that the existence asserted lies within the range of potential perception.

Berkeley's two alternatives to *percipere*—*velle* and *agere*—extend the notion and the area of activity, but they add nothing new in principle. Berkeley added them on the facing page opposite the original entry, presumably some weeks later. They represent, I imagine, a slight shift in emphasis on a different matter. As Berkeley developed his notion of distinct mind to match his revised conception of real sensible body, he concentrated more and more on the active aspect of the mind; the will became the primary element, and the passive understanding dropped to second place. My guess is that the addition of *velle* and *agere* reflects this shift of accent. The words bring out the latent content of *percipere,* but introduce little or nothing that is esentially new. They are applications of the *esse est percipere* rather than extensions of it. In actual life *percipere* is ever on tiptoe, ready to pass on into will and action. I see the car, and I want to buy and drive it, and I do so, or I refrain from doing so.

During the second stage Berkeley came to recognize possible perceiving and possible percepts as parts of the perceptual situation. He in effect extended the Principle to cover the *posse percipere* and the *posse percipi,* accepting the reality of dispositions to perceive and of objects we might perceive but are not perceiving. The development was part of his drastic revision of his earlier view of body, and is reflected in the following considered statement, which concludes the four sections of the *Principles* (§§ 45–48) in which the point is discussed,

> It does not therefore follow from the foregoing principles, that bodies are annihilated and created every moment, or exist not at all during the intervals between our perception of them.

I come now to the second half of the entry (PC # 429), quoted above, "The horse is in the stable, the Books are in the study as before." It is a cryptic remark, which at first sight has nothing to say to the words that precede. But there is an organic connection. The whole entry concerns Existence; it is the fourth of the twenty-nine entries in the second notebook with the marginal sign "E" for Existence. In the first half of the entry Berkeley is reflecting on active existence, the existence of active beings; in the second half he reflects on possible existence, the existence of things we are not actually perceiving, but might perceive if we took the appropriate steps. Just above, in the first of the entries labeled E, Berkeley wrote:

> I must be very particular in explaining wt is meant by things existing in Houses, chambers, fields, caves etc wn not perceiv'd as well as wn perceiv'd. & shew how the Vulgar notion agrees with mine when we narrowly inspect into the meaning & definition of the word Existence . . . (PC # 408)

In his remark about the horse in the stable and the books in the study, he is doing what he had just said he would do; he is trying to explain what is meant by things existing when they are not perceived. He is trying to show that the vulgar notion about them agrees with his—interpreted from the standpoint of the New Principle. And whatever we may think of the vulgar notion, no one will say that it includes the *nonexistence* of the unperceived perceivable.

The problem of *body,* of which the problem of the unperceived perceivable is a part, occupied Berkeley's attention from the beginning of his first notebook almost to the end of the second, and he may not have reached his full and final solution (represented by the entries ## 800, 801, and 802) when he made the entry about the horse in the stable and the books in the study; but he was certainly well on the way to it; for these are his working instances of the unperceived perceivable. "You ask me whether the books are in the study now wn no one is there to see them. I answer Yes. . . ." (# 472) He referred to the horse in # 427, stating that "We see the Horse it self . . . it being an Idea & nothing more." There is no second or material horse over and above the horse we see and touch and ride or back. We see the horse itself, not a mental copy or a somatic copy. The horse is an idea; it is an immediate object of sense. There it is in front of my eyes. I cannot doubt its existence, any more than I can doubt my own existence. It exists. Its *esse* is *percipi.* The groom comes, leads the horse away, locks him up in the stable, puts the key in his pocket, and off with him. Now, Dr. Berkeley, the horse in the stable and the books in the study are unperceived; do they still exist? "Yes, Sir," replies Berkeley, "the horse is in the stable and the books are in the study, as before."

What goes for the inanimate books and the living horse goes for all sensible things. The Berkeleian idea of sense is not a momentary existent, like a dream or the imagined dagger-in-the-mind; it is not something that ceases to be when it is no longer dreamed or imagined. On the contrary, the Berkeleian idea of sense is a continuing existent, still perceivable, still in relation to perception, even when it is not actually perceived. Accordingly, Berkeley's New Principle, if it is sound, must expand so as to cover the perceivable as well as the actually perceived. And so it does.

That which is actually perceived by man was Berkeley's first concern. All students of perceptual theory begin with the actual. Naturally enough the *esse* is *percipi* has always been the focus of interest in Berkeley's philosophy. It gives Berkeley's account of the meaning of the word *exist* when man says it of what he is actually perceiving. But Berkeley obviously could not stop short there; he had to follow where the argument led; he had to state what *exist* means when man says it of things he is not actually perceiving, but might perceive on taking the appropriate steps. Accordingly, on his first mention of his New Principle in print, before he has said anything about the universal spirit, Berkeley begins with a clear statement about what man actually perceives, and at once follows it up with an equally clear statement about what man might perceive. He says that the perceivable exists, but denies that it exists without any relation to perception, and he states definitely what *he* means by the existence of the perceivable. Here are his words:

> The table I write on, I say, exists, that is, I see and feel it; and if I were out of my study I should say it existed, meaning thereby that if I was in my study I might perceive it, or that some other spirit actually does perceive it. . . . For as to what is said of the absolute existence of unthinking things without any relation to their being perceived, that seems perfectly unintelligible. Their *esse* is *percipi*, nor is it possible they should have any existence, out of the minds or thinking things which perceive them. (PHK § 3)

Berkeley's expanding thought about existence necessitated an expanded formula. *Esse* is *percipi* is incomplete. To cover active existence Berkeley himself made the necessary addition to it: *esse est percipere* (or *velle* or *agere*). So far as is known he made no addition to the formula to cover the existence of the possible; but when he came to the point, he did make the addition to his philosophy. We must therefore make what is implicit explicit, and complete the formula, if it is not to misrepresent the full content of the philosophy. As was pointed out above, in the very entry (# 429) in which Berkeley adds *percipere* to the formula he says that the horse is in the stable, and the books in the study as before; though unperceived they exist; they are not nothing;

they have not been annihilated; they exist; they might be perceived; their *esse* is *posse percipi.*[3] Again in the first printed mention of the formula, Berkeley expressly brings the perceivable table under the formula, saying "I might perceive it." (PHK § 3) If I *might* perceive it, it *might* be perceived. It is therefore fully in keeping wth Berkeley's thought and his words to add *posse* to both limbs of his Latin formula. Accordingly, I venture to set forth his completed New Principle in the quadrilateral, *Esse est percipi, aut percipere, aut posse percipi, aut posse percipere.* To exist is either to be perceived or to perceive, or to be able to be perceived, or to be able to perceive.

I am taking verbal liberties with Berkeley's famous formula; but I plead in defense that I am only following out the logic of his case. Berkeley himself added to the formula the words *percipere* or *velle* or *agere,* and by implication he added *posse percipere* and *posse percipi,* both in his notebooks and in the *Principles.*

A recognition of the incompleteness of the *esse* is *percipi* by itself, and of the need to allow the formula to expand and complete itself, may ease some difficulties felt by readers of Berkeley's *Principles,* and may lead to a juster appraisal of his revised immaterialism. In particular it eases the difficulty about the meaning of the word *exist;* it puts the accent on the affirmative aspect of his philosophy; and it offers a balanced and comprehensive picture of the perceptual situation with which we work and in which our lives are cast from the cradle to the grave. I deal with these three points *seriatim* in the rest of this essay.

The Meanings of "Exist"

First, about the meaning of the word *exist.* The completed Principle offers a choice of four meanings according to the context, whereas the *esse* is *percipi* ties us down to one. According as the context indicates active or passive existence, actual or possible existence, *exist* may mean to perceive or to be perceived, to be able to perceive or to be able to be perceived. The four meanings are cognate, and turn on the one notion, but the choice of meanings does ease the situation and lessen the arbitrary look of Berkeley's *dictum,* though it does not go to the root of the matter. The four alternatives confine existence to the perceptual situation, and leave unanswered the (for Berkeley) all-important question, Has the word *exist* any meaning outside that situation, that is, unconnected with perception?

In an attempt to answer this question I searched Aristotle's *Metaphysics.* He has much to say about existence, and he credits the word with "many senses." (1077b; cf. 992a) He shows that men use the word in various ways, but not that it has many meanings. The norm of existence for him, is the

[3] See also entries ## 445–446, where, speaking of squares or points that may be perceived in a circle, or made out of it, Berkeley says that they "are actually in it, i.e. are perceivable in it."

passive existence of sensible things, for example, "the shape of a bronze sphere exists." (1070a) He accepts supersensible existence, for example, the active existence of the First Mover. His standing problem is where to place ideas and mathematical objects, which "exist apart." One meets vague adjectival usages, such as "health exists" (1070a), and cases where the word adds emphasis, but means virtually nothing. Topics of discussion are habitually described as existing, that is, existing in the mind; but, so far as I could see, Aristotle has made no attempt to establish existence outside the mind; and even his matter turns out to be potentiality (1050a), a state relative to possible perception.

For modern usage one turns to the dictionaries. The *Oxford English Dictionary* may fairly be quoted in support of Berkeley, especially as regards the original meaning; it says that the word *exist* comes from the late Latin "ex(s)istere, to stand out, be perceptible, hence to exist." It comments on the late appearance of the Latin original, which does not occur in Cooper's Latin–English dictionary of 1565. The English derivative had not been long established when Locke and Berkeley used it, and a complete departure from its original meaning in so short a time is unlikely. The dictionary specifies four heads of derivative meanings: (a) to have place in the domain of reality, (b) to have being in a specified place or under specified conditions, (c) to have life or animation, to live, and (d) to continue in being.

The terms used here—*the domain of reality, being, life,* and *animation*—are vague, but they all seem to me to express, or at least to imply, a reference to active percipience or passive perception. Life, organic life, is no exception. *I exist* can mean *I live,* and often does so, because life is the bearer of percipience, and, if one may judge from one's own case, the will to live is basically the will to perceive. In *willing* to live one wills the heart to beat and the blood to circulate; one wills the organic machinery to function as a means to the ends of percipience. The struggle for existence, in essence, is the struggle to perceive and to continue perception.

But dictionaries and authorities apart, what does the word *exist* mean today in ordinary talk, if it does not mean what Berkeley says it means? Two possibilities occur to me. Neither is satisfactory, though there may be a grain of truth in both.

Perhaps the word *exist* has no meaning of its own, but takes its meaning from its context. Perhaps it means nothing, because it can mean so many things. That account is too paradoxical. The word is colored by its context, as Berkeley saw; but its meaning varies within limits, and those limits appear to be set by the factors in the perceptual situation.

The other possibility is more plausible. Could the very opposite of the Principle be true? Could it be that the root-notion of existence is that of standing *outside* the mind and being *un*perceived? Berkeley's sharp eyes fell on this possibility, and he twice refers to it in his notebooks, styling it "the Reverse of the Principle." In entry # 304 he wrote, "The Reverse of ye

Principle introduc'd Scepticism," and in # 411 he calls it the chief source of skepticism, folly, contradictions, and inextricable puzzling absurdities. The reverse of the Principle is, of course, *esse est non-percipi,* to be is to be unperceived. Berkeley has left us no analysis or refutation of it—which, considering the care he bestowed on the demonstration of the Principle, is strange. Perhaps he thought it too Pickwickian for philosophical treatment, and of course he knew the limitations of semasiology; he knew that in some measure words mean what the users say they mean; he recognized that men often do make assumptions about existence, which are tantamount to reversing the Principle. "Bare existence" out of all relations to percipience is one such assumption. In our less philosophical moments we picture it vaguely as a sunless limbo, like chaos before the *fiat lux.* We conceive it dimly as a neutral state in which things *are* prior to perception, and to which they return after perception. Such pictures and concepts are of the twilight of reason. Bare existence is *bare,* bare of meaning. Can trained thinkers think of it as a reality? *We* are trained to watch our own perceivings and percepts. *We* know well that we perceive the perceivable. Can *we* think down to a state of bare existence, quite without relevance to mind? I don't think I can. Trained or untrained, percipient minds cannot divest themselves of their percipience, nor think away the inherent relevance of their objects. The meaning *on* things, their relevance to mind, like living light, is indefectible. We can close this book; we can shut our eyes; we can put out the lights; but we cannot think the book down to a dud or neutral state of bare existence; we cannot rob its letters and words and the other reals that compose it of all their significance for mind. The same holds of the whole book of nature. Its *esse* is *percipi* in that sense, and no one can think it down to a state of bare existence, in which its *esse* becomes *non-percipi.*

The completing of the Principle should complete, it seems to me, the rejection of the reverse of the Principle. If *esse* cannot fairly be made to mean *non-percipi,* a fortiori it cannot fairly be made to mean *non-percipere,* or *non-posse percipi,* or *non-posse percipere.* If to say the table exists cannot mean that it is *not* being perceived, a fortiori to say it exists cannot mean that it *could not* be perceived. If to say that Socrates exists cannot mean that he is not perceiving, a fortiori to say that Socrates exists cannot mean that he could not perceive. The frank acceptance of possible existence as possible perception removes the main objection to accepting *esse* as *percipi.* People are afraid that if they admit that the word *exist,* applied to sensible things, means *to be perceived,* they are banishing the perceivable from the real world, and reducing the status of sensible things to that of (in Kant's words about Berkeley) "mere products of the imagination." Those fears are groundless. The books unperceived are in the study, and the horse unperceived is in the stable, as before, when with Berkeley we reject the reverse of the Principle, and accept the *posse percipi* and the *posse percipere* as constituent parts of the completed Principle.

Affirmative Immaterialism

Berkeley's philosophy is a grand affirmation. This is my second point. I am not running away from his bold denial, or belittling it; his philosophy is nothing if not immaterialist. His denial of unknown, unknowable matter was of first importance in its day; and though the notion of matter is more fluid today, the issue he raised is very much alive, as is shown by the attention paid to the *Principles* by Russian philosophers. Philosophies, however, do not live by polemic alone. Berkeley's thought would not have lived and flourished for two centuries and a half, had not readers sensed the affirmation behind the denial. The *esse* is *percipi* is the key to the denial; since to be is to be perceived, Berkeley argued, matter, which *ex hypothesi* cannot be perceived, *non est*. The completed Principle, without weakening that denial, brings the affirmation to the forefront. In the light of it we see that Berkeley so denied the existence of matter as to affirm the real existence of sensible things, perceived and perceivable, and of living, active, spiritual beings that perceive them, or may do so. In a word, Berkeley's immaterialism is an affirmation of sense and spirit, and there is much wisdom in what he has to say about both heads of reality.

Berkeley's epistemological approach is realist, not idealist. His theory of sense-perception is direct, two-term, and positive, and far more satisfactory, it seems to me, than any variety of the representative theory. It dissipates illusions, and rules out any permanent radical skepticism, assuring us that what we see and touch, when we see and touch, is there to see and touch. Berkeley's world of sense is an ordered world of significant reals, subject to natural law and adapted to perceiving and conceiving mind, as ordinary folk take it to be. Berkeley's world of spirit is a society of embodied minds or souls or selves, who live and learn, and may become wise and good, as ordinary folk believe.

Much more might be said, of course, on all these points; but even in the outline sketch given above they add up to an affirmative philosophy that enables the thinker to move with ease and poise about the tasks of life and in the realms of thought. The *esse* is *percipi* represents only the negative aspect of that philosophy; it was the decisive and distinctive part of the Principle for Berkeley in his wonder-year; and so it has been ever since for historians and teachers of philosophy. But the fact remains that it is *part* of the Principle only, and not the whole. We must take it along with its complementary parts, if we are to do full justice to the system.

Real Body and Distinct Mind

Lastly, Berkeley's completed Principle makes for a balanced and comprehensive realism. In the pages of his second notebook we can watch the philosophy maturing as the Principle expanded. *Percipere* is added to *percipi,* and, in effect, *posse* to both. At the same time the whole range of existence is transposed into the key of perception, and the perceptual situation begins to dominate the philosophy. As Berkeley took into his ken the subject perceiving with the object perceived and the possible behind the actual, so his original panpsychism fell away, and was gradually replaced by a philosophy of real body and distinct mind.

Exclusive attention to the *esse* is *percipi,* on the other hand, makes for the idealist misinterpretation. *Esse* is mistranslated *essence,* and the formula is taken to mean that the essence of things is mental, and that we produce the ideas we perceive. Kant must have argued along these lines when he reached his conception of Berkeley as a dogmatic idealist who treated objects in space as mere products of the imagination.

Berkeley passed through the mentalist stage, and for some months held that all was mind; but even then he was no *idealist,* except in journalese jargon. Human knowing to him was always a finding, not a making. A fortiori he was no idealist when he found the other of mind. His realism consisted in his direct awareness of the sensible, and the characteristic of his realism is inwardness; he viewed sensible and sentient from within the perceptual situation, together but distinct. The astronomer sees the Milky Way from within; we others see it from without, or think we do. The table I see is not in my head; it is out there, along with the Milky Way. Quite so; but it is not outside the Perception Way, if Berkeley is right; for it is within the galaxy of mind. In other words, Berkeley treats perception as a microcosm; he made it a window on the universe; and thus he sought, and maybe he found, a total appraisement of the perceptual situation.

A striking passage in the *Third Dialogue* (DHP 251) well illustrates this method. Berkeley imagines himself present at creation, and he interprets it in terms of percipience. He sees "things produced into being; that is, become perceptible, in the order described by the sacred historian." Those words mark the end of a crisis in his dialectical development (see PC ## 60, 293, 436, and 723). Moses says that God created things before He created Adam—which could not be if the things created were only Adam's percepts. To create Adam on Friday and Adam's percepts on the previous Thursday were beyond the powers of omnipotence. Berkeley offers a choice of explanations; there may have been intelligences before man, or the things may have been produced "in a desert where nobody was present." In either case things were created *to be perceived,* and beginning to be was to "become perceptible." The speculation thus contains a clear recognition of the *posse percipi* as real, and shows Berkeley's thought expatiating in a vast perceptual situation.

Percipience is a far-flung wonder, familiar and close to us, coterminous with man, presumably coterminous with life. Its pattern of awareness is pervasive, found with variations in sensation, imagination, memory, thought, and the higher work of mind. Can it be only a freak achievement of privileged animals on the earth?

Berkeley explained it in terms of universal spirit. He looked out at the object perceived, vast, passive, yet radiant with meaning, and then he looked in at his self, the active subject perceiving; and he concluded that *"haec non sine numine dei."* Berkeley was one of those masters of "justness and extent of thought [who] are withal used to reflect." (PHK § 154) The shuttle movement of his thought to and fro marks his discussion of the existence of God in the *Principles.*[4] His argument goes deep, and the superficiality and artificiality sometimes ascribed to it are due to misunderstanding. Berkeley had recourse to deity, we are told, to bolster up a tottering metaphysic; his chairs and tables would vanish the moment he shuts his eyes only for God who imprints ideas of them on our minds, and, in effect, makes us think we see and touch things not really there at all. In point of fact, Berkeley did not conceive deity along such lines. Berkeley's God is not a passive receptacle for ideas-in-waiting, nor a cosmic conjuror, nor a *deus ex machina;** He is a universal spirit, active, great, and good, in whom we live and move and have our being. Long before he published the *Principles* Berkeley had come round to the common-sense view of continued existence. He regarded his furniture as lasting, as in fact it was and is. I myself have seen the table he wrote on; his family has it still. It is there to see and touch, and it remains there to see and touch, when nobody is about; it is made that way. From his common-sense world of significant reals Berkeley rises, when he wants to or needs to, as easily as a jet plane. He argues to God from the presence, reality, and significance of sensible things, not from their supposed absence or unreality. He turns to other controls to support the argument, switching from the object to the subject. He reviews the intercourse of minds, the bond of spirit, and the community of perceivings. He distinguishes perceiving by sense from imagining. He marks the effects on us of the wills of our fellow men, and he contrasts those ideas with "the far greater part of the ideas or sensations, perceived by us." (PHK § 146) These latter, he thinks, are of such a character that the reflective mind cannot fail to read in them evidence for universal spirit.

The argument is balanced and comprehensive, and it follows the lines of the completed Principle. It might be sketched, as follows: As I am to the ideas I frame, as you are to the ideas you excite in me, as we are to the ideas we excite in one another, so is the universal spirit to the ideas that constitute the works of nature. Berkeley puts it best, perhaps, in these words:

> Whereas some one finite and narrow assemblage of ideas denotes a particular human mind, withersoever we direct our view, we do at all times and in all places perceive manifest tokens of the divinity; every thing we see, hear, feel, or any wise perceive by sense, being a sign or effect of the Power of God; as is our perception of those very motions, which are produced by men. (PHK § 148)

[4] See especially PHK §§ 26, 36, 56, 146–148, and compare St. Thomas's famous Five Ways—a fine phalanx of argument, but static compared with Berkeley's, because based almost entirely on the nature of the object.

* [For a different view see Professor Farooqi's chapter, p. 132.—Ed.]

II

Berkeley and the Possibility of an Empirical Metaphysics*

IAN T. RAMSEY

What help can Berkeley give us toward the construction of an empirically based metaphysical theology? That is the question that lies behind this essay. I hope to show that there are to be found in Berkeley all the ingredients for an empirical metaphysics, and that, in particular, had Berkeley developed his doctrine of notions the misunderstandings of Berkeley's position might have been fewer, and the novelty of his position would have been more striking than it was. At various points in the discussion we shall see how relevant Berkeley's suggestions are to contemporary empiricism—whether to its growing interest in metaphysics or to the concern it has generated in religious language.

Locke and Berkeley: Ideas and Notions

Undoubtedly, an exposition of Berkeley best starts by recalling Locke. But we must be cautious about taking this dependence on Locke too uncritically. It is sometimes said, for example, that Berkeley accepted un-

* This article incorporates, in a much revised and rearranged form, a contribution to the XIth International Congress of Philosophy, 1953, and a sermon preached in that year at the Berkeleian Commemoration at Trinity College, Dublin, which was subsequently printed in *Hermathena,* # 82 (1953), 113–127. I hope that meanwhile I have benefited from further reading both of Berkeley and of articles, especially, those by my friend Harry M. Bracken—even where my views do not entirely coincide with his.

reservedly Locke's doctrine of Ideas as "particular objects" of sensation and reflection, and that with this assumption he criticized Locke's doctrine of abstract ideas as a meaningless absurdity. But such a summary statement either overlooks Berkeley's doctrine of notions altogether or thinks that it is a somewhat inconsistent afterthought, and those are positions which, though commonly held, are nevertheless, as I hope to show, quite indefensible.

Admittedly, Berkeley, in his early years, more or less accepted a position very similar to that of Locke, whether it be Locke's doctrine of meaning or his associated theory of ideas. Not that Locke is entirely clear and uncomplicated, still less unambiguous, in these matters, but for our purposes we may summarize Locke's relevance as follows. For Locke, the significant "use of words is to be sensible marks of ideas."[1] And such ideas, he has already told us, are the particular objects of sensation or reflection. "External material things as the objects of sensation; and the operations of our own minds within as the objects of Reflection, are, to me, the only originals from whence all our ideas take their beginnings."[2] Similarly, Berkeley can say: "All significant words stand for Ideas" and "All ideas come from without or from within. If from without, it must be by the senses . . . if from within they are the operations of the mind . . ." (PC # 378) Here for Berkeley was his original starting point with Locke; but it was one that Berkeley soon found need to develop.

To begin with, Berkeley was genuinely puzzled about these "ideas of operations," or, more strictly, these ideas that for him must be operation-pictures. He asks, "Qu: whether it were not better *not* to call the operations of the mind ideas, confining this term to things sensible." (PC # 490)

The immediate difficulty arose from his conviction that all ideas are "inert" or "passive." How, he asked, could there be an idea of an operation? For this would have to be for Berkeley an image of activity, an operation-picture, something which at one and the same time had to be both active and passive. How could anything be both active and passive in this way? Is not the idea of an operation of the mind self-contradictory? "I have no idea of a Volition or act of the mind . . . for that were a contradiction."[3] (PC # 663)

Berkeley was so troubled about these operations of the mind that his first reaction was to try to make do with nothing but "things sensible," and to construct a theory of knowledge from ideas of sensations alone. But with Locke's criterion for the significant use of words such a bold venture made nonsense of many words with which Berkeley was loathe to dispense. Indeed, it seemed to him that these words in many ways completed our talk about ideas. For instance, we speak of ourselves, not as *being* ideas but as *having* ideas, as being active about ideas, and so on. (DHP 223) It was to do justice

[1] Locke, *Essay Concerning Human Understanding*, Book III, Chap. 2, § 1.

[2] *Ibid.*, Book II, Chap. 1, § 4.

[3] See PC # 176a: "The grand Mistake is that we think we have Ideas of the Operations of our Minds. certainly this Metaphorical dress is an argument we have not."

to the claims of these other words that in the second edition of the *Principles* he introduced the new term "notion" in relation to them. He says:

> So far as I can see, the words *will, soul, spirit,* do not stand for different ideas, or in truth, for any idea at all, but for something which is very different from ideas, and which being *an agent* cannot be like unto, or represented by, any idea whatsoever. Though it must be owned at the same time, that we have some notion of soul, spirit, and *the operations of the mind,* such as willing, loving, hating, in as much as we know or understand the meaning of those words.[4] (PHK § 27)

Here are significant words—"will," "soul," "spirit," and speaking more generally, the phrase "operations of the mind"—that do not fulfill Locke's condition for significance and yet are not nonsense. Berkeley finds the same puzzle about the word "person." He has said: "Qu: about the Soul or rather person whether it be not compleatly known" (PC # 25), and later, after reminding himself of Locke's dictum, "All knowledge onely about ideas" (PC # 522), he says next: "It seems improper & liable to difficulties to make the Word Person stand for an Idea, or to make ourselves Ideas or thinking things ideas." (PC # 523)

"Will," "soul," "spirit," "person," "operations of the mind"—none of these words or phrases stands for ideas, and yet all of them are significant. What account is Berkeley going to give of them? How is he going to explicate this term "notion"? What can we make of his doctrine of notions, even if it is sometimes a matter of piecing suggestions together and going beyond, though never contrary to, what Berkeley explicitly says?

My first point will be that, not surprisingly, Berkeley did not have in his own day the logical equipment to deal with his novel contention, so that the exposition of what we might call his "notionalized empiricism" is bound to be somewhat ambiguous and misleading. But granting that difficulty, my second point will be that there still remains something of fundamental importance to which a doctrine of notions does justice when it also modifies Locke's epistemology in the most thoroughgoing way, and presents us with the novel possibility of an empirical metaphysics.

Notions and Activity

First, then, I shall suggest that Berkeley was muddled when he talked about notions of the will, soul, mind, spirit, person, *and* of activity ("operations of the mind"); and muddled in a way that has misled his commentators. Instead of seeing "operations of the mind" or "personal activity" as that to which the doctrine of notions essentially referred, both Berkeley and then, not surprisingly, his commentators rather talk of our notions of the will, soul, mind, spirit, and so forth, to the consequent neglect of the activity factor. Yet, as we have seen, it was Berkeley's logical puzzlement about activity that first set him

[4] Italics after the first line added.

thinking in a way that took him ultimately so far away from the Locke with whom he began.

For example, Professor Jessop says (and of course with some reason) that notion is used "for the mental as object."[5] Likewise, in a footnote to § 89 of the *Principles,* Professor A. C. Fraser says that by the use of the term notion, Berkeley recognizes "independent substance in Spirit, while he rejects it in Matter,"[6] as if Berkeley were talking about some sort of parallel objectivity in each case. It is in this vein that Fraser can say that Berkeley's main argument is that "I am *conscious* of permanence or substance in the Ego, but not in the things around me,"[7] and that this is evident in the *Third Dialogue.*

Now, insofar as Berkeley talks like this, insofar as he thinks of the "mental as object," he is undoubtedly drawing a parallelism between notions and ideas (mental and material respectively), which in other places he wishes most decidedly to reject.[8] Nor need we deny that in some places Berkeley does speak in this misleading way. If we look, for example, at the *Third Dialogue,* which Fraser mentions, and especially at pages 231 to 233, we easily notice the extent to which Berkeley's case is both complicated and confused by his negative inability to find a grammar for notions, and so by his consequent use of idea-logic and faculty psychology ("my . . . thinking principle") to discuss them. We can see, in other words, how Jessop and Fraser's interpretations are possible and, as far as they go, justified. But it is not the whole story, and Berkeley is never *so* confused as to lose his way altogether. For when Philonous is questioned on this very point of "spiritual substance" what is his central defense? It is that the notion of spirit is not "repugnant" or "inconsistent" as is talk about material substance, because spirit is *active;* and with this goes an appeal to "reflexion" and what has been called earlier "a reflex act." Here is the positive and permanent claim of the doctrine of notions: first, that the phrase "personal activity" is logically odd as contrasted with talk about ideas, with discourse which has typically a descriptive logic; and second, that there is metaphysical significance in the fact of "reflexion" and in the activity this "reflexion" reveals.

So we need not be unduly worried that Berkeley talks of notions of the mind, soul, spirit, and person, and of the will, besides talking of a notion of activity. This misleading and somewhat puzzling way of speaking only arises because Berkeley's thought forms are not equal to the originality of his doctrine of notions. But that is no reason whatever why we should strive to perpetuate the inadequacies that Berkeley could not help but commit. We ourselves can recognize that for Berkeley the interest of words like "mind," "soul," "spirit," "person," and "will" was that, insofar as they do not stand for

[5] Editor's footnote to § 27 of PHK.

[6] A. C. Fraser, *Selections from Berkeley* (Oxford: 1891, 4th edition), 106.

[7] *Ibid.,* 106.

[8] PHK § 142: "*Spirits* and *ideas* are things so wholly different. . . ."

ideas, they are all alike distinctive in referring to agency or activity. The heart of Berkeley's doctrine of notions is the notion each of us has of his own activity.

Notions and Self-disclosure

This brings us to my second point. What I am now urging is that Berkeley's importance as an empirical philosopher lies in his noticing that an adequate empiricism not only has to have its "particular objects" or (in his sense) "ideas" with their appropriate language, which is typically descriptive, but must also characterize each of us with an awareness of our own activity, which by descriptive standards is an epistemological and logical curiosity. We each have, he would say, a notion of ourselves as active. We use words about our activity significantly, and yet no ideas, in the sense of particular objects, exhaust their meaning. "The knowledge of my ideas" is "immediate"; of my activity it is by "inward feeling" or "reflexion." (PHK §§ 145 and 89) Again, in the *Third Dialogue* to which we have already referred, he says, "you neither perceive matter objectively as you do an inactive being or idea, nor know it, as you do your self by a reflex act." (DHP 232) We are reminded of his phrase in *De Motu: "conscientia quadam interna"*—"a certain internal consciousness." (§ 21)

The point is that an adequate empirical epistemology demands not only Locke's ideas but also this curious experiential fact about ourselves. What I suggest is that we are aware of our activity in the sense in which this is significant for Berkeley's doctrine of notions, as and when there is what Berkeley calls an "inward feeling" or a "reflex act" (which I would call a self-disclosure) around some ideas, ideas of sensation in Berkeley's (and Locke's) sense. When we give a nodding assent to some story, that kind of assent is something which calls for no account in terms of notions. But as and when in reading some story we come to ourselves, as and when some story provokes us to action, being discourse that directs us to act,[9] then it deals in words that are not merely descriptive but have the logic of notions.

Indeed, Berkeley comes close to suggesting that every word (or sentence) will have both a descriptive and a "notional" logic. There may be sentences whose logic is largely, and on the face of it, wholly descriptive, such as "The cat is on the mat," "The penny is brown." There may be sentences whose logic is largely, and on the face of it, wholly "notional," such as "That's nice," said in order to register our reactions to something. Certainly the particles of grammatical punctuation are notional, directing us to do something. Unpunctuated prose may fail to impress us; particles by themselves will most likely bewilder us. But prose and particles together create intelligibility (in Locke's sense) and *also* direct our activity in "following the argument." Any assertion

[9] See *Alciphron* 292.

which we affirm, as distinct from merely "mouthing," must combine notions and ideas. Thus, the unit toward which Berkeley's thinking pointed was not an idea, or even ideas together with minds, but personal activity terminating in ideas, activity about ideas, the kind of unit given in a situation of self-disclosure. Notions and ideas were mutually implicating elements of every genuine assertion. Here indeed is a logical version of the old maxim *esse* is *percipi* when this was expanded (as it always had to be) to tell the full story, into *esse* is *percipi* or *percipere*. The unit of existence for Berkeley's thought is activity about ideas, *percipere* with *percipi*.

So Berkeley's appeal to notions was an appeal to a self-disclosure that discloses what I am beyond the "ideas"—ideas of sensation, which are given by descriptive discourse, more precisely by scientific discourse—when I am distinctively active. Here in the notion I have of my activity is the paradigm of transcendence, and the word "I" or "self"—insofar as it explicates this—has no descriptive logic and describes no object; rather, it occurs in assertions that, if I may use J. L. Austin's phrase, have the logic of performative or illocutionary utterances. These are assertions that talk of what is happening when it is happening. The word "I" hints at, points to, what is distinctive about what is happening to whoever is using a sentence containing the word "I" to talk of his activity.

Berkeley in his doctrine of notions is pointing to the empirical curiosity of the situation in which I come to myself in being active, and to the need to talk about this self-disclosure in a way that is logically peculiar by comparison with descriptive sentences.

I suggest that so to ground notions in a self-disclosure that arises around ideas when we are stirred to be active about them, might help us to understand better what Berkeley says—for example, in *Principles*—when he remarks that a spirit or "myself" is a "thing" wherein they (ideas) exist (PHK § 2), or again that ideas are "supported by, or exist in, minds." (PHK § 89) As the background to these remarks, Berkeley might have said that his ideas were abstract parts of an active whole, a situation which might for the moment be described as "my activity." It would then be something not altogether unlike Bradley's "positive . . . whole of feeling,"[10] about which Bradley indeed might have said that we had no "idea" but only a "notion." For he saw that it could not be an externalized particular, and to some degree he discerned that "Absolute" had to be given a curious use. Further, if we look at Bradley's argument we shall see similarities between his "immediate experience," "immediate feeling" and what I have called a disclosure situation.[11] It is true that such a suggestion is a long way from the Locke-Hume tradition, but as anyone who has read G. E. Moore's "Refutation of Idealism" in his *Philosophi-*

[10] F. H. Bradley, *Essays on Truth and Reality*, Chap. VI, 189.

[11] See I. T. Ramsey, *Religious Language* (London: 1957), 52, 54, 62, and Ramsey (Ed.), *Prospect for Metaphysics* (London: 1960), Chap. X, 163–164.

cal Studies will know, it is not difficult to make Berkeley's point of view look very silly on an eighteenth-century epistemology restricted to ideas. At any rate, I do not think that Berkeley would have disallowed any "notion" of "whole" or "situation" which such a suggestion as I am making might involve. It is true that for Berkeley a mathematical "unity" is nothing, because an abstract idea, but that is just the point; is "whole," as notionally given, likewise an abstract idea? Pringle-Pattison is singularly revealing where he says of unity in Locke *and* Berkeley, that it is a "notion."[12] But Berkeley's own words, which he has just quoted, specify unity as an abstract idea. My suggestion is that inasmuch as Berkeley wants notions *besides* abstract ideas, to that extent he could have allowed for a whole and a unity which was not a mathematical unity.

Abstract Ideas, Innate Ideas, and Relations

At this point, something should be said about Berkeley's attitude to abstract ideas. In the beginning—and it is a position not without its echoes even in Locke—Berkeley insisted that such objectivity as characterized "abstract ideas" must be worked in terms of externalized particulars. There were no special things called "abstract ideas" to which general words referred. The only objectivity which abstract ideas could have was that of particular ideas. Abstract ideas were no special sort of idea with some special factual reference. That part of Locke's theory he wholeheartedly rejected.[13] But he allowed like Locke at one point[14] that abstract ideas might reasonably relate to groups of particulars or to a particular used generally. But in the end, going far beyond Locke, he granted that insofar as abstraction involved activity on our part, to that extent general words might relate to some features of particular ideas "conceived asunder" (ALC 293; cf. PHK Intro. § 10) and so have a "notional" reference. In this way, by reference to the activity that abstraction involves, there might be a reasonable rehabilitation of some abstract ideas. But all other abstract ideas, such as "substance" or "pure space," would be mere verbiage and refer to nothing. (PHK § 116)

Berkeley may thus sometimes speak approvingly of abstract notions, but insofar as they are notions they never merely have the externalized objectivity belonging to ideas, or arising from ideas that had been considered together or asunder. They have a factual reference all of their own, for they involve that self-disclosure in activity we have mentioned above.

[12] A. S. Pringle-Pattison (Ed.), *Locke's An Essay Concerning Human Understanding* (Oxford: 1924), 63*n*.

[13] Locke, *Essay,* Book IV, Chap. 7, § 9. See PHK Intro. § 13. Cf. *Alciphron* (First and Second editions) VII, § 5, in *Works, Vol. III,* Appendix, 332.

[14] *Ibid.,* Book III, Chap. 3, §§ 6–7. See PHK Intro. §§ 12, 18. Cf. *Alciphron* (First and Second editions) VII, § 7, in *Works, III,* Appendix, 334–335.

This is confirmed, I suggest, by his remarks about innate ideas. In talking of innate ideas we are talking significantly, Berkeley would say, yet not talking in any way about something that is a function of externalized particulars. Here is a word used significantly, yet not analyzable into the objective feature of ideas. If our general contention is correct, innate ideas must then have the status of notions, and that indeed turns out to be the case. In *Siris* (§ 308), innate ideas and personal activity are closely linked. Incidentally, I need hardly say that these reflections would support any claim that there was not that major change of attitude in *Siris* which some have felt driven to postulate.

To see how these reflections could broaden out to justify an empirical metaphysics, let us next glance at what Berkeley says about relations. At the start he is very puzzled as to whether relations are ideas or not.[15] But it is significant that his views about relations crystallize with his doctrine of notions. In the end he argues that relations are *reasonably* abstract,[16] precisely because they involve an act of the mind. (PHK § 142) Now, certainly relations involve "an act of mind," but they may do this in two ways: insofar as (to talk crudely) the mind groups terms together; or insofar as the discernment of relations is always the occasion of a self-disclosure. If there is any reason to think of such a self-disclosure as reminiscent of Bradley, then we might have had in Berkeley, had he ever developed his theory of relations so far, something strangely anticipatory of Bradley's doctrine of relations. Meanwhile, neither Bradley nor Berkeley made a distinction between those relations that arise from conceiving particulars together or asunder and an *ultimate* self–other relation that must be demanded as a condition for any knowledge and any language at all, though I think that Berkeley at least implied this distinction whereas Bradley denied it. If we have a notion of anything besides ourselves, its "objectivity," presumably somehow given to us in a situation which subjectively is one of self-disclosure, will, like that of ourselves, be something other than the "objectivity" which belongs to ideas, and its logic will have to be appropriately odd.

That is a point I will take further very soon. Meanwhile, let us pause to recall retrospectively that when Berkeley introduced notions as well as ideas, and began to elaborate the wider empiricism which we may call a notionalized empiricism, it was to grapple with what seemed to him insuperable difficulties about Locke's "operations of the mind." Notions, as I have argued, highlighted the significance of personal activity, which for Berkeley was transcendent of the spatiotemporal insofar as it was other than but presupposed by the spatiotemporal "ideas of sensation" toward which it was directed. Of such activity we are aware, I have suggested, in a disclosure whose generation

[15] PC ## 461, 540, 545, 735.
[16] PHK § 89, and ALC 305, 307.

is the aim of such discourse about ideas as directs us how to act. Such discourse is then, by descriptive standards, logically peculiar, and of this peculiarity Austin's doctrine of performatory force may offer us some clue.

God

I hope now to show that such reflections can illuminate much of what Berkeley says about other selves and God, which, to make Berkeley generally consistent, must be given a philosophical status having close kinship with that of ourselves. Indeed, now that we have seen the possibility of grounding a transcendent "I" in the self-disclosure which characterizes activity about ideas, we have already taken one step towards the possibility of an empirical metaphysics. Let us now see how Berkeley makes his further moves towards theism.

We may begin conveniently by imagining that Berkeley was confronted with a question often raised in our own day: What is the logic of the word "God"? What kind of empirical anchorage can be given to God-sentences?

In answer to such questions, someone might hazard the guess that the word "God" is like the words "matter," "absolute time," "absolute space" of some physicist-philosophers or mathematicians. At this, of course, Berkeley the antagonist of "abstract ideas" would protest violently. Anticipating a Russell he would protest, as he does in *Alciphron,* against the "current opinion that every substantive name marks out and exhibits . . . one distinct idea separate from all others." (ALC 293) Some names refer to nothing whatever. They are just brawling. For example, "matter" and "absolute space" refer to *nothing*—at most they are pleasing noises and in these cases there are not even notional overtones. Make "God" logically similar to such words or phrases (as Kant, to some extent, did when he made "God" an Idea of Reason used regulatively) and you have words without meaning, a theology but no God, and "polemical divines" are warmed by nothing but the hot air of their own making. (ALC 103) It is not so much that there are no abstract ideas—though Berkeley may often express it thus—it is rather that the words referring to such abstract ideas as these are empirically bankrupt. On this account, it will be remembered, Berkeley criticizes Malebranche, who "builds on the most abstract general ideas which I entirely disclaim." (DHP 214)

It might, however, be objected, not least in the light of our earlier discussion, that Berkeley does not take so negative an attitude to all abstract ideas, some of which may have an empirical grounding by being founded in various ways on "particular things." (ALC 305) May not "God" have a similar sort of reference to "particular things"? Here might seem to be the possibility of some kind of "secular theology," such as has a certain amount of appeal in our own day. But if "God" referred to an abstract idea in this sense it would refer significantly to nothing else but to such "particular things"; and this

Berkeley cannot allow. Berkeley is adamant that the significance of "God" is *not* reducible to any group of such "idea-particulars." Why? The reason is, for Berkeley, plain and explicit, and it takes us at once to the point behind his doctrine of notions. If we may say so without irreverence, sauce for "any other spirit" must be sauce for God as well and "these being *active,* cannot be represented by things perfectly inert, as our ideas are." So says Philonous in the *Third Dialogue.* (DHP 231, italics added) What possibility then remains? The word "God" is not a word referring to some altogether "abstract idea" or else it would be merely noise; nor is it a word that, being more respectably "abstract," reduces to, and so relates wholly to, "ideas." For that would give us nothing but a secularized theology. What, then, is its logical setting?

We approach an answer by recalling what Philonous says a sentence or so afterwards: "I know what I mean by the terms *I* and *myself,*" and their factual anchorage is what he calls a "reflex act." (DHP 231–232) Now, as we have seen, this logical oddity of "I" and this empirical curiosity called a "reflex act" are both signified by his introduction of the word *"notion."* We each have a "notion" of our own activity. The point is made again in the *Alciphron.*

> An active . . . spirit cannot be an idea . . . words which denote an active spirit do not stand for ideas. And yet they are not insignificant neither; since I understand what is signified by the term I, or *myself,* or know what it means, although it be no idea, nor like an idea, but that which . . . operates about them. Certainly it must be allowed that we have some notion that we understand, or know what is meant by, the terms *myself, will, memory, love, hate,* and so forth: although, to speak exactly, these words do not suggest so many distinct ideas." (ALC 292)

Likewise, we have a *notion* of God, and this arises when we survey the world from the standpoint of what Berkeley has taken to be his ultimate unit of thinking. Here is Berkeley's answer to the question of the logic of "God" I raised earlier. Ideas in the case of our own activity point to ourselves in a moment of self-disclosure. When we now survey the world with its immense number and variety of ideas, and use these occasions of self-disclosure as a catalyst, may there not occur a cosmic disclosure, in which the finitude of self-disclosures is obviously surpassed? If the exercise has been successful we are then aware, as Berkeley might have said, of the activity of God, which discloses itself to us through the vast and variegated pattern of ideas that constitute the universe.

So I think we shall be misled, both historically as to his intentions and philosophically as to his importance, if we claim that Berkeley the theologian is mainly memorable as being the author of a novel proof of God's existence; if we merely commemorate him for increasing the number of traditional proofs by one—possibly in two, maybe three, versions. For we have it from Berkeley himself that for him the greatest virtue of his natural theology was that it did *not* present men with the intricacies of an argument. Says

Philonous in the *Second Dialogue:* "You may now, without any laborious search into the sciences, without any subtlety of reason, or tedious length of discourse, oppose and baffle the most strenuous advocate for atheism." (DHP 213) It is a fact, remarks Berkeley (with perhaps a certain irony), that "divines and philosophers had proved beyond all controversy, from the beauty and usefulness of the several parts of the creation, that it was the workmanship of God." (DHP 212) Even so, that we may now set "aside all help of astronomy and natural philosophy, all contemplation of the contrivance, order and adjustment of things" and "from the bare existence of the sensible world" infer an "infinite mind," is, as he notes, a *"peculiar advantage."*[17] Nor need we be unsettled by his use of the word "infer." In *Alciphron* he has an alternative expression: "at all times and in all places" we perceive "sensible signs which *evince* the being of God" (ALC 147), and in the *Principles* he remarks that men only disbelieve by "stupidity" and "inattention"—when "blinded with excess of light" or upon "a wilful shutting of the eyes." (PHK §§ 149, 154) No doubt he tried to make the same point—that he is commending no subtle intricate argument, no novel proof—by his continual use of words like "plain" and "immediate." What Berkeley in effect appeals to is a cosmic disclosure which he hopes the whole Universe will generate for us once we have had, each in our own case, that self-disclosure of our own activity about ideas, which lies at the heart of his doctrine of notions. We believe in God as and when the whole world "comes alive" in a cosmic disclosure that occurs around the "ideas" of the Universe to give us a notion of God.

Here is Berkeley's route to an empirical theism, and to a position midway between Malebranche and the "Minute Philosophers." As we have noticed, not only had Malebranche his "abstract general ideas," but with these went a mystical disregard and philosophical belittling of the "world of sense." True, Berkeley might say with Malebranche that "in God we live and move and have our being." (DHP 214) But for Berkeley part of the reference of this word "God" was to particular ideas—to that external world which Malebranche belittled, when he supposed that we could have independent access to God's essence by a pure intellect which by-passed the external world. On the other hand, Berkeley was no "reductionist." Not all empirical reference was exhausted by ideas of sensation; "God," ethical words like "love" and "hate," metaphysical words like "freedom," all have some sort of reference to disclosures, whether cosmic or finite, disclosures that, while they include ideas, are not restricted to them. To suppose otherwise would be to write off distinctively personal words in a way that Berkeley from the start had refused to do. So, to take up our original point, we "see" God, not in Malebranche's sense, which might be said to be completely unintelligible, nor altogether in the sense in which we "see" "ideas." "Seeing God" is not

[17] DHP 212, italics added.

to be modeled in terms of sensing a "collection of ideas"; this is intelligible but inadequate. Nor do we see him by discerning somehow or other his "essence"; that is altogether *un*intelligible, says Berkeley. The "metaphysical hypothesis of our seeing all things in God by the union of the human soul with the intelligible substance of the Deity" is something "which neither I, nor anyone else could make sense of." (ALC 159) Rather do we see God "as plain as we see any human person whatsoever" and he "daily speaks to our senses in a manifest and clear dialect." (ALC 159) "In Him we live and move and have our being" (Acts 17:28)—a quotation that occurs so often in Berkeley's works as to have been called his "favorite quotation." (PHK § 66 and note) We see God as we see man; God and people are what we meet. But we do not meet just "bods," nor is a personal encounter the same as the physical crush of a queue.[18] Notional awareness of spirits and God is characterized by ideas, but not adequately. Such is the background to Berkeley's claim in *Alciphron IV* that the world is "divine visual language"; and to this claim, which I mentioned above, that nothing is more "evident" than the existence of God—"plain" and "immediate." (ALC 155–162) Berkeley himself uses the parallel of God and persons in *Alciphron:*

> . . . in a strict sense, I do not see Alciphron, but only such visible signs and tokens as suggest and infer the being of that invisible thinking principle or soul. . . . Even so, in the selfsame manner . . . I do . . . behold and perceive by all my senses such signs and tokens . . . as suggest, indicate and demonstrate an invisible God . . . (ALC 147)

and here too he remarks, as elsewhere, that the reason God is not discerned is that familiarity breeds, if not contempt, at least blindness. (ALC 155–156) Too often we look on glass, and look no further. What Berkeley hopes to do is to provide currency for us to "espy the heavens," to see God through it.

Broadening our theme at this point we may notice that such reflections as these help us better to see the significance of the text from Jeremiah 2:13 which Berkeley places at the front of *Alciphron:* "They have forsaken me, the fountain of living waters, and hewed them out cisterns that can hold no water." The minute philosophers, the "men of strong heads," the minimizers with a vengeance, had forsaken an *actively* encountered God—a *living* God—and instead had taken hold of *static* ideas—stone cisterns of their own making, but broken and partial, and quite unable to hold the (living and active) water it was their intention to contain. An active "God," because the word referred to *more than* ideas, they denied; religion claiming to "inspire" dutiful behavior they called "a State trick" (ALC 107); "all stings of conscience and sense of guilt"—those moral experiences that likewise are logical

[18] This would be Berkeley's line of reply to Antony Flew's discussion on "Death" as found in the short-lived journal *University,* Vol. 2, # 2 (Blackwell's, Spring 1952). See also the discussion between Flew and myself in the *Hibbert Journal,* 54 (April 1956), 242–250, and 54 (July 1956), 330–338, where the argument involves some discussion of Berkeley's position.

oddities grounded in disclosures, they reduced to "prejudices and errors of education"; man was no agent; he was "a machine . . . a curious piece of clock-work." (ALC 107) This was unbelief and atheism par excellence; and Berkeley triumphed over it insofar as he measured not only its force but also its inadequacy, insofar as he saw the need not only for ideas but also for notions. He was a skeptic, "minute" indeed when it came to ideas of the operations of the mind, *but more.*

Discourse about God: Berkeley's Recipe for Combining Intelligibility and Mystery

Yet Berkeley's difficulties are by no means over, and I would now like to indicate how this broad philosophical approach to natural theology, this union of ideas with activity-notions, stood him in excellent stead when he faced contemporary controversies on traditional themes. Of these we will select only two: first, the problem of theological anthropomorphism: that though human predicates are needed for intelligibility, yet they are naively inadequate for devotion.* They leave room for neither mystery nor transcendence, if these can be properly distinguished. Second, the problem of having Christianity both reasonable and distinctive.

We will begin with the problem of anthropomorphism. Amongst the comparatively few who were moved by St. Paul's preaching was, we are told, Dionysius the Areopagite, and legend (though I fear only legend) associates him with what Berkeley calls in the Fourth Dialogue of *Alciphron* "a very singular style"; God is *"above all* essence and life," *"above all* wisdom and understanding." (ALC 166, italics added) Here is "negative theology" with a vengeance; and in it is implied a permanent problem that also happened to be the center of a contemporary controversy in Dublin. Can theology be both intelligible and transcendent, reasonable yet mysterious? In 1696 there had appeared Toland's *Christianity not Mysterious,* a book that, starting from Locke's views in *Reasonableness of Christianity,* contrived to make Locke even plainer and more intelligible than he had himself intended.[19] For Locke had allowed for the possibility of "mystery," of truths "above reason," though he had done little to treat of them adequately. Toland was not long in completing Locke's job of "underlaboring" so well as to get rid (so he thought) of this rubbish, too. In opposition to Toland, Peter Browne, soon to become Provost of Trinity College, Dublin, urged that "mystery" could be defended by some doctrine of analogy; but Archbishop King of Dublin some twelve

* [For a similar observation, see Professor Farooqi's chapter, pp. 126 f.—Ed.]

[19] Cf. Alexander Pope's suppressed couplet in the *Essay* on *Man:*

What partly pleases, totally will shock
I question much if Toland would be Locke.

years later went further and fared worse—talking of the "metaphorical" use of words in relation to God. Here were extremes meeting in controversy: "minute philosophers" like Toland at best denying mystery to defend intelligibility; theologians like King defending mystery, but at the cost of an unintelligible theology. Now Berkeley is notable for having in his doctrine of notions, which includes but goes beyond ideas, a middle way. Further, if the Angelic Doctor and Provost Browne do not object to each other's company,[20] we may say that though Berkeley's outlook had express sympathies with the doctrine of analogy common to them both, it was a genuine alternative with its own philosophical merit.

For Berkeley could talk about God in the language of ideas with something of the same appropriateness, and something of the same qualifications, that were evident when he used public language about himself. For just as his own "reflexive act," his own self-disclosure, was concerned with ideas; so was theology capable of intelligible expression; and just as that "act" was more than the ideas in which it terminated, so the "mystery" and transcendence that theology demanded were made possible, and the demands of devotion justified. "Person" when used of ourselves, has something of the intelligibility and the mystery that belongs to theology in general.[21]

The Distinctiveness of Christianity: Berkeley's View of Grace

So to the second problem and to perhaps the greatest difficulty that a Christian philosopher must face: what philosophical defense could Berkeley give of the distinctive claims of Christianity?

As early as St. Paul's Sermon at Athens it had become clear that the transition from natural theology to revealed theology was exceedingly problematical. The Athenians showed an interested respect while Paul expounded a natural theology, but at the mention of the resurrection they

[20] Cf. Berkeley's own remark, ALC 170: "This doctrine, therefore, of analogical perfections in God, or our knowing God by analogy, seems very much misunderstood and misapplied by those who would infer from thence that we cannot frame any direct or proper notion, though never so inadequate, of knowledge or wisdom, as they are in the Deity; or understand any more of them than one born blind can of light and colours."

[21] We may regret that Berkeley never worked out more fully the logical parallels between God and persons. As PC ## 713–715 reveal, it was largely in order to avoid misunderstanding and so as "not to give the least Handle of offence to the Church or Church-men." With such an original doctrine as Berkeley's, readers were more than likely to suppose that his parallel of God and persons denied the three persons in one God, characteristic of the Chalcedonian definition. It is only in *Siris* that we have any explicit hints from Berkeley and then he is still somewhat cautious, though no doubt old enough not to care about misunderstandings of which by then he had had more than his desert.

mocked. This was too much to swallow from a University preacher. And in Berkeley's own time the difficulties had been heightened indeed. Just before *Alciphron* appeared, Tindal had produced, in 1730, *Christianity as Old as the Creation or the Gospel a Republication of the Religion of Nature:* Christianity so "reasonable" that its only distinctiveness was to support the themes of a "natural religion." Christianity might claim, as was urged some ten years later, to supply "free agents with new arguments";[22] it might claim to give new sanctions for old duties; but the resurrection was only an argument for immortality "from eyesight."[22] Can Berkeley do better justice to its traditional claims for distinctiveness?

For many pages *Alciphron* does not give us any reason to think he can. The earlier dialogues (apart from the Fourth we have noticed) seem merely to commend negatively and positively the Christian religion as no more than a "principle of happiness and virtue." It is true that enough water has flowed down the Liffey, not to say other rivers in West and East, to make this plea for interpenetration of morality and religion more impressive than it once was, though for some philosophers, and perhaps an increasing number of them, it barely conceals some crucial difficulties. But whatever view we take of the relations of morality and religion we shall certainly find no clues to the distinctiveness of Christianity here. Again, Berkeley's discussion of the Scriptures, while for his own day advanced, defends them against various attacks only at the cost of stressing their similarities to other ancient writers. As for miracles, they are admittedly inexplicable; and will never be the foundation of faith, though they may be its "object."[23] Where then is the distinctiveness of the Christian claim to be found? Here is the challenge par excellence. What is Berkeley's answer?

We come to the last of the seven dialogues in *Alciphron,* and we have not gone far in it before we find both the full measure of the problem, and Berkeley's important answer to the crucial question it embodies. The question and the answer alike concern "Grace."

Grace is the main point in the Christian dispensation . . . Christians are said to be heirs of grace, to receive grace, grow in grace, be strong in grace, to stand in grace, and to fall from grace. . . . Christianity is styled the covenant or dispensation of grace. And it is well-known that no point hath created more controversy in the Church than this doctrine of grace. What disputes about its nature, extent, and effects, about universal, efficacious, sufficient, preventing, irresistible grace, have employed the pens of Protestant as well as Popish divines,

22 A. A. Sykes, *Principles and Connection of Natural and Revealed Religion* (1740), 100, 249.

23 Berkeley was distinctive amongst eighteenth century writers in giving no apologetic significance to miracles. Undoubtedly, as Jessop remarks, this was partly because for Berkeley God's activity was to be discerned everywhere. But this only underlines Berkeley's real difficulty: granting God is everywhere active, how is he distinctively and specially active in miracles?

of Jansenists and Molinists, of Lutherans, Calvinists, and Arminians, as I have not the least curiosity to know, so I need not say . . ." (ALC 289 f.)

Thus Alciphron claims. But only because there is to be a plague on them all. For "what is the clear and distinct idea marked by the word grace?" (ALC 290) None. Christian doctrine is meaningless.

How does Berkeley deal with this problem? There is an important and significant omission from the Seventh Dialogue in the third edition of the *Alciphron.* Originally Berkeley's main answer to the problem, which he gave in §§ 5–7, was in effect that "grace" worked like a general abstract idea: "words become general by representing an indefinite number of particular ideas" (ALC 335)—that is a familiar story to which I have already made reference more than once. But sometimes no particular idea turns up. There is a blank, and "not finding particular ideas" (ALC 335) yet having no doubt some sort of "hunch" that there is a series of particulars round the corner, we suppose some "abstract general idea" even more curious than usual. So grace, while yielding a blank, might nevertheless have a sort of dispositional significance. Now, such an argument after three sections seems singularly negative and inadequate. Grace yields a blank; so sometimes do abstract ideas; yet this does not prevent them having some kind of factual reference to particular ideas—so grace may have the same. Small wonder that Berkeley omitted these sections from his third edition.[24]

For first, by itself, the argument would imply that "grace" might after all be given an adequate "public" analysis—a possibility which he has by implication rejected in § 4. Alciphron can gladly say "Grace taken in the vulgar sense, either for beauty, or favour, I can easily understand." (ALC 290) There is no difficulty here. Rather does the controversy concern grace "when it denotes an active, vital, ruling principle." (ALC 290) And this, in the earlier editions, is given but a brief and subordinate treatment. So the unfortunate impression might arise, developed over three sections, that "grace" was just like any abstract idea, and, especially remembering our remarks at the start, the need for a theology of notions (which is really Berkeley's novel and major point) might not be at all clear. Small wonder that Berkeley felt the original three paragraphs, with the emphasis their length gave, to be unsatisfactory and indeed compromising. So not surprisingly they are omitted from the third edition, and when the original argument is summarized at the beginning of the present § 5, its original sections are greatly abbreviated and somewhat significantly modified. True, the example of count-

[24] So here I differ somewhat from Professor Jessop, who remarks of the omission that it "seems to me to be an artistic improvement, for the three sections must have appeared to most readers to be an unnecessary digression." He concludes that the new paragraphs have "the advantage of not making an argument for *Christianity* rest wholly on Berkeley's own and ill-received philosophy." (ALC 291, note) If I am right, Berkeley was rather seeing the importance of his doctrine of notions for elucidating and defending the Christian concept of grace.

ing, when numbers may miss ideas, is taken to show that perhaps "grace" might in some similar way refer to particular ideas—although not "every time" does the word "grace" "excite the ideas" which it signifies. (ALC 291–292) But this point (while in its way important and, as far as it goes, necessary, to provide such idea-reference as theological language needs to have) soon disappears into the much more important one: that such an example of numbering suggests that "a discourse . . . that directs how to act" (ALC 292) may have an important significance even though the relation to ideas is problematical.

Here is Berkeley on old, firm, familiar ground at last. "Grace" is not logically like "number" but rather like "numbering." "Grace," being a construct from activity, involving activity, is notionally given. The word "grace," like "God," is significant though its distinctive reference extends beyond ideas. The "grace of God"—"God specially active"—as characterizing the objective constituent of a cosmic disclosure (and this time a cosmic disclosure that arises around the elements of the Christian dispensation, such as the passion and crucifixion of Jesus of Nazareth, or the Sacraments) shares with the self-disclosure of my activity the same odd logical status and empirical reference. Each phrase contains words that are "significant although they do not stand for ideas." (ALC 292) Each phrase characterizes such part of a disclosure as is not reducible altogether to idea-particulars. Berkeley might well have concluded that "grace," as a special characterization of "activity," will only be talked about in terms of ideas which exhibit even more logical impropriety than customarily belongs to talk about "activity" in any case—and though this is certainly to go well beyond Berkeley,[25] perhaps miracles are precisely those odd event-patterns which endeavor to do this. But such points we cannot develop now; we can only note that Berkeley consistently concludes with the view that Christian doctrines are associated with this *special* characterization of an active encounter with God, precisely as God's activity characterizes the world in general. Meanwhile, all this talk of God's activity has obviously some reference to particular ideas, but it always denotes more than these ideas; and so always denotes this "more" in some mysterious fashion. Christians may "be allowed to believe the divinity of our Saviour or that in Him God and man make one Person" precisely insofar as such "faith" becomes a "real principle of life and conduct" (ALC 298), which it does when the logic of faith is in part that of notions having performatory force. Creedal affirmations can only be made adequately in the context of Christian behavior. If it be true that "in him we live and move and have our being," it is also true, to use another of Berkeley's favorite texts, that "great is the mystery of godliness." (I Timothy 3:16)

In a final broadening of vision, let us reflect that Berkeley properly gives the same logical placings to "grace" and to "force"—both are constructs from

[25] See, for example, note 23.

"activity." For as we saw earlier, all genuinely significant words will no doubt not only refer to particular ideas, but also demand some reference to "activity," especially when we recall that relations involve an "act of the mind." (PHK § 142) Here is the possibility of *Siris,* though it be only an outline of a genuine "chain of reflexions," nevertheless a comprehensive view, taking us from tar water to the Trinity—with language having at all times some reference to disclosures—whether finite or cosmic—that at one and the same time offer themselves for, and yet ultimately elude, the philosopher's mapping. Here is the possibility and range of the empirical theism Berkeley sponsors, and here also is the original path towards it along which his doctrine of notions points—a path it might be worthwhile for others to trace.

III

The Origin of Berkeley's Paradoxes*

COLIN M. TURBAYNE

The Problem

"So many instruments . . . hid, as it were behind the scenes . . ."—(PHK § 64)

After all this time Berkeley's philosophy still astonishes by its oddness. Although gifted with an impressive lucidity of style, Berkeley could not avoid presenting his central assertions as paradoxes. In the Preface to the *Principles of Human Knowledge* he admits: "There are some passages that, taken by themselves, are very liable (nor could it be remedied) to gross misinterpretation, and to be charged with most absurd consequences." In the *Essay Towards a New Theory of Vision* he says that he finds it almost impossible to deliver the "naked and precise truth without great circumlocution, impropriety, and (to an unwary reader) seeming contradictions." (§ 120) Here, doubtless, are examples: "Collections of ideas constitute a stone, a tree, a book, and the like sensible things" (PHK § 1); "All those bodies which compose the mighty frame of the world, have not any subsistence without a mind" (PHK § 6); "When we do our utmost to conceive the existence of external bodies we are all the while only contemplating our own ideas" (PHK

* I am indebted to Professor John Stewart for valued discussions on some of the points in this paper.

§ 23); "The only thing whose existence we deny is that which philosophers call matter or material substance" (PHK § 35); "We eat and drink ideas and are clothed with ideas" (PHK § 38); "Strictly speaking, we do not see the same object that we feel" (DHP 245); "Different persons may perceive the same thing, or the same thing or idea [may] exist in different minds (DHP 247); "Distance or outness is [not] immediately of itself perceived by sight (PHK § 43).

Such paradoxes, of the same order as "The child is father of the man" and "No man born of woman can harm Macbeth," constitute part of Berkeley's strength, but also his weakness, for they lay him wide open to attack and easy conquest. In uttering them he commands attention, but he takes an enormous risk, for they generate in the literal-minded reader first, that "momentary amazement and irresolution and confusion"[1] that prompts him to ask and exclaim: "How could this be? The words are wild!"; then the denial of their literal truth; and finally, at times, an attack on Berkeley's sincerity. Indeed, Leibniz suspected "the man in Ireland" of seeking notoriety by his "paradoxes."[2]

It is often easy to force the literal meaning and hence the absurdity present in any paradox. At some times it is extremely difficult to discover the submerged meaning, especially for the literal-minded reader and the advocate of robust common sense. Fully aware of the presence of the paradoxes, Berkeley frequently implores his readers not to "stick in this or that phrase" but to collect his meaning from the whole "scope and tenor and connection" of his discourse. Thus, in the context of the whole play we may be able to collect the real meaning of the utterance that pleased the literal-minded Macbeth. In similar fashion we may be able to discern the real meanings of assertions such as "We eat and drink ideas" that so disturbed those other Scotsmen, Baxter, Beattie, and Reid, that they thought Berkeley meant that we eat and drink our own mental states.* But what is the explanation of the paradoxes? What was the mechanics of their production? How did Berkeley come to produce such notions "so far out of the common road"? The key to the solution of these problems is to be found, I believe, in Berkeley's sustained use of a powerful device, the language model.

We know that he uses this model to help him *illustrate* some of his views in optics in the *Essay Towards a New Theory of Vision* and a few of his views in metaphysics in the *Principles of Human Knowledge*. But does he use it to help him *work out* his theories in these subjects? If he does, then we have a plausible explanation of the origin of the paradoxes, for what is a

[1] David Hume, *An Inquiry Concerning Human Understanding* (London: 1748), sec. XII, part 1, note.

[2] *"Suspicor esse ex eo hominum genere qui per paradoxa cognosci volunt"*: letter to DesBosses, March 15, 1715, in *Opera Philosophica*, ed. J. E. Erdmann (Berlin: 1840), 726a.

* [For a discussion of Beattie's relation to Berkeley, see Chapter XIII.—Ed.]

tame and obvious truth in the language of the model often becomes odd or anomalous when translated into the language of the thing.

Accordingly, the hypothesis that I test here in part is that it was Berkeley's use of his language model, enabling him to discover and display, first, the structure of vision, and then the structure of reality, that issued in his paradoxes and gave to his whole system its astonishing originality as well as its appearance of oddness.

It would not be possible, however, in the space available to me to reveal the nature of the linguistic apparatus used in both the *Essay* and the *Principles.* My purpose here is to test the hypothesis in so far as it relates to vision and to show its relevance to Berkeley's metaphysical views.

The Model and the Theory of Vision

"For having now my method by the end still as I pull'd it came."—John Bunyan

How does Berkeley use his language model? I define "model" in terms of "metaphor." By "metaphor" I mean the presentation of facts belonging to one sort in the idioms appropriate to another, or the representation of the facts *as if* they belonged to one sort when they actually belong to another.[3] If a metaphor is extended and its features spelled out and applied, we have what I shall call a "model." The paradigm of this procedure is given by Plato in his *Republic.* Having decided that man is a state, Plato first builds his state by spelling out features that he needs, then deduces corresponding features in man, and finally submits these conclusions to independent testing and appraisal. Plato is here making use of one of two procedures, both of which were invented by the Greeks as the best ways of delivering science: the analytical or hypothetico-deductive method and the synthetical or axiomatic method. These names mark "the difference," in Aristotle's words, between "arguments *to* and those *from* the first principles," respectively (*Nicomachean Ethics* 1095a)[4] Plato himself, although he described both procedures, showed a preference for the former.

What is the role of the model? Is Plato using it as an aid in scientific discovery, or merely for didactic purposes? If we take his analytical account in the *Republic* at its face value, then this essay towards a new theory of man is a record of thinking undergone in making his discoveries: "As we are not remarkably clever," we look first at the model where our subject is "easier to make out," then we can go on to "look for" and, hopefully, discover

[3] My definition of "metaphor" is much the same as Gilbert Ryle's definition of "category-mistake" in his *The Concept of Mind* (London: 1949), 8, 16. This view of metaphor is developed in Colin Murray Turbayne, *The Myth of Metaphor* (New Haven: 1962), Chap. I, III.

[4] For an account of the methods of analysis and synthesis, see *The Myth of Metaphor,* Chap. II.

it in the thing (*Republic* 368). Time out of mind he exhibits his pattern of discovery by showing how the model offers new ideas to him. But we cannot forget that the *Republic* is a play written by a consummate playwright, perhaps long after its composition in his mind. In this case, Plato uses his model merely to expound his views, meanwhile, giving the appearance of reporting discoveries, because this is the best way of teaching. In the case of Plato, therefore, it is difficult to answer the question.

My definition of "model" is consistent with the well-known definition of "model" as merely another theory, an alternative interpretation of the calculus of the theory. The standpoint of the former is the analytical method, while that of the latter is the method of synthesis. Plato did not leave a version of the *Republic* presented in the style of Euclid's *Elements*. If he had done so, it would have contained few scholia dealing with political matters, for these would have been redundant. It is left to the curious student, however, to present the material of the *Republic* as two different theories, a theory of man and a theory of the state, in which the vocabularies of the two theories (except for some logically basic expressions that remain constant) are kept separate. In practice, however, the vocabulary of the model tends to rub off, as it were, onto the vocabulary of the thing.

Consonant with my hypothesis, Berkeley, right at the start of his career, already critical of the received solutions to the traditional problems of philosophy, was inspired with the idea that the phenomena of nature constitute a language. Having pulled out various features of the structure of language common to such languages as English, Greek, and Latin, which he knew well (a process aptly described by John Bunyan in the passage at the head of this section), he proceeded to look at the world, transformed, as it were, by the new spectacles he had just put on. Then he began to describe the nature of his new spectacles as well as the nature of the bright new world he could see through them. His descriptions were of four different types, of which the first two, A and B, are basic. Here are some examples drawn mainly from his accounts in optics, the science of vision:

A. *Language of the Theory*	B. *Language of the Model*
1. "The extension, figures, and motions perceived by sight are specifically distinct from the ideas of touch called by the same names, nor is there any such thing as one idea or kind of idea common to both senses." (NTV § 127)	1. "There is no similitude or resemblance betwixt words and the ideas that are marked by them." (*Draft* § 12)
2. "And to ask [a man blind from his birth at first sight] of the two bodies he saw placed on the table which was the sphere, which the cube,	2. (a) "A Chinese, upon first hearing the words 'man' and 'tree' would [not] think of the things signified by them." (ALC 155)

were to him a question downright bantering and unintelligible." (NTV § 135)

(b) "There must be . . . repeated acts to acquire a habit of knowing the connection between the signs and things signified; that is to say, of understanding the language." (ALC 155)

3. "It is evident that no idea which is not itself perceived can be the means of perceiving any other idea." (NTV § 10)

3. "When I [understand] your meaning by your words, must I not first hear the words themselves?" (ALC 151)

4. "The very same visible appearance [of the moon] as to faintness and all other respects, if placed on high, shall not suggest the same magnitude." (NTV § 73)

4. "A word pronounced with certain circumstances, or in a certain context with other words, has not always the same import and signification that it has when pronounced in some other circumstances or different context of words." (NTV § 73)

The examples of type A are four well-known items of Berkeley's theory of vision. 1 is the "main part and pillar" thereof (TVV § 41); 2 amounts to the answer "No" to the celebrated Molyneux problem;[5] 3 is a point of departure from geometrical optics; and the role of 4 in the solution of the Moon Illusion is obvious. Berkeley did not write a book on language. Nevertheless, the collection of statements of type B in his writings constitutes his account of syntax and semantics. That so many statements of this type appear is owing to his happy choice in models. If A1 is the "pillar" of his theory of vision, perhaps its analogue, B1, is the pillar of his theory of language. Strictly speaking, types A and B have two divisions, of which I have given examples of only one. There are statements of the current theories of vision and language, and statements of Berkeley's rival theories of vision and language. Thus, under type A it is to be understood that there appear such statements as: (a) 1. "We suppose an identity of nature, or one and the same object common to both senses" (TVV § 47); (a) 2. "The blind man here mentioned might know a square surface as soon as he saw it" (NTV § 133), that is, "Yes" to the Molyneux problem; (a) 3. [Brain events are] a means for the soul [by which we perceive objects] without in any way having to know (*connaitre*) or think of (*penser*) [the means]."[6] Similarly, under type B there should appear statements of a rival theory of language.

[5] The problem, sent by William Molyneux to his friend, John Locke, in 1693, was published by Locke in his *Essay Concerning Human Understanding* (2nd edition, 1694), II, ix, 8. For an account of its significance, see *The Myth of Metaphor,* 109–112, and George Berkeley, *Works on Vision,* edited with a commentary by Colin M. Turbayne (Indianapolis: 1963), xxix–xxxi.

[6] Descartes, *La Dioptrique,* appended to *Discours de la Méthode* (Paris: 1637), VI.

Although the vocabularies of the two different theories—those of his theory and of his model—are readily distinguishable, Berkeley usually conjoins them to make similes or comparisons, or combines or fuses them to make metaphors or identifications.

C. *Explicit Comparisons or Similes.* Berkeley frequently conjoins corresponding items of A and B, using conjunctions such as "just as," "as . . . so," and "in the same manner as," to produce, for example:

a. "The proper objects of sight . . . suggest . . . various qualities of tangible objects . . . just as words suggest the things signified by them." (ALC 154)

b. "I see . . . that rock only in the same sense that I may be said to hear it, when the word 'rock' is pronounced." (ALC 155)

D. *Metaphors.* Often he discards the device of explicit comparison in favor of metaphor. This involves making an utterance having the same reference as a statement of type A but with the difference that some of the type B vocabulary replaces that of type A:

a. "God speaks to man by outward sensible signs." (ALC 149)

b. ". . . understanding the language . . . of the eyes." (ALC 155)

c. "Men who do not think . . . confound in this language of vision the signs with the things signified." (ALC 156)

d. "We are not so apt to confound other signs with the things signified . . . as we are visible and tangible ideas." (NTV § 144)

e. "The characters of divinity are large and legible throughout the whole creation." (TVV § 7)

This device gives Berkeley the value of two sentences for the cost of one, as well as, in Dr. Johnson's words, "two ideas for one." Such economy, although it pays rich dividends, can also be expensive.

The Model and Discovery

> *"I began by dropping the picture theory of language and ended by adopting the language theory of pictures."*—Nelson Goodman[7]

Fortunately for the curious student who seeks to understand the relationship between Berkeley's language model and his theory of vision, there are available to him three accounts written in different styles and with different points of emphasis.

[7] "The Way the World Is," *Review of Metaphysics,* 14 (September 1960), 55 f.

Since the *Essay Towards a New Theory of Vision* is written in the analytical style as a work of scientific discovery using the hypothetico-deductive method described by Plato, Berkeley does not here present his theory. He offers an argument *towards* a conclusion, which he states near the end as follows:

We may fairly conclude that the proper objects of vision constitute a universal language of the Author of nature. (§ 147)[8]

Most of the assertions are type A assertions made in the language of the theory. More than a dozen paragraphs contain type C assertions or similes, but only in four paragraphs near the end does Berkeley abbreviate some of the similes to make actual identifications or metaphors of type D, mixing into his type A vocabulary such words as "sign," "thing signified," "language," "voice," "speaks," and "ambiguity" from type B.

As might have been expected, Berkeley's egregious *Essay* was poorly received in England. Twenty-three years later he produced his second account of vision in the fourth dialogue of *Alciphron* (1732). Here he refers to the reception of his earlier work: "The paradoxes of which theory, though at first received with great ridicule by those who think ridicule the test of truth, were many years after surprisingly confirmed by a case of a person made to see who had been blind from his birth." (ALC 161*n*) The case referred to is the experiment performed by Cheselden in 1728.[9] One of the "paradoxes" confirmed I have already stated (see A2 above). Perhaps because his theory had thus been "vindicated," Berkeley presents this second account with the utmost freedom and verve. Nowhere else does he reveal so much of the machinery of his thought about vision. That is to say, the whole account is richer than any other in the linguistic vocabulary of the model. But whereas in the *Essay* this vocabulary had been used largely to make similes, in this account it is used to make metaphors. That is, statements of type D are prevalent.

In his third and final account, the *Theory of Vision or Visual Language showing the immediate Presence and Providence of a Deity Vindicated and Explained* (1733), Berkeley for the first time presents his theory, that is, he offers it as a work in accordance with the axiomatic or synthetical method. "In the synthetical method of delivering science," he says, "we proceed in an inverted order, the conclusions in the analysis being assumed as principles in the synthesis." (TVV § 38) This work, then, unlike the *Essay*, is an argument *from* a principle:

[8] Fourth edition, 1732. In the first edition of 1709, the phrase "a universal language of the Author of nature" read "the universal language of nature."

[9] *Philosophical Transactions*, No. 402. See also Berkeley, *Theory of Vision* § 71, and M. von Senden, *Space and Sight* (New York: 1960; tr. Peter Heath from German edition of 1932), 224–235. See note 5.

I shall therefore now begin with that conclusion, that vision is the language of the Author of nature, from thence deducing theorems and solutions of phenomena. (TVV § 38)

By thus stating his principle Berkeley provides himself, right at the start, with his new vocabulary for vision. The reader expects that Berkeley, if he is using the language metaphor entirely as a didactic device, will now go on to present his theorems using the vocabulary of "sign," "signify," "thing signified," "ambiguity," and so on. But Berkeley does not do this. It is true that the vocabulary is used, but it is used sparingly, and largely at the start. The total number of metaphors and similes is far smaller than in the *Essay*. In general, the theorems are stated using the literal vocabulary of vision. It is as if Berkeley, while composing his system, has in front of him a page listing descriptions of language which he translates into descriptions of his subject, vision.

Now there is nothing in Plato's *Republic* that enables me to answer the question "Is Plato using his model of the state as an aid in discovery?" in the affirmative. The *Republic* is a play, and we, the audience, are merely to make believe that Socrates receives suggestions about the nature of man from the features he has fed into his model. Such make-believe is entirely consonant with the belief that Plato is using political institutions as valuable pedagogical illustrations.

Similarly, there is nothing in Berkeley's *Essay* alone that enables me to answer the corresponding question in the affirmative. But in Berkeley's case we have available not just one account but several accounts. Accordingly, in line with my hypothesis that he is using his language model to help him solve problems in vision, one would expect Berkeley to drop many of the linguistic illustrations of the *Essay on Vision* when he comes to present the *Theory of Vision:* certainly they would be redundant in the latter systematic presentation although not in the former presystematic or analytic account. In fact, as already noted, this is the case: nearly all the theorems in the *Theory* are stated in the technical language of vision. One would also expect an author who has made a discovery to leave undisclosed some of his apparatus or machinery. Specifically, in the *Essay* one would expect to find some important items of the theory unaccompanied by their linguistic analogues, and one would hope to find the latter elsewhere. That this expectation is also realized in the facts is noticed when we consider the type A and type B statements listed in the previous section. All the type A statements are taken from the *Essay* but only A4 occurs together with its linguistic analogue. For the remaining type B statements we must look elsewhere.

Consider, first, the argument of which A1 and A2 form a part. This is a central argument of the *Essay*. Although its conclusion forms the "pillar" of the theory of vision (TVV 41), Berkeley chooses not to illustrate it with corresponding features of his language model. The structure of the argument may be exhibited as follows:

1. $(x)(y)\{(Vx \cdot Ty) \rightarrow [(x = y) \rightarrow (Sxy \cdot \sim Exy)]\}$ (NTV § 133)

for which we find an equivalent rendering in the same section:

$(x)(y)\{(Vx \cdot Ty) \rightarrow [(x \neq y)(Sxy \cdot \sim Exy)]\}$ (NTV § 133)

2. $(x)(y)[(Vx \cdot Ty) \rightarrow \sim (Sxy \cdot \sim Exy)]$ (NTV § 135)

$\therefore$ 3. $(x)(y)[(Vx \cdot Ty) \rightarrow (x \neq y)]$ (NTV § 127)

On one interpretation of these symbols we get an argument in the vocabulary of the theory. Thus, interpreting "V" as visible extension, figure, or motion, and "T" as the corresponding tangible extension, and so forth; and reading "=" as "homogeneous with" or "qualitatively identical with," "≠" as "heterogeneous with" or "specifically distinct from," "S" as "suggests to a person," or "enables a person to recognize," and "E" as "repeatedly experienced with" or "associated with," we get an argument similar to Berkeley's. On another interpretation of the same symbols we get an argument in the vocabulary of the model which, in order to clarify Berkeley's meaning, I render first in my own words:

A. *The Argument of the Theory*

[1] "If [extension, etc., e.g.] a square surface perceived by touch be of the same sort with a square surface perceived by sight, it is certain the blind man here mentioned might know a square surface as soon as he saw it." (NTV § 133)
or:
"Either . . . visible extension and figures are specifically distinct from tangible extension and figures, or else the solution of the problem [of Molyneux] given by these two thoughtful and ingenious men [Locke and Molyneux] is wrong." (NTV § 133)

[2] "To ask [the man born blind and made to see] of the two bodies he saw placed on the table which was the sphere, which the cube, were to him a question downright bantering and unintelligible . . ." (NTV § 135)

B. *The Argument of the Model*

[1] [If the signs of a language were pictures of the things signified, then we could interpret them, that is, tell what they signified, although they had not been ostensively defined for us.] If there were "similitude or resemblance betwixt words and the ideas that are marked by them," then a foreigner to a language, for example, "a Chinese, upon first hearing the words 'man' and 'tree,' would think of the things signified by them . . . [without] time and experience, by repeated acts, to acquire a habit of knowing the connection." (*Draft* § 12 and ALC 155)

[2] [We cannot interpret the signs, that is, tell what they signify, unless they have been ostensively defined for us.] A foreigner to a language, e.g., "a Chinese, upon first hearing the words 'man' and 'tree' would [not] think of the things signified by them . . . There must be time and experience by repeated acts to acquire a habit of knowing the connection." (ALC 155)

[3] ∴ "The extension, figures and motions perceived by sight are specifically distinct from the ideas of touch, called by the same names." (NTV § 127)	[3] ∴ [The signs of a language are not pictures of the things signified.] "There is no similitude or resemblance betwixt words and the ideas that are marked by them." (*Draft* § 12)

The argument of type A in the *Essay* has as its second premise Berkeley's negative answer to the Molyneux problem and as its conclusion the heterogeneity of the objects of sight and touch. As one expects, the argument is transformed in the *Theory*. Since the latter is a deductive system, conclusion [3] now becomes a premise which, together with the inverse of [1] (obviously assumed by Berkeley) entails [2]. Thus in the *Theory* Berkeley's famous solution to the Molyneux problem is explained or proved on the basis of heterogeneity, rather than premised, as in the *Essay,* to establish heterogeneity. But in either case, if he were using his language model purely for didactic purposes, how much illumination he might have shed upon his arguments by presenting the parallel arguments of his language model! The argument of type B is not found in the *Essay* or the *Theory*. Its ingredients are found as an argument sequence only in *Alciphron*. The sequence is that of the *Theory:* [3] is premised as: "What I mean is not the sound of speech merely as such, but the arbitrary use of sensible signs, which have no similitude or necessary connection with the things signified" (ALC 149), which, together with the inverse of [1] (again assumed by Berkeley), entails [2] as a "consequence." (ALC 155) Although [3] is perhaps the chief lesson of Berkeley's writings on vision, and although it is stated frequently in the "material" mode, versions in the "formal" mode are rare. There are only abbreviations in the *Essay* and *Theory,* and these are extraneous to the argument I have been considering. I have used the version of the *Draft* because of its succinctness.

Similar remarks apply to the next pair of statements listed as A3, and B3 in the preceding section. Clearly these are parallels, as is shown when Berkeley's original "E" proposition, "No idea which is not itself perceived can be the means of perceiving any other idea," and its analogue are rendered in the same form. Their common structure may be exhibited as:

$$(x)\ [(Ix \cdot \sim Px) \rightarrow \sim (\exists y)\ (Iy \cdot x \neq y \cdot Sxy)]$$

or as:

$$(x)(y)[(Ix \cdot Iy \cdot x \neq y) \rightarrow (Sxy \rightarrow Px)].$$

On one interpretation of these symbols, reading "I" as "is an idea," "S" as "is a means of perceiving," and "P" as "is perceived," we get a statement of the theory of vision. When partially reinterpreted, reading "S" as "is a sign of" and "P" as "is heard," we get a statement in the terms of the model. However, the two interpretations may be represented in statements closely resembling Berkeley's own as follows:

[A3] If an idea is the means of perceiving another idea, then it must be perceived.

[B3] If it is by your words that I perceive [understand] your meaning, then I must first perceive [hear] your words themselves.

Although Berkeley omits [B3] from his major works, he includes it in *Alciphron* as an illustration of [A3]. In the *Essay* the latter is preceded by "It is evident that." But it is by no means immediately evident, as Berkeley claims, for Descartes and others hold a contrary view. Indeed, these rival views characterize Empiricism and Nativism in optics, and the acceptance of [A3] by his audience is of extreme importance to Berkeley. On the other hand, [B3] *is* immediately evident, and perhaps Berkeley has unconsciously shifted the self-evidence of [B3] to [A3]. If [B3] is a truism, its acceptance by Berkeley's audience as an obvious, though not an amazing, truth might reinforce the acceptance of [A3] as an extremely important, though far from obvious, truth. Yet Berkeley refrains from using such an aid in his major works.

It is clear that part of what Berkeley is claiming about language in [B3] is that if anything is actually functioning as a sign, that is, is being interpreted or understood, then it must be heard or otherwise directly perceived. He is claiming in this place not that language must have a sayer and a sayee, but that nothing is actually spoken or written unless it is heard or read. The stop sign is still at the bottom of the street and the books are in the study as before, but they are only bits of wood, cardboard, paper, paint, and ink unless they are noticed. If they are not noticed, they cannot be the signs or words of a language. In short, Berkeley is claiming here that the *esse* of signs is *percipi*. In the theory of vision only the phenomena of vision are signs, but in Berkeley's theory of reality, presented in the *Principles* and re-presented in his last book, all "the phenomena of nature, which . . . form a most coherent, entertaining, and instructive discourse," are signs (SIR § 254). Accordingly, since "all the choir of heaven and furniture of the earth, in a word, all those bodies which compose the might frame of the world" are nothing but the signs of a language, it becomes a truth "so near and obvious to the mind" of Berkeley that they have to be perceived. (PHK § 6)

Why does Berkeley refrain from using his model to illustrate these difficult and dark sayings? We know that he uses it in many clearer and easier cases, and we know that he possesses the linguistic apparatus needed for the elucidation of these particular items. The argument of the *Essay,* in which the solution of the Molyneux Problem is used to establish heterogeneity, is steeped in paradox. The premise and the conclusion are surely the most paradoxical statements in the whole account of vision. Yet how mild and obvious they become when translated into the language of the model! The paradoxes vanish. Similar remarks apply to the conversion of the amazing paradox of

Berkeley's philosophy, the *esse* of the world is *percipi,* into the tame truth that words must be heard or read. If the reader would be persuaded to accept these esoteric doctrines, surely he "would think it a godsend if someone pointed out that the same inscription was written up elsewhere on a bigger scale, so that he could first read the larger characters and then make out whether the smaller ones were the same." (*Republic* 368) Why, then does Berkeley not provide his audience with the larger characters as well as the smaller ones?

The facts do not fit well with the hypothesis that Berkeley is using his model primarily for teaching others. The more likely story is that he is using it primarily for teaching himself and only secondarily for teaching others. In other words, the primary role of his model is to offer him hints on how to extend his theory. While working out his ideas he has constantly before his mind, and probably before his eyes on paper, the ingredients of a theory of language. Whenever he encounters a difficult problem in vision or in metaphysics, he transforms it into a problem of language, and is often able to reach an astonishingly adequate solution. But here lies the danger. What had been an obvious truth about language frequently becomes, when translated back into the language of nature, a shocking paradox. At some times Berkeley chooses to exhibit his apparatus or machinery by presenting similes, but more often he leaves it hidden. Why exhibit all the linguistic apparatus when it has already done its job? A tailor does not leave all the tacks and the pattern in the finished suit.

IV

Berkeley and Skepticism

F. W. MCCONNELL

That we are living in an age of skepticism is no longer simply true. It is a truism. But the skeptic has always been with us and a significant contribution to thought was both Berkeley's exposure of the assumptions and logical structure of skepticism and his vigorous, cogent attack on this position.

In his day the skeptics and materialists were called the "free thinkers," and Berkeley also labeled them "minute philosophers" because they were so narrow in their outlook. Like many contemporary skeptics, they hailed freedom of thought but were slaves to antireligious prejudices, and "would hope to prevail by ridicule" when they could not do so by reason. (ALC 319) But there was no lack of erudition. They certainly "had read much and written much" even though they had "thought little." (ALC 323) Since many were vague even about their skepticism and materialism they were "considered enigmatical and profound." (ALC 320) Did they need be so vague? Hardly. "Thus much is certain: either there is or is not a God"; there is or is not immortality; consciousness is or is not physical. (ALC 322) One could at least expect commitment here.

Again, like many of his contemporary counterparts, the free thinker, Berkeley complained, lacked the courage of his convictions. Would he refuse to condemn the assassin of a great political leader as morally wrong or turn his back on patriotism? Hardly. In a cowardly sort of way he would still cling to his outmoded moral and religious scruples. "If such a man doth not see his true interests he wants sense: if he doth but dare not pursue it, he wants courage." (ALC 93) Nor would he have the courage to condone others who would take him seriously and apply his teaching to their practical life. "Can anything be more inconsistent than to condemn in practice what is approved in speculation? Truth is one and the same: it being impossible a thing be practically wrong and speculatively right." (ALC 74)

Like skeptics of the twentieth century, the minute philosophers labeled thinkers of an older generation as "oldfashioned writers." Yet, "instead of thought, books and study most free-thinkers are the proselytes of a drinking club." Even worse "their principles are often settled, and decisions on the deepest points made, when they are not fit to make a bargain." (ALC 96)

Making "great pretensions to thinking" but showing "little exactness in it" (ALC 324), the skeptic and materialist would display great courage in defending their cause, a cause, incidentally, quite popular since the Renaissance. Yet they were particularly silent about charity and political and social justice. (ALC 83–87) But why not? Was it not one of their spokesmen, Mandeville, who proclaimed that nature and uncontrolled impulses, left to themselves, would bring about a great society? Then, as now, many free thinkers were not only dogmatic but snobs "known only to the better sort and would sound strange and odd among the vulgar." (ALC 54)

Of course, for skeptics and materialists, religion and ethics are the results of "a confederacy between the prince and the priesthood to subdue the people." (ALC 209) Moral principles are simply a "state trick." If a free thinker had some inclination to defend a religious perspective, to keep status he would have to screen out any religious meaning in his interpretation of God. Even "Hobbes allowed a corporeal God: and Spinoza held the universe to be God. . . . I could wish indeed that the word *God* were quite omitted." (ALC 163)

But all was not black. At least some of the minute philosophers were so only in disguise, wishing to spread dissension in order to implant new truths. Like some communists of today the Jesuits of Berkeley's time were "pleased with the growth of infidelity . . . hoping it may make way for them." (ALC 110)

Since "vanity, disgust, humour, inclination . . . are often known to make infidels," whatever may be said for reason, they are not to be cured by it. (ALC 326) Nevertheless Berkeley engaged a lifetime in defending a Christian theism against skeptics and materialists, not of course to convert them, but to guide reasonable persons with an interest in Christian belief. The fact that his philosophy was inspired by a religious interest does not make it any less true than the thinking which discovered many of our antibiotics, inspired though it may have been by the motive of fattening hogs more economically. "Truth is the cry of all but the game of few." (SIR § 368)

Unable to accept the impossible belief that God created out of nothing a "corporeal substance which hath an absolute existence" Berkeley was convinced that the interpretation of nature as "the divine language" was superior to the more vulnerable teleological arguments. (DHP 256) Single-minded to the end in defending reason against skepticism he believed that irrationalism in religion was most dangerous. "Can anything be more dishonorable to religion than the representing it as an unreasonable, unnatural, ignorant institution? God is the Father of all lights, whether natural or revealed." (ALC 325) Nor was Berkeley ever apologetic in his defense of Christian theism. Thoroughly convinced that he had a neat and invulnerable philosophical system Berkeley declares:

> Sensible things do really exist: and if they really exist, they are necessarily perceived by an infinite mind: therefore there is an infinite mind, or God. (DHP 212)

Since an infinite mind is necessarily inferred from the bare existence of the sensible world one "may now, without any laborious search into the sciences, without any subtlety of reason, or tedious length of discourse, oppose and baffle the most strenuous advocate for atheism." (DHP 213)

Nor could Berkeley be satisfied with any "peace by appeasement" between religion and science. God must be shown to be active in the world and what could be more revealing of God's activity than our very sensations that God discloses to us? Theism must compete with materialism as a "world hypothesis."

Since a theist must be concerned with truth, Berkeley was compelled to wage an attack on all forms of skepticism, and it is with this attack that this paper is concerned. The skeptic is either responsible, being supported by reasons, or arbitrary. It was with the former type that Berkeley was primarily concerned—the skeptic who realized the inconsistency and foolishness of denying any reliable knowledge, but who believed he could rationally deny certain types of knowledge for good reasons. The following are the types of skepticism in which Berkeley was mainly interested:

The Belief That Sensations and Logic Are Relative to Human Beings and Incapable of Describing All Possible Worlds

This reasoning tacitly assumes that real things are external and antithetical to both our senses and thought, and this of course is what Berkeley challenges. Has the skeptic shown that the object is anything more than a sensation or a group of sensations, which by definition exist in and for a mind? How can the skeptic assume an external relation to thought when all thinking, including that of the skeptic, presupposes the trustworthiness of reason? What is implied in Berkeley's challenge is the fact that if the relation between thought and reality were capricious there would be no confidence in the power of reason to disclose the true nature of things. If the skeptic were to defend the disparity between thought and nature he would have to assume the harmony between his thinking and the supposed real state of affairs, which in his case is just the disparity of thought and nature. In short, to defend his belief the skeptic must assume what he denies, and if he refuses to defend it he indulges in a bit of intellectual promiscuity.[1]

To continue with what is implied in Berkeley's reasoning: If the skeptic assumes that our truth is not valid for other orders of being he must make at least three assumptions: (1) that these hypothetical beings exist, (2) that their truth contradicts ours, and (3) in case of contradiction, they are right and we are wrong.[2] The skeptic who raves against "truthing" ought to consider what is involved in the assumption that there are objects external and unrelated to thought. Deny the law of identity and no one could meaningfully refer to these hypothetical beings and objects, for they would be simultaneously nonhypothetical beings and nonobjects.

The Belief That There Are Equally "True" Ways of Describing Things, None of Which Is to Be Necessarily Preferred

While this belief is implicit as well as explicit in many skeptical outcries and is passed off with a great air of profundity, is it skepticsm? Hardly, at least not in this form. Nature, like love, has many faces and as long as our descriptions harbor no contradictions and are equally comprehensive one's choice would depend upon his purposes. The fact that the universe has many characteristics is no more a support of skepticism than is the fact that persons display many qualities an argument against the science of psychology. What does cause skepticism, Berkeley believes, is the attempt to reduce secondary sense qualities to primary ones and make these existentially and causally supreme. Such an attempted reduction of the universe of color, smell, sound, and touch to the colorless, insipid one of mass in motion rests either on the dogma of "substance" or on a bias in favor of the priority of some corporeal stuff.

Certainly, for Berkeley, the universe may have many characteristics, described equally well by different disciplines. He would not deny that with different senses we would see different things and that the same thing could be described differently from a broader perspective. What he does deny is (1) that we would see things which would contradict what we do see and (2) that either the senses or thought can have an extra-mental existence. (DHP 238–240)

The belief that the universe may have varied characteristics described by

[1] See DHP 173, and ALC 129–130, 141–143, and 170–173.

[2] For a treatment of this see B. P. Bowne, *Studies in Theism* (New York: 1879), 9–61.

different intellectual systems becomes skeptical—or better, nihilistic—when one affirms either that (1) two contradictory systems can both be true or (2) the law of identity is relative to us. Both assertions contradict themselves. The first presupposes the noncontradicted truth of that system from which such a ridiculous statement would follow, and the second presupposes the nonrelative truth of the law of identity for its own truth. That responsible persons really come dangerously close to the first of the above positions, I quote from a molecular biologist:

> Again, neither the scientific nor the religious interpretation is the truer. If the theologian argues that everything was made by God . . . then the scientist will argue back that chance chemical reactions created men with brains, including those theological brains which can conceive of a God who made everything. The impasse is permanent and within their own systems of communications the scientist and theologian are equally right.[3]

He seems to forget that chance chemical reactions also produced his own brain which is supposed to be doing some really true thinking in describing the real state of affairs of the impasse between science and philosophy. What chance chemical reactions produce right thinking brains? In short, is philosophy everyone's business?

The second form of skepticism may be found in articles by E. Nagel and T. Lavine.[4]

Berkeley knew that philosophy emerges when contradictions arise between different systems and spent his lifetime defending the truth of a rational theism as against an opposing mechanistic interpretation. Modern philosophy itself has been primarily engaged in the attempt to resolve the contradictions that emerge between the presuppositions and developments of the physical sciences on the one hand and the religious and moral interests on the other.

The Belief in Hidden Entities or Forces That "Explain" the Object

We often hear scientists and laymen alike saying that we do not really know what electricity is. What does this mean? Do they believe that some discovery of a hidden mechanism would give us illumination? Would such knowledge solve the mystery? Hardly. If not, what possible kind of knowledge would? Are we not seeking a kind of certainty which comes with self-consciousness and can never be gained elsewhere? What Berkeley contends is that the only

[3] Paul B. Weisz, *The Science of Biology* (New York: 1963), 15.

[4] See E. Nagel, "Logic without Ontology" in Y. H. Krikorian, *Naturalism and the Human Spirit* (New York: 1944), 210–242, and Thelma Lavine, "Naturalism and the Sociological Analysis of Knowledge," *ibid.,* 183–210.

possible understanding of phenomena such as electricity and other natural phenomena is simply more of the same type we already have—an increased knowledge of their effects, that is, their actual or inferred sensations, and how these are related to other phenomena (sensations). There is mystery enough in life without having to add more by appealing to hidden entities. With the belief in hidden "entities" comes the attempt to "save the appearances" but this is a losing game, for the "thing in itself" forever eludes us. With regard to such "entities" Berkeley had in mind particularly "substance." A substantialist must argue that either the physical object has the sense qualities we perceive or it has not. If it has these qualities, Berkeley believes, its function has been destroyed. For substance was to serve as a unity or a support of sense qualities. To attribute to it the multiplicity of perceived qualities is to restate the problem that the hypothesis of substance is supposed to solve. Yet if substance lacks these qualities, he maintains, we are dealing with an unknowable. How can something correspond to red and not be red? What job can "substance" do that sense cannot perform better? In short, does a rose have to be anything more than the plain man takes it to be—colored, fragrant, figured, and the like. One would starve eating the "real" bread of the realist, which is without color, taste, odor, and all of those other qualities we attribute to it. (DHP 229) Berkeley, of course, is criticizing the view which would reduce nature with its sensuous variety to that "night view" of matter in motion, which leaves it quite destitute of anything really worth appreciating.

With regard to hidden "forces," these are quite demobilized in Berkeley's *De Motu*. We neither perceive such forces nor can we intelligibly infer them from what we do perceive. What we perceive in the explosion of an atomic bomb, for example, are the sensations of heat, light, movement, and the like. These sensations will do anything the hidden "forces" will do in destroying the human race. Of course there is something behind the sensations insofar as they are included in the context of consciousness, whether that of the finite or the Ultimate Mind. The sensations we generally associate with things are caused by God while the more confused disorderly ones, as in a dream, are caused by us. (DHP 236–245)

The above analysis must not be taken to mean that Berkeley totally discounts the categories of causality and substance. Since both economy and evidence demand that we go no further than sense in interpreting objects, the only type of causality remaining would be volitional, which Berkeley believed we actually experience. Whether we really experience it is not the issue here, but rather the fact that Berkeley did insist upon some type of causality. Ultimately causality is attributed to God's will and relatively it is attributed to the will of sentient organisms.

No doubt there is real difficulty when one attempts to square Berkeley's concept of volitional causality with his belief that there is no necessary connection in things. Literally this would mean that there is no necessary relation between my willing to write this article and the actual writing of it, which is absurd. What he probably meant by his ridicule of necessary connection was that consequents are not logically entailed in antecedents. But there are other types of necessary connections than the purely logical ones, such as whole–part and means–ends relationships, which he did recognize.

What Berkeley does with regard to substance is simply to re-define it in terms of a unitary, self-identical agent rather than some vague support or stuff. The category of personality became for him the real meaning of substance as well as the key to his whole philosophy. In shifting the emphasis from the subject–predicate to the whole–part conception, from the abstract to the concrete universal, he anticipated Hegel.

His fear of the subject–predicate description of things was caused by the attempt of materialists to convert classes, such as substance, matter, and force, into physical realities. That the subject–predicate description had its linguistic and classificatory values, Berkeley, in spite of his nominalistic leanings, would readily grant.

The Illusiveness of the Senses: the Copy Theory of Knowledge

The belief that perceptions are copies of the "real" object is a persistent source, Berkeley believes, of our distrust of our senses. If they are copies, how do we ever know that they are truly copying the "real" thing? What are they supposed to copy? Hidden "forces," "substance," "matter"?[5]

Berkeley believed that he alone truly championed the cause of common sense, by attributing to the object those very sense qualities which "the plain man" believed belonged to it. He was a true spokesman of "ordinary language," or better, ordinary men. After all, the "plain man" would rather eat a piece of sensible bread than "ten thousand" pieces of the "real" or "material" bread of the scholastic or physical realist. (DHP 229)

It may be objected that he goes beyond naive realism both in his refusal to attribute substance or thinghood to objects and in his belief that nature has no existence apart from an ultimate mind. With regard to the first point, he does not deny substance if understood to mean a coherent unity of sensations within the context of a self-identical, unified consciousness, human or divine.[6] He denies only the "unintelligible" kind of the physical realist.

As to the plain man finding Berkeley's mentalism objectionable, is not Berkeley's metaphysics the logical conclusion of common sense? When digging around the roots of the "common" man's thinking do we not perceive that the real object is regarded as that which is socially verified and consistently and coherently thought about? Neither of these involve an extra-mental existence.

[5] See DHP 199–208, 227–230, 246–248.
[6] See PHK §§ 24, 26, and 27.

Nor can it be objected that his view cannot account for error. What is error on any theory but an acquiescence in incoherent, inconsistent objects (sensa)? To prove his point Berkeley resorts to that perennial source of philosophical as well as psychological insight—the dream.

> But the ideas perceived by sense, that is, real things, are more vivid and clear . . . and have not a like dependence upon our will. There is therefore no danger of confounding these with the foregoing: and there is as little of confounding them with the visions of a dream, which are dim, irregular, and confused. And though they should happen to be never so lively and natural, yet by their not being connected, and of a piece with the preceding and subsequent transactions of our lives, they might easily be distinguished from realities. In short, by whatever method you distinguish *things* from *chimeras* on your scheme, the same, it is evident, will hold also upon mine. (DHP 235)

Can we trust our senses? Of course. When we observe order among our senses we infer mind, human or divine. We have, Berkeley believes, as much right to infer a Supreme Mind from the visual signs of nature as we do to infer human minds from the auditory signs of the spoken word. Yet people are unreasonable.

> Hence, a common man, who is not used to think and make reflections, would probably be more convinced of the being of a God by one single sentence heard once in his life from the sky than by all the experience he has had of this Visual Language, contrived with such exquisite skill, so constantly addressed to his eyes, and so plainly declaring the nearness, wisdom and providence of Him with whom we have to do. (ALC 161)

The Belief in Materialism and Mechanism

Why did Berkeley regard materialism as a form of skepticism? For one thing it harbors a belief in occult entities neither sensed nor rationally inferred.[7] In addition, it destroys our trust in the secondary sense qualities because they are derivative and therefore less real than the primary ones. The materialist "will have them to be empty appearances, I real beings. In short, you [the materialist] do not trust your senses, I do." (DHP 245) Materialists also proclaim that things produce thoughts. Consequently thinking becomes mechanical and no one could know whether he had been physically conditioned to think truly. Not only skepticism but fatalism would follow.

Significant is Berkeley's clear comprehension of the logic of materialism. He recognized the merger of the scholastic belief in substance and the new theory of matter in motion. Substance, which for the scholastic was a kind of a unitary ground of things, was converted by Berkeley's materialist contemporaries into a material stuff to the degree that Berkeley could use the terms substance and matter interchangeably.

7 See DHP 243–248.

Combining matter with other class terms, such as force, motion, space, and time, Berkeley found the materialists well armed with a set of abstractions that were to "explain" everything. But "explain" in what sense? Then, as now, materialists parted company. Some would literally reduce the secondary qualities, and of course consciousness itself, to the primary ones of matter and motion and their derivatives, which alone were the stuff of the universe. Others would make the former causally dependent on the latter.

The logic of materialism never seems to change. Berkeley's attack assumes subtle forms and it is the source of most of the later arguments directed against materialistic philosophies. I will deal with what I regard as important arguments not only explicitly stated by Berkeley but implied in his whole philosophy.

A. Substance and absolute space, time, and motion. Berkeley's argument against substance has already been discussed. What is it but a class term and how can class terms exist in anything but the mind of their conceiver?[8] No one perceives space and time any more than he eats fruit. He perceives spaces and times just as he eats particular apples and pears. (De Motu §§ 5–7, 23, 24, 26) What would motion be apart from moving objects (sensa), or space apart from colors and the tactile sensations? As there can be no motion, space, and time in general, there can exist no absolute motion, space, and time, and the treatment of these abstractions as things Berkeley regards as one of the pernicious aberrations of philosophy.[9]

B. The reduction of nature to mass in motion: the secondary identified with the primary qualities. The primary qualities, Berkeley claims, are not only impossible without the secondary, but are no less sense qualities than the secondary ones. Berkeley's belief that the primary qualities which are identified with matter, such as figure, extension, and motion, are no less sense qualities than the secondary, can easily be tested in the classroom. Ask a schoolboy what the real shape of a penny is. Realizing that its shape depends upon the position of the perceiver, he will reply that it depends upon how you look at it. Exactly, Berkeley would retort. Its shape depends upon the observer and to talk about "real" shapes is as meaningless as to talk about "real" apples. No one was ever nourished by "real" apples nor was he ever intellectually edified by believing in such entities.

Equally important is his contention that it is meaningless to call a color or sound a motion. If matter is motion then "real sounds may possibly be *seen* or *felt,* but never *heard,*" as motion belongs to sight and touch. (DHP 182)

If secondary qualities cannot be considered rearrangements of the primary ones, even less can other conscious events be considered such. "It seems

[8] See DHP 192–193; DeMotu §§ 47–49, 63, 66; SIR §§ 269–272.
[9] DeMotu §§ 52–53, 55, 58; SIR §§ 269–272.

plain that motion and thought are two things as really and as manifestly distinct as a triangle and a sound." (ALC 311)

Berkeley, a persistent foe of converting classes into things, believed that classifications are apt to play tricks on us and it was this as much as anything that was behind his nominalism. But his fear is justified. Simply that both color and motion can be classified as objective referents does not mean that color is a kind of a motion any more than the fact that hogs and cows can be classified as animals means that a hog is a kind of cow. This type of reduction is out of the question. Red is not blue, thoughts are not things. The only kind of reduction possible is one in which diverse qualities are considered aspects of a more fundamental thing. Yet, strangely enough, more recent physiological psychologists do identify consciousness with physiological processes. If the physicists or chemists will not permit a violet light wave to be colored, or a sound wave to be loud, or an apple to be sweet, why is the physiological materialist permitted to call a physical process thoughtful or emotional or witty?

But one wonders whether, instead of reducing mind to matter, the materialist has really spiritualized matter by endowing it with conscious qualities. What the matter of the physicist and chemist cannot do the matter of the physiological materialist can well do. A brain that does quite a bit along the mental and emotional lines is no longer the brain assumed by the molecular biologist.[10] The materialist's brain smacks of animism—or better, panpsychism. Was it not a founding father of scientific method who complained about the lingering "spirits" in nature?

The closer we get to physical conceptions the more obvious becomes the impossibility of reaching the conscious life. Of course, if physical processes are endowed with sentience it takes little ingenuity to get such processes to account for consciousness. The pioneers of the physical sciences purged physical nature of mind and the secondary qualities but the champions of contemporary behaviorism, suffering from the excesses of their materialism, would re-spiritualize it. Would that they be more moderate and spare science the embarrassments of hylozoism.

What these behaviorists would do to matter Berkeley would regard as unthinkable. Matter for him is the organization of lifeless, mindless, inert sensations. The only active principle Berkeley considered was the will of God, and to a lesser degree, the will of man and perhaps other sentient beings. The fact that these sensa were always within the context of some consciousness does not make them animated. Berkeley internalizes the dualism between the mind and the object, a feat accomplished later by the German idealists, particularly Hegel.

Why has reductionism been so commonly held? Why have mass, motion, extension, and the like been regarded as ontologically ultimate and consciousness as something either less real or a form of mass in motion itself? Most of us

10 Cf. B. P. Bowne, *Metaphysics* (New York: Revised, 1898), 301–314.

believe that nature existed prior to finite sentient beings. But this proves nothing unless it is shown that physical nature, that is, the coherent body of sensations, could exist prior to consciousness in general, that is, a conscious ground or ultimate mind. And this proof is not forthcoming. Why then the existential priority of the primary qualities? Berkeley suggests that pain and pleasure are not so closely attached to the primary qualities of extension, figure and motion, as they are to heat and cold, tastes and smells. But, as he shows, this would not make them the less sensory. (DHP 191 f.) He also believed with Descartes that sight is basic to science because it reveals "clear, distinct, various, agreeable, and comprehensive" sensations. (ALC 306) Implicit in Berkeley's statement are other reasons. Motion and extension are more universal than the qualities of touch, color, and scent, which may vary according to conditions. And, in addition, the primary qualities are measurable. Gravitation was known before Newton but the discovery of its quantitative law was what gave it significance.

Berkeley's point is simply this: The fact that heat and color and the other secondary qualities have their "mechanical equivalents" is no more a reduction of these to length, time, mass, motion (and change) than does the fact that convicts can be numbered imply a reduction of convicts to number. As F. R. Tennant humorously suggests, primary qualities for dogs would be those of smell and for eels they would be electrical sensations. Could they but scientifically reflect, they would have respectively an olfactory and electrical theory of matter. For a supersonic being, length would be determined by notes and the violin would become a calculating machine.[11]

The practical and scientific utility of the quantitative aspects of life make it difficult to believe not only in the higher qualities but in the things unseen. (SIR § 330)

C. The causal primacy of matter. The belief in the causal primacy of matter vanishes when matter is reduced to sense qualities that for their very meaning must exist in the broader context of consciousness. Berkeley's argument is convincing against any realism which would involve the belief that nature could exist apart from consciousness in general, that is, an ultimate mind (God).

But can God exist apart from nature? Berkeley has not established the causal primacy of God's will either. At best he has shown the coexistence of will and sensa, energy and matter, within the context of the eternal consciousness, and in this scheme God's will could be determined as much by the "brute facts" of sensations as these could be determined by his will. In fact it is conceivable, though not too believable, that we could have in God's personality a kind of psychological determinism, the general consequences of which would lead to a theological determinism. In studying Berkeley we are never quite sure as to the status of sensa. Sometimes God's will is

[11] F. R. Tennant, *Philosophical Theology,* Vol. I (London: 1935), 359.

limited simply to stabilizing and organizing these. At other times he seems to imply that they are creations of God's will. In fact we are never certain whether they are eternal data within the consciousness of God or whether they are simply caused in our minds by the divine will. A solution here is crucial to an understanding of the degree of causal priority we apportion to the power of God.

Berkeley utilized other arguments of varying weight against the materialist belief in the causal priority of matter. If conscious phenomena are determined by physical behavior how could one be free enough to judge impartially the truth of the materialists' contention? Everyone must see "the ridicule of proving man no agent, and yet pleading for free thought and action, of setting up at once for advocates of liberty and necessity." (ALC 316 f.)

Again, how can you get the effect out of the cause if it is not implicitly contained in the cause in the first place?

> [How] can that which is *unthinking* be a *cause* of thought? You may indeed if you please, annex to the word *matter* a contrary meaning to what is vulgarly received; and tell me you understand by it, an unextended, thinking, active being, which is the cause of our ideas. But what else is this, than to play with words, and run into that very fault you just now condemned with so much reason? I do by no means find fault with your reasoning, in that you collect a cause from the phenomena: but I deny that the cause deducible by reason can properly be termed *matter*. (DHP 216)

This, a later thinker, Borden P. Bowne, who thought of himself as a "Kantianized Berkeleian," believes to be the real "failure of impersonalism."[12] Either the cause must provide for the effect or not. If it does then we no longer have simply matter but a matter pregnant with the potentiality of mind. Is it any wonder that a matter with a mind potential could develop a mind that is actual? On the other hand, if the cause does not provide for the effect how is it to be accounted for? We would then have a groundless becoming. The belief that something cannot come from nothing is a deep-seated conviction implicit not only in the principles of sufficient reason and conservation, but ultimately, I believe, in our conviction that no fact can be understood apart from the whole.

Berkeley criticized the belief in the causal primacy of matter also on the grounds that it is unempirical. No one has ever perceived a cause.[13] He perceives sensations, the ground or cause of which, depending upon how one interprets Berkeley, is the ultimate consciousness on which all sense phenomena depend. Sensations certainly follow sensations but is it not odd to say, for example, that a sensation of touch causes a sensation of vision? Could solidity cause figure, or a color? Could a motion cause a mind when it is nothing but a sensation of mind, that of both God and human beings?

If physical causes cannot be perceived can they be coherently inferred?

[12] See his *Personalism* (Norwood: 1908), 217–268.
[13] DeMotu §§ 41, 43, 55–56; DHP 222–223.

Just what would these forces be that no one ever sensed? Perhaps just forces. But this is a word denoting nothing in particular. The only nonperceived force or power we know anything about is that of will, not occult physical forces of mechanisms.

Berkeley introduced a final argument at great risk of consistency. Matter cannot cause mind and its secondary qualities because, anticipating Hume, there is no necessary connection between antecedents and consequents. But is this really an argument against the "causal efficacy" of matter? The important question concerns the temporal sequence. If a headache always follows a blow on the head, do I care that technically the blow was not a "metaphysical" agent? The headache is not eased by telling me that there is no necessary connection, logical or otherwise, between the two events. Now, if the materialist can show that all psychic events follow physical antecedents, he has won a practical victory—if not, technically, a philosophical one. The physiological determinist could still adopt a Berkeleian interpretation and the shift would be one from a materialistic determinism to a theological one. But it seems impossible experimentally to prove physiological determinism true, for the simple reason that experimentally it could never be proved false. Any experimental evidence gained could be interpreted to mean that a physical event always precedes, and in this sense, determines, a conscious event, just as a religious believer could always interpret a physical event, no matter how detrimental, as a providential one.[14] Neither the religious hypothesis of providence nor the materialist belief in physiological determinism is a scientific hypothesis for the same reason—they cannot experimentally be proved false.

What is more, as A. E. Taylor points out, the fact that later stages may be deduced from earlier stages of the physiological process without considering its mental complements is no justification for the materialist to go on and argue that these processes would be what they are without their psychological accompaniments. And, as Taylor goes on to say:

> Either our Physiology must remain rigidly faithful to the fundamental postulates of mechanical science, or not. If it is faithful to them, its descriptions of human action must rigidly exclude all reference to teleological determination by reference to conceived and desired ends. *I.e.* we must treat human conduct as if it were fatally determined apart from any possible influence of human choice and intention, and thus stultify that whole work of historical and ethical appreciation . . . the *raison d'être* of Psychology as a science.[15]

D. Physiological determinism. Physiological determinism as a special form of materialism has already engaged our attention. Although Berkeley's belief

[14] Cf. M. Cohen and E. Nagel, *Logic and Scientific Method* (New York: 1934). "Thus the theory that whatever happens is the work of Providence . . . is not verified, if after the 'happening' we can interpret the event as the work of Providence . . .", 211–212.

[15] A. E. Taylor, *Elements of Metaphysics* (New York: Seventh Edition, 1961), 320.

that there is no necessary connection (probably in the sense of logical entailment) was not a good argument against physiological determinism, he used others that were much better.

He emphasized the fact that persons experience freedom and the importance of freedom in the life of the spirit—that is, the life of religion, morality, and art.[16] In spite of the fact that such an experience or feeling could be physically determined, the argument carries some practical weight. Better is Berkeley's contention that the materialist begs the question because he conceives mind in physical terms and makes it a resultant of so many pushes and pulls. Even the more subtle type of psychological determinism assumes the physical analogy in supposing that the personality is the end product of so many competing psychological forces, motives, with the strongest winning out, as though the personality as a whole had nothing to do with either the directions or the intensities of these motives.

> Your arguments proceed upon an erroneous supposition, either of the soul's being corporeal, or of abstract ideas . . . You might as well suppose that the soul is red or blue as it is solid. You might as well make the will anything else as motion. . . . You distinguish in all human actions between the last decree of the judgment and the act of the will. You confound certainty with necessity. You inquire, and your inquiry amounts to an absurd question—whether man can will as he wills? (ALC 317)

Berkeley's argument has been developed by Stout and Ward.

Perhaps more interesting is the question of how physiological determinism would be conceived if Berkeley's metaphysics were true. Then the brain, along with everything else regarded as belonging to the physical world, would become sensations in the mind of God or sensations produced by God, depending on how Berkeley is interpreted, and physical determinism would assume the form of a theological fatalism. But Berkeley is not willing to yield this much. With his interpretation of nature Berkeley believed that physiological determinism would be ridiculous.

> Now, I would fain know whether you think it reasonable to suppose, that one idea or thing existing in the mind, occasions all other ideas. And if you think so, pray, how do you account for the origin of that primary idea or brain itself? . . . When therefore you say, all ideas are occasioned by impressions in the brain do you conceive this brain or no? If you do, then you talk of ideas imprinted in an idea, causing that same idea, which is absurd. If you do not conceive it, you talk unintelligibly, instead of forming a reasonable hypothesis. (DHP 209)

Such reasoning is the germ of an argument exploited by Stout and Bowne: since secondary qualities and mind have been taken out of the physical realm, how can the physical system cause them? They are irrelevant to the system, physically unreal. If the physical scientist is unable, on his own principles, to say that matter causes heat, sound, or color, since these have been relegated

16 See ALC 313–318.

to the less real existence of minds, how can he say that the physical processes cause these minds? True, a vibrating instrument produces a vibrating nerve, but a vibrating nerve is a motion and not a sound. The same reasoning applies to color. Matter as the movable explains only motion and aggregation. As long as we remain on the physical level nothing more is possible.[17]

E. The atomic theory. I include a brief discussion of the atomic hypothesis because many regard it a special form of materialism and particularly incompatible with Berkeley's philosophy. Whether the atomic theory is materialism depends upon one's interpertation of it in light of a world view. What concerns us is the fact that it could easily be made to square with Berkeley's metaphysics. Even if the universe were someone's dream a scientific description of the uniformities of the proportional and sequential relationships of the dreamed objects, plus whatever theories would be contrived to represent these, or even "explain" them for that matter, would be possible. All that would be necessary would be some order and coherence among the objects dreamed, animate or inanimate.

On Berkeley's system the belief in atoms, or better, fundamental particles, presents no problem. If these particles "in principle" can be sensed then they have the same ontological status as a chair or table. They are sensa and "to be is to be perceived," that is, in the mind of God. If they cannot be sensed what are they? Physics, as the logical positivists have rightly observed, deals with actual or possible sensations. All else is metaphysics, good or bad. If these elements cannot be sensed, not because a technical difficulty, permanent or temporary, such as the grossness of our sense mechanisms, prevents it, but because a logical inconsistency makes such perception inconceivable, then we are dealing with the nonphysical forces. The only nonphysical force we know is that of will.

If these particles are interpreted exclusively in terms of energy, then of course we are dealing with actual or possible sensations. Do we need to go beyond the primary and secondary sensations in describing the atom bomb? Only, Berkeley believed, to the extent that these sensations must have their ground within the context of the consciousness of the Ultimate Perceiver.

In conclusion let me say that Berkeley believed his metaphysics would be an asset rather than a liability to science. He persistently argued that materialism is detrimental not only to the cause of religion, morality, and art, but to the cause of science as well.

> In natural philosophy, what intricacies, what obscurities, what contradictions hath the belief of matter led men into! To say nothing of the numberless disputes about its extent, continuity, homogeneity, gravity, divisibility, etc., do they not pretend to explain all things by bodies operating on bodies, according to the laws

[17] See G. F. Stout, *Mind and Matter* (New York: 1931), 128; and James Ward, *Naturalism and Agnosticism,* Vol. II (London: 1903), 97–128, 160–202.

of motion? and yet, are they able to comprehend how one body should move another? . . . Have they accounted by physical principles for the aptitude and contrivance, even of the most inconsiderable parts of the universe? But laying aside matter and corporeal causes, and admitting only the efficiency of an all-perfect mind, are not all the effects of Nature easy and intelligible? If the phenomena are nothing else but *ideas;* God is a *spirit,* but matter an unintelligent, unperceiving being. If they demonstrate an unlimited power in their cause; God is active and omnipotent, but matter an inert mass. If the order, regularity, and usefulness of them can never be sufficiently admired; God is infinitely wise and provident, but matter destitute of all contrivance and design. These surely are great advantages in *physics.* (DHP 257 f.)

V

Berkeley's View of Spirit

I. C. TIPTON

"Berkeley's observations about 'spirits' have received, perhaps, more attention than they deserve; for the fact is that he had formed hardly any views at all on problems about the mind and its doings."[1] So says Mr. Warnock in his book on the philosophy of George Berkeley. He shows that he means what he says by himself devoting no more than two pages to outlining and criticizing what Berkeley has to say about spirit and our knowledge of it. So in this paper we shall not so much be criticizing what Mr. Warnock has to say—he has given his reason for saying very little—but rather the assumption that lies behind his cursory treatment of this aspect of Berkeley's philosophy.

The assumption is far from being an uncommon one. Berkeleian scholars and historians of philosophy generally tend to the view that what merit there is in Berkeley's system lies in the fact that he provided a thoroughly empirical analysis of the material world—the world of apples, trees, stones and chairs and even of motions, physical forces and gravitational pulls—whereas he merely accepted that the traditional account of spiritual substance as it was represented in Locke's philosophy was itself basically sound. Berkeley the empiricist, the story goes, stopped being an empiricist when it came to mind. His importance and position in the history of philosophy is often pointed to by saying that whereas Locke stopped being an empiricist when it came to material substance and spiritual substance, Berkeley stopped only when it came to spiritual substance. After this it was left for Hume to do for spirit what Berkeley had done for matter.

[1] G. J. Warnock; *Berkeley* (Baltimore: 1961), p. 204.

An Objection in the Dialogues

Two facts might make us want to look a little more closely at this really too simple picture. The first is that in the third of the *Dialogues* Berkeley himself put forward an objection to his own account of spirit in terms quite as uncompromising as any used by critics today. In this passage Hylas, the materialist, considers the statement of the Berkeleian, Philonous, that God must be considered as the ultimate cause of all our ideas of sense. Against this, Hylas charges that as ideas are essentially passive objects and as God is essentially an active Being, it is as inherently impossible that we should have knowledge of God as it is that we should have knowledge of matter. He sums up:

> Since therefore you have no idea of the mind of God, how can you conceive it possible, that things should exist in his mind? Or, if you can conceive the mind of God without having an idea of it, why may not I be allowed to conceive the existence of matter, notwithstanding that I have no idea of it? (DHP 231)

The answer Philonous gives—that the knowledge we can have of God is based firmly on that knowledge each of us does have of himself as a spiritual entity—has seemed to many to be wrong at its very starting-point. And Berkeley must have realized that this might be questioned, for in the third edition he added a long passage in which Hylas is made to press the objection now against the claim that we have immediate knowledge of a finite self as a spiritual being. In concluding his answer to this objection, Philonous claims: "There is therefore upon the whole no parity of case between spirit and matter." (DHP 234) Obviously, then, Berkeley did realize that there was an apparent problem here, and, just as obviously, he *thought* that he had an answer.

"S-entries" in the Philosophical Commentaries

But there is a second fact that might make us want to look once more at the belief that Berkeley was more or less completely naive in his acceptance of the Lockian view of spiritual substance. For though it is true, as is regularly pointed out, that Berkeley says relatively little about spirit in the published works, it is equally true that he has a great deal to say about it in the *Philosophical Commentaries,* those notebooks he filled during the years 1707–1708 in preparation for his first major publications. Here, among almost a thousand often difficult and obscure entries that were intended solely for the author's own use we find one hundred and thirty-six marked with the marginal sign "S," the sign Berkeley used to mark entries concerned with "Soul" or "Spirit." Berkeley obviously gave *some* thought to problems connected with spirit and our knowledge of it, and there is obviously *something* to be discussed.

If we look just a little closer at the S-entries in the *Commentaries* we are immediately struck by the nature of their distribution. They are not spread anything like evenly over the pages of the two notebooks but are in fact very largely concentrated in the second, one hundred and twenty-one appearing there and only fifteen in the first.[2] Indeed, in the last fifty-two folio pages over one third of the entries are marked with this sign. It seems, then, that the *Commentaries* do contain a fairly close study of the concept of spiritual substance, but that this study was started relatively late.

By the time he had filled the first of his notebooks Berkeley had worked out his case against material substance to his own satisfaction, and he had even gone so far, in entry # 378, as to draft out in note form a summary of his arguments as he intended they should appear in what he there calls his "Treatise." Almost as an afterthought it seems to have dawned on him that his immaterialism would be incomplete if it consisted solely of an attack upon matter and failed to include a defense of the concept of spiritual substance. Indeed, it seems to have been only some time after he had begun the second of these preparatory notebooks that he realized that it had become of urgent importance that he should be able to work out a coherent account of mind and of our knowledge of it and that lack of such an account would certainly undermine the rest of his thesis.

Locke's Account

He must have thought hard about what Locke had to say about spiritual substance, and he may have realized that this was far from being straightforward. In the first place, Locke was quite definite that we have intuitive knowledge, the very highest kind of knowledge, each of us of his own self. Thus, in the fourth book of the *Essay* he argues that no analysis of our experience is complete without our taking into account the immediate apprehension each of us has of a self distinct from other objects of knowledge:

> As for our own existence, we perceive it so plainly and so certainly that it neither needs nor is capable of any proof. For nothing can be more evident to us than our own existence. I think, I reason, I feel pleasure and pain: can any of these be more evident to me than my own existence? If I doubt of all other things, that very doubt makes me perceive my own existence, and will not suffer me to doubt of that. For, if I know I feel pain, it is evident I have as certain perception of my own existence, as of the existence of the pain I feel: or if I know I doubt, I have as certain perception of the existence of the thing doubting, as of that thing which I call 'doubt.'[3]

[2] The position is rather more complicated than this suggests. Three of the S-entries in the first notebook appear as corrections on the verso page, and I take it that they were written relatively late. Another three entries so marked have nothing to do with spirit. Berkeley seems to have planned at first to use the sign "S" for "Space." Against this, a number of entries in both notebooks would have been marked as being concerned with spirit if Berkeley had not decided that the thoughts expressed in them were unhelpful or wrong. In such cases he uses the sign "+."

[3] J. Locke, *Essay, Concerning Human Understanding,* Bk. IV, Chap. IX, § 3.

The passage is obviously strongly reminiscent of Descartes' *cogito* argument. Perhaps the only difference is that what Locke claims to know intuitively is the existence of a thing or being which he calls "self," whereas Descartes claims rather to know intuitively the truth of a proposition which connects the fact of thought to the necessary existence of a self. It is interesting to note also that in the sections which follow this Locke claims, as Berkeley was later to claim, that this intuitive knowledge of a self is a necessary precondition of the mediate knowledge each of us can have of God. Locke gives no arguments for the existence of the self, and in one of these sections we find him saying that if anyone chooses to remain skeptical on this issue he may safely be left "until hunger or some other pain convince him of the contrary." Though Locke himself eschews the use of the word "argument" in this context, it will be convenient for us, for the sake of a label, to refer to what Locke says here as "the argument for the person."

But opposed to this very positive aspect of Locke's teaching there is an aspect that resulted from his attempt to answer the question left unanswered by the argument for the person: the question as to the nature of his self that is intuitively known. And it is this aspect that might be expected to have worried the young immaterialist. The self in its essence, Locke says, is a substance which, although it must be supposed to exist as a substratum for things we do immediately apprehend, is itself never so known. For Locke, spiritual as well as material substance was a "something-I-know-not-what." In one passage, after pointing out that we have no clear and distinct idea of material substance but that we find it necessary to "suppose" its existence, he says:

> The same happens concerning the operations of the mind; viz. thinking, reasoning, fearing, &c., which we concluding not to subsist of themselves, nor apprehending how they can belong to body, or be produced by it, we are apt to think these the actions of some other substance, which we call 'spirit'; whereby yet it is evident, that having no other idea or notion of matter, but something wherein those many sensible qualities which affect our senses do subsist; by supposing a substance wherein thinking, knowing, doubting, and a power of moving, &c., do subsist; we have as clear a notion of the substance of spirit as we have of body; the one being supposed to be (without knowing what it is) the *substratum* to those simple ideas we have from without; and the other supposed (with a like ignorance of what it is) to be the *substratum* to those operations which we experiment in ourselves within.[4]

Neither material substance nor spiritual substance, Locke points out, is an object of immediate knowledge, but anyone inclined to be skeptical about spiritual substance is warned that by the same token he might as well be skeptical about material substance—the exact opposite of the position Berkeley found himself in. We can refer to this argument as "the argument for the substratum-self."

[4] *Ibid.*, Bk. II, Chap. XXIII, § 5.

This near skepticism of Locke about material substance would have delighted the young Berkeley, but at the same time he would certainly have recognized the challenge implicit in the statement that the concept of spirit was as problematic as that of matter. It was no use rejecting one "something-I-know-not-what" and dogmatically including the other in his system. "Our knowledge," Locke had said, "is equally obscure, or none at all in both." Notoriously, Locke's position had got him into considerable difficulties. He had considered, for example, whether the same "person" could at different times be allied to different substances, and he had even questioned whether God might not have superadded the power of thought to matter. If spiritual substance was to be included in Berkeley's system, then he had to give an account of our knowledge of it that left no room for such questions and, in general, no room for skepticism.

At the time when he began to fill the first of the notebooks it seems Berkeley did accept more or less uncritically that there was some sort of distinction to be made between the self as it is intuitively known and the self as a supposed substratum. The first he generally calls "person" and the second he calls "soul." Entry # 14 is particularly interesting in this respect, for here Berkeley argues, in the spirit of Locke's teaching, that the immortality of the person can be conceived of without our supposing the immortality of the soul:

> Eternity is onely a train of innumerable ideas. hence the immortality of ye Soul easily conceiv'd. or rather the immortality of the person, yt or ye soul not being necessary for ought we can see.

The hesitation over terminology is typical of Berkeley's thought during this period. Indeed, one of the primary sources of confusion when it comes to study of the various entries in his *Commentaries* is that so many key words—words such as "idea," "perception," "thought," "mind," and "understanding"—only come to have the precise meanings they have in the published works as Berkeley's thought develops. Settled terminology came only with settled doctrine.

The Two-edged Sword

Berkeley's realization that he might be wielding a two-edged sword and undermining the concept of spiritual substance at the same time as he sought to undermine that of material substance was not forced on him merely by a consideration of the tendency of the arguments of a philosophic predecessor. More insidiously he found that in formulating his attack on material substance—admittedly largely in Lockian terms—he seemed to have left himself no room for any account of the self at all. In order to appreciate just what Berkeley's difficulties were in this respect it will be convenient to look at the first eleven propositions of the "demonstration" of the nonexistence of matter as contained in entry # 378. They read:

1 All significant words stand for Ideas
2 All knowledge about our ideas
3 All ideas come from without or from within.
4 If from without it must be by the senses & they are call'd sensations.
5 If from within they are the operations of the mind & are call'd thoughts.
6 No sensation can be in a senseless thing.
7 No thought can be in a thoughtless thing.
8 All our ideas are either sensations or thoughts, by 3.4.5.
9 None of our ideas can be in a thing wch is both thoughtless & senseless. 6.7.8.
10 The bare passive reception or having of ideas is call'd perception.
11 Whatever has in it an idea, tho it be never so passive, tho it exert no manner of act about it, yet it must perceive. 10

By the time he came to publish, Berkeley was to reject much of what is contained in these eleven propositions, but what is immediately obvious is that the "demonstration" is designed with one end only in view—the undermining of the concept of material substance. Yet if Berkeley had considered its wider implications he would have seen that the whole thing was self-defeating. For spiritual substance, the thinking subject implicit in propositions 6, 7 and 11, is neither a sensation nor a thought as these are defined in propositions 4 and 5, and it follows from propositions 1 and 2 that the word "thing" in this context is meaningless and that spiritual substance is not an object of knowledge.

At this point we should certainly note that as it is formulated here the demonstration leaves no more room for the intuitively known person than it does for the unknown spiritual substratum. But the fact is that Berkeley could quite easily have modified the demonstration so as to make it allow the significance of the word "person" while retaining its cogency against the concept of matter. From this point of view it seems that there were two possibilities open to him. He could have said either that we have through immediate intuition an "idea" of the person and added a rider to proposition 5 to the effect that such an object is included among ideas we have "from within," or, alternatively, he could have modified proposition 1 by substituting the words "objects open to immediate apprehension" for "ideas." Adopting this second alternative he would have had to modify proposition 2 to the same effect, and he would then have had to state that such objects include ideas, as detailed in propositions 3–5, and also the intuitively known person.

For the Lockian there would have seemed to have been little to stop the adoption of the first of these alternatives; the recognition, that is, of a further class of ideas. It was one of the weaknesses of Locke's epistemology that he used the word "idea" in so wide a sense (or in so many senses) that for him, with "idea" defined as an object of knowledge, the statements expressed in Berkeley's first two propositions were virtually analytic. Berkeley *could* have claimed that just to recognize the intuitive character of self-awareness was *ipso facto* to recognize a further class of ideas.

It was, of course, the second of these possibilities that Berkeley was eventually to adopt. Indeed, he was to go further and to make the term "idea" cover not sensations and thoughts, but sensations only, together with their representations in imagination. But early in the second of the notebooks it is clear that he is considering limiting the use of the term in some such way. Particularly important from this point of view are entries # 522 and # 523, for here he does seem to recognize the double action of the two-edged sword as it concerns material substance on the one hand and the person (not the substratum-self) on the other. In the first of these entries he simply notes down the axiom he had used as proposition 2 in his demonstration, this time attributing it to Locke in order to show that it is now being put forward for examination rather than being simply asserted. Thus:

> All knowledge onely about ideas. V. Locke B.4 c.1.

The entry is marked with the marginal sign "M" (for "Matter"), which shows that Berkeley fully recognized the usefulness of this axiom as the blade of the sword whose main function had been achieved in the annihilation of the concept of matter. But the objection to the axiom that follows in the next entry does recognize the other sharp blade of the sword, and, significantly, this entry is accompanied by the marginal sign "S":

> It seems improper & liable to difficulties to make the Word Person stand for an Idea, or to make our selves Ideas or thinking things ideas.

Although Berkeley does not say here what the difficulties he envisages are, it is certainly reasonable to conjecture that he was unhappy about describing the self which is primarily that which knows and only secondarily an object of knowledge in the same terms as other objects, which are always and essentially objects of knowledge *for* mind.

Here, and in entry # 490 where he considers the possibility of not calling the operations of the mind "ideas" but restricting this term to the sensible, Berkeley seems to be on the verge of jettisoning the "axiom" and of narrowing the connotation of "idea" so that the proposition becomes not analytic but simply false. In fact, however—although there is a tendency from this time on to call the operations of the mind "volitions" rather than "ideas"—this step had to wait until he had nearly completed this second notebook. The axiom is in fact reaffirmed as late as entry # 639.

But if there were ways in which Berkeley could accommodate Locke's "person" in his system, it seems clear that he could not similarly have accommodated the substratum-self. For spiritual substance was not supposed to be something that was an object of immediate apprehension but rather it was put forward only as the object of supposition. And, as Hylas was to point out and as many critics of Berkeley's position have since pointed out, if you allow one such supposition there is no reason for you to refuse to allow another. If spiritual substance as described by Locke is built into the system there can be no grounds for refusing to recognize that material substance may exist. As Locke saw, and as Berkeley certainly saw, the two concepts stand or fall together.

The Attack on the "Substratum-self"

Perhaps it is only the shifts and changes in Berkeley's terminology that have prevented critics from realizing that in the *Commentaries,* Berkeley engages in an attack on the Lockian concept of spiritual substance with all the vigor that is generally associated only with his attack on the concept of material substance. His terminology is undoubtedly confused at this period, but when he talks of "mind," "soul," and "understanding" in a remarkable group of entries, ## 576–581, which have been seen as an adumbration of Hume's skepticism, there can be no doubt that it is the substratum-self rather than the person to which what he says is strictly relevant. There is a danger that because in these entries Berkeley refers to the mind as a "congeries of perceptions," whereas later and in the published works he refers to mind always as something essentially distinct from its perceptions, his argument here might be thought of either as merely representing a false turning in his road to a satisfactory philosophy and thus as little more than a curiosity, or else that he might be thought to be giving the point away that, whatever he was to assert dogmatically in his published works, strict logic and his empiricist principles required him to deny the existence of a self distinct from the "ideas" he recognized in proposition 4 and 5 of his demonstration (PC # 378).

Neither of these interpretations would be justified. The "mind" and "soul" are attacked at this stage in the *Commentaries* simply because they are supposed to represent an *unknown* and *unknowable* substratum of volitions and ideas such as we have found Locke supposing. In the published works these words always stand for the self as an agent that is known through all other experience. Of this known self we find Berkeley writing in entry # 547:

> We have an intuitive Knowledge of the Existence of other things besides our selves & even praecedaneous to the Knowledge of our own Existence. in that we must have Ideas or else we cannot think.

It is not *this* self that is to be attacked in later entries.

Berkeley's objections to the supposition of any spiritual substance, substratum, or entity conceived of as being essentially inaccessible and hidden to direct apprehension are interestingly similar to those he uses against the existence of material substance. Here we can only consider in summary form what he goes into in considerable detail. We must know this supposed entity either through some "sense" or by reason. Do we know it by some internal sense? In answering this question there is first of all the familiar Berkeleian device of the direct challenge, which in this case is contained in entry # 579:

Consult, ransack yr Understanding wt find you there besides several perceptions or thoughts. Wt mean you by the word mind you must mean something that you perceive or yt you do not perceive. a thing not perceived is a contradiction. to mean (also) a thing you do not perceive is a contradiction. We are all in this matter strangely abused by words.

Here too is the claim that a word is insignificant unless it has a basis in immediate experience.

Introspection, then, does not help us. Could it help us? Is it merely a deficiency in our actual cognitive equipment that accounts for our failure to perceive such an entity? The answer to these questions involves the same principle that Berkeley uses in the *Commentaries* and the published works against the supposition that an "extra sense" might help us to perceive material substance. In entry # 672 he says:

Say you the unknown substratum of Volitions & Ideas, is somthing whereof I have no Idea. I ask is there any other Being wch has or can have an Idea of it. if there be then it must be it self an Idea wch you will think absurd.

The absurdity lies, of course, in the fact that spiritual substance is considered necessary as a substratum or support for ideas, and if it could be itself known as an idea it would itself need an unknowable support. Following this suggestion through leads us inescapably to an infinite regress.

Berkeley could expect champions of spiritual substance to agree that the supposed substratum was not the object of direct awareness. Their position would be, as we saw to be the case with Locke, that it was necessary to suppose the existence of such an essentially hidden support. The possibility remains, then, that the ground for the belief may properly be found to lie in reason. Besides giving the answer that we have already seen—that it is absurd to suppose the existence of something which is not in principle perceivable—Berkeley challenges right at the gates of his adversaries by claiming, as he does in the case of material substance, that it is not at all necessary or helpful to work with such a concept. Thus, in entry # 637 he says:

Say you there must be a thinking substance. Somthing unknown wch perceives & supports & ties together the Ideas. Say I, make it appear there is any need of it & you shall have it for me. I care not to take away anything I can see the least reason to think should exist.

And with this Berkeley's case against an unknown and unknowable spiritual substratum is almost complete. But he does go just a little bit further, for, characteristically, he does try to account for the fact that it has been thought necessary to suppose the existence of an occult spiritual substance, and he finds the answer in the way we talk about mind.

It was always clear to Berkeley that one of the most common causes of error in our thought about the mind and its operations is that we are forced all the time to use metaphor. As early as entry # 176 of the *Commentaries* we find him saying:

> Speech metaphorical more than we imagine insensible things & their modes circumstances &c being exprest for ye most part by words borrow'd from things sensible. the reason's plain. Hence Manyfold Mistakes.

This thought is expressed time and time again in the published works.[5]

In ordinary day-to-day conversation we are quite ready to use phrases such as "I had it in mind to visit London," "a thought crossed my mind," and "I call to mind the last time I saw Arthur." Similarly, it is only slightly more sophisticated to talk of "a stream of consciousness," or of "the private world of my thoughts." Yet in all these usages there is a strong element of metaphor, and useful metaphor at that for they all succeed in conveying something meaningful to the hearer. Perhaps it is only when the philosopher comes on the scene that such talk becomes dangerous, for he may be prone to ask questions such as "What is this 'mind' that the thought crossed?" and "What is the nature of this 'private world'?" and it will prove very difficult to provide him with an answer. It is at this stage that we may find ourselves talking about hidden substrata and "mind stuff." Certainly, however natural it may be to talk of a "stream of consciousness," it will not do for the philosopher to take the metaphor so seriously that he starts looking for the spiritual bed and banks. Surely it was because he was aware of the danger of taking such quests seriously that Berkeley talked of mind as a "congeries of perceptions."

In another entry, # 581, Berkeley gives an illustration of how we are "abused by words." Thus:

> Say you the Mind is not the Perceptions. but that thing wch perceives. I answer you are abus'd by the words that & thing these are vague empty words wthout a meaning.

It is necessary to insist that Berkeley is here still concerned with the mind as it passively receives ideas, and with this granted it is easy to see what he means in this entry. Once again, he claims, the philosopher is guilty of verbal confusion, for he supposes that in considering the mind as "that which perceives" the word "that" must stand for some substantial entity or "thing." He is misled by the word, for the pronoun need not function in that way.

An illustration may help to make this clearer. If we consider the statement that "the peas are in the saucepan" it is obvious that the peas on the one hand and the saucepan on the other are both real entities. Further, if we talk of "that which holds the peas," the word "that" does signify a real entity—the saucepan. Suppose now that we consider the statement that "the horses are in the herd" (admittedly not a very likely statement). Here the case is quite different, for horses are not in herds in the same way as peas are in a saucepan, if only because when the peas are taken away the saucepan remains whereas if the horses are taken away the herd goes with them. And because saucepans

[5] See especially PHK 144, ALC VII, § 13, SIR § 171. See also Locke's *Essay*, Bk. III, Chap. 1, § 5.

and herds are different types of entity, the word "that" is behaving quite differently in the phrase "that which contains the horses" from the way it is in the phrase "that which contains the peas." To suppose otherwise is to commit what Professor Ryle would call a "category-error." We may suppose, then, that Berkeley has spotted a particularly interesting type of category-mistake when he suggests, in effect, that minds are more like herds than they are like spiritual saucepans.[6]

Berkeley and the Person

In the short space we have taken it has been impossible to do real justice to Berkeley's attack upon the notion of an occult spiritual substratum of volitions and ideas. For the same reason it will be impossible to do justice to his development of the notion of a person. Here it must suffice to say that one very important step was made before Berkeley completed the notebook. He had always supposed that mind was completely passive in its reception of ideas. We saw this in proposition 10 of the demonstration we have cited. And while he believed this, he called the mind as it perceives or passively receives ideas the "understanding." As we saw, when he tried to give some meaning to the word when this faculty was considered as something having an existence distinct from its perceptions, he could find no substantial content. Now, in a sense he did continue to believe that the mind was inactive in sense perception, for he saw that sensory ideas were impressed upon the mind (another dangerous metaphor here) from without and independently of the agent's volition. But what he did come to see was that passive reception could never be experience, and that there could be no experience unless the mind was active about what was received from without. Thus we find him saying, in entry # 791:

> While I exist or have any Idea I am eternally, constantly willing, my acquiescing in the present State is willing.

And with this comes a new view of the understanding. Thus, in entry # 821: "Understanding is in some sort an Action." All is now ready for his "mature" view of mind.

In entry # 854 he says:

> Will, Understanding, desire, Hatred etc so far forth as they are acts or active differ not, all their difference consists in their objects, circumstances etc.

We now find him talking of an agent-self that is known in and through all other experience and that he at first calls variously "spirit," "will," and "mind." The word "person" is rejected in this context in entry # 713, apparently because Berkeley was aware of the special implications of the term in discus-

[6] It should be emphasized that Professor Ryle would have much to say against Berkeley's own concept of mind.

sions of the Trinity. He consistently avoids the term in the published works until he overcomes his scruples in *Siris*.

When Berkeley came to answer the objection he put into the mouth of Hylas in the *Dialogues,* he certainly felt himself to be standing on very firm ground. Hylas, who is very Lockian in his assumptions, has two preconceptions that prevent him from seeing the point Philonous is trying to make. In the first place, he simply cannot see that the Berkeleian is using the term "idea" in a sense very different from that in which Locke had used it. For the Berkeleian, to say that we have an immediate and intuitive knowledge of spirit and its operations though we have no *idea* of these is meaningful only because the word is now used in a restricted sense and refers only to the passive objects of perception. In the second place, Hylas finds it very difficult to see that the spiritual substance Philonous is championing is not Locke's unknown substratum-self but something more akin to Locke's *person*.

In his answer as it stands completed in the third edition, Berkeley, through Philonous, makes his position quite clear:

> How often must I repeat, that I know or am conscious of my own being; and that I my self am not my ideas, but somewhat else, a thinking active principle that perceives, knows, wills, and operates about ideas. I know that I, one and the same self, perceive both colours and sounds: that a colour cannot perceive a sound, nor a sound a colour: that I am therefore one individual principle, distinct from colour and sound; and for the same reason from all other sensible things and inert ideas. (DHP 233 f.)

He insists that this knowledge is "immediate" and "intuitive" and that it is gained "by a reflex act."

Often, but by no means always, Berkeley avoids the term "spiritual substance," preferring for the obvious reason to use simply "spirit." Insofar as he recognizes the propriety of the terms "substance" or "support" it is because these can be given a meaning in terms of "perception." Thus we can say that a spirit "supports" ideas if we mean by this that a spirit "perceives" ideas. Beyond this, his main point is that there is no comparison to be made between material substance and spirit. Here he makes the same points against material substance that we saw he was prepared to make against any concept of a substratum-self, while at the same time insisting that these objections have no cogency against his own concept of spirit. He claims, that is, that we do not perceive any such existent; that the notion of an unperceived existent involves a contradiction, and that the concept is at any rate a useless one which does nothing to help account for any of our actual experiences. The case is different with spirit, for this is something known so that without such a concept no account of our experience can be complete.

Enough has now been said for us to see that it is a gross oversimplification to suppose that Berkeley simply accepted Locke's account of spiritual substance. It is not intended here to defend Berkeley's own concept. There are fundamental objections to it that we can now see; there are objections to points of detail that perhaps he should have seen, and there are objections, or difficulties rather, that he certainly did see. He saw and fully accepted, for example, that the existence of spirit could not be abstracted from its cogitation or thought, and thus that it was impossible to conceive of spirit as existing but not perceiving. That this consequence became connected in his mind with difficulties he experienced with the concept of time is another story.

Some alleged difficulties are spurious. Certainly, when Berkeley says that we have a "notion" of spirit he is not, as has sometimes been supposed, putting forward a mediate object of knowledge between the knowing subject and self-knowledge. What he does insist on is that we are *immediately* aware of a perceiving subject existing through all our changing experiences. In the published works and in the *Philosophical Commentaries* he has perhaps more to say in defense of this than is generally supposed.

VI

Berkeley and "Things"*

AUGUSTO GUZZO

Esse *Is* Percipi: *"Things" Divinely Made to Be Perceived and Minds to Perceive Them*

In the *Principles,* Berkeley writes:

> As to what is said of the absolute existence of unthinking things without any relation to their being perceived, that seems perfectly unintelligible. Their *esse* is *percipi,* nor is it possible they should have any existence out of the minds or thinking things which perceive them. (§ 3)

In *Siris,* we find:

> Natural phenomena are only natural appearances. They are therefore, such as we see and perceive them. Their real and objective natures are, therefore, the same —passive without anything active, fluent and changing without anything permanent in them. (§ 292)

In *Siris,* then, he does not alter the doctrine of the *Principles,* but clarifies it, specifying how he understood it towards the end of his life. As Professor Jessop says in his Introduction to the *Principles,* "the possibility that may be excluded is that he came to have misgivings about the truth of his distinctive doctrines."[1] Jessop grants that "*Siris* undoubtedly represents a big change of

* Translated from the Italian by T. E. Jessop.

[1] A. A. Luce and T. E. Jessop (eds.) *The Works of George Berkeley* (London: 1949), Vol. II, from the Editor's Introduction, 7.

mood, interest and emphasis," because there "the sense of mystery, which had affirmed itself combatively in *Alciphron* and the *Analyst*, has become a settled mood. He now feels as well as knows that *omnia exeunt in mysterium*."[2] It may be said, however, that this sense of mystery was not foreign to what Jessop calls the "clean, stripped, athletic pages of the *Principles*."[3]

In the early period of Berkeley's thinking there was a point at which he considered that a mind is only the sum of its perceptions (PC # 587), just as he had reduced body to the sum of its qualities; but he turned his back on that view and took his stand on the position that mind has solidarity and personality (PC # 788), whereas sensible things have neither persistence nor indivisibility. In the *Principles* he started from the vision of a universe consisting of stable perceivers and a flux of percepts, and sees these two sorts as bound together by the relation of perception, not a merely accidental one but constitutive, forging a bond that is essential: "things" are made in order to be perceived, and minds in order to perceive what is presented to them by the Author of both minds and "things." The task of the philosopher is to detect this divinely willed scheme, in which "we live and move and have our being"[4] not to explain or justify it, for we cannot deduce it by any a priori reasoning but only become aware of, accept, and admire it. In this sense we are born, live, and die in the mystery of universal reality (a most clear mystery, though not to reason), which is held together by the perceptual relation, apart from which neither minds nor "things" have either existence or meaning.

Various Meanings of Berkeley's Percipi

"*Esse* is *percipi*" was for Berkeley a general principle, but the term *percipi* there has a variety of meanings.

In the first place he sharply distinguishes sensation from imagination. It is one thing to perceive the sweet and the cold, another to imagine them "at pleasure." (PHK § 28) Although he calls both what is perceived and what is imagined "ideas," he does not put them on the same level. (PHK § 30) The ideas of imagination depend on my will:

> I find I can excite ideas in my mind at pleasure, and vary and shift the scene as oft as I think fit. It is no more than willing, and straightway this or that idea arises in my fancy: and by the same power it is obliterated and makes way for another. This making and unmaking of ideas doth very properly denominate the mind active. (PHK § 28)

[2] *Ibid.*, Vol. V, 18.

[3] *Loc. cit.*

[4] St. Paul in Acts 17:28, the text which Professor A. A. Luce observes Berkeley "seems to use at the turning point of his arguments" in PHK § 149, DHP 214 and 236, ALC 159 f., PC #827, and the *Guardian* essay on "The Christian Idea of God."

The ideas of sense do not depend on my will:

> Whatever power I may have over my own thoughts, I find the ideas actually perceived by sense have not a like dependence on my will. When in broad daylight I open my eyes, it is not in my power to choose whether I shall see or no, or to determine what particular objects shall present themselves to my view; and so likewise as to the hearing and other senses, the ideas imprinted on them are not creatures of my will. (PHK § 29)

If, then, Berkeley's principle holds of both, we must say that the being of sensations consists in their being sensed, and of images in their being imagined. For an image to exist it is *sufficient* that it be imagined, but for a sensation to exist it *must* be sensed—sensation implying a dependence of my mind on that which makes me sense, while imagining means the mind's own free play. *Esse* is *percipi* has in these two cases not merely different but opposite meanings: perceiving as sensing means being acted on, receiving ideas, as imagining means acting, producing ideas.

There are further meanings of *percipi* besides these two basic ones. Take, for example, the following passage:

> By sight I have the ideas of light and colours. . . . By touch I perceive, for example, hard and soft, heat and cold, motion and resistance. . . . Smelling furnishes me with odours, the palate with tastes, and hearing conveys sounds . . . and as several of these are observed to accompany each other, they come to be marked with one name and so to be reputed as one thing. (PHK § 1)

Here we have an example of what Locke called "complex ideas." So far as these are simple collections of simple ideas their *esse* is *colligi*. The perceiving of them is not sensing but forming; yet not imagining, because not forming "at pleasure," for the forming depends on the fact that "such and such ideas are attended with such and such other ideas in the ordinary course of things," on the "set rules or established methods wherein the mind we depend on excites in us the ideas of sense, which are called the Laws of Nature." (PHK § 30)

Another different instance is the apprehension of "notions," sharply distinguished from "ideas" in the second edition of the *Principles*. In the first edition he had thought it enough to write:

> So far as I can see, the words will, understanding, mind, soul, do not stand for different ideas, or in truth for any idea at all, but for something which is very different from ideas, and which, being an agent cannot be like unto, or represented by, any idea whatsoever. (PHK § 27)

In the second edition he added to that sentence, not changing his point but making it more precise: "Though it must be owned at the same time that we have some notion of soul, spirit, and the operations of the mind such as willing, loving, hating, inasmuch as we know or understand the meaning of those words." These notions, too, we perceive in ourselves. To perceive them is to know them, so that their *esse* is their being known. He had said in the first edition, "All our ideas, sensations, notions, or the things which we perceive, by whatsoever names they may be distinguished, are visibly inactive." (PHK § 25)

Further, Berkeley's whole endeavor in the *Principles* is to *demonstrate* his immaterialism. There are a posteriori arguments, but Berkeley tells us that there is no need to go through them in order to defend "what has been, if I mistake not, sufficiently demonstrated *a priori*" (PHK § 21), for the materialists' assumption that we conceive bodies as existing unconceived is "a manifest repugnancy" (PHK § 23). The *esse* of a philosophical doctrine thus consists in "*demonstrari.*"

In short, all the operations of the mind—sensing, imagining, forming ideas of "things," making particular ideas function as universals, willing, inferring, demonstrating—fall under our direct awareness. To have them is to be intimately aware of them, to *ap*perceive them. In such cases "*esse* is *appercipi.*"

It is evident, then, that Berkeley's principle that the perceptual relation does not merely happen to *esse* but constitutes it, holds in all instances, but with various meanings of *percipi* (and correspondingly of *percipere*).

Meanings of Percipi *as Involving Mental Activity of* Percipere

Of the meanings so far distinguished, all except the first (sensing) involve activity, initiative, on the side of the human mind. To that extent those mental operations approximate to willing, which Berkeley contrasts with the passivity of sensing the natural phenomena presented to us by God for our perceiving. We must now ask what Berkeley means by speaking of sensing as passive. Is it strictly the sensing that is passive? Here we must proceed carefully, since Berkeley did but outline his teaching instead of carrying it through to completion, as a professional philosopher would try to do.[5] Although we must not slip into making him say what he does not intend, we need not hesitate to introduce clarifications, though not actually in his text, that appear to be necessary to make his explicit teaching tenable and to safeguard the reasons that led him to maintain it, despite its paradoxicality, throughout his life. We may do so not to reform Berkeleianism or to move away from it, but to keep in line with it.

What is meant by "sensation"? A fact? Yes, apparently, if it is passive. Yet if it is passive fact it has no thinking in it, and thus falls under Berkeley's general criticism of anything supposed to exist outside of any relation to thought. (PHK § 3). To avoid that criticism, sensation must be conceived as

[5] Cf. T. E. Jessop's remark: "Perhaps his philosophizing was but a pastime of genius, one only of the brilliant things with which he strewed his life." (*Works,* Vol. II, 7)

in the mind that perceives it. There, however, it is as much a sensing as something sensed. As the latter it is received by the mind that perceives it; as the former it is a complex active judgment about the distance, size, and position of what is sensed. That sensation as sentient is judgment is not said in the *Principles* but is clearly shown to be such in the *Essay Towards a New Theory of Vision* (though not one of the innovations of this work, for, as Luce remarks in his introduction to the *Essay,* it "is at least as old as Aristotle, and . . . was freely accepted before Berkeley wrote").[6] What Luce calls the "principle of mental interpretation" is not invoked in the *Principles* because here Berkeley was concentrating on sensation as sensed. Still, that this is inseparable from sensing follows from his general principle that nothing—least of all what is sensed—is conceivable apart from its relation to thought. In his *Theory of Vision Vindicated* of 1733, "meant to bring its basic assumptions into line with the philosophy of the *Principles,*"[7] he used "apprehensions" and "judgments" as synonyms. (TVV § 65, 69)

It is thus clear why Berkeley said that sensation as sensed is passive, while convinced that as sensing it is active judging. On the one hand it is "given," by the Author of the universe, to the mind that perceives it. On the other hand the mode of receiving proper to a mind is mental interpretation or judgment. Hence Berkeleianism is not actualism, for which the mind creates the content it senses; nor absolute phenomenalism, for which the sensed content moves of itself into the mind; nor ideism, for which the mind perceives only its own ideas and is never able with or in these to arrive at the natural phenomena offered to it by the Author of them. Berkeleianism is a realism of sensation as sensed, and neither contradicts nor is contradicted by the idealism of sensation as sensing. What is sensed is "given," and the sensing receives it by interpreting it. In this way Berkeleianism is a theism for which the activity of finite minds in interpreting the sensible contents given to them is a likeness, though a finite one, of the infinite activity of the infinite Mind, which is the Author of the two inseparable parts of reality, the natural phenomena to be sensed and the minds fitted to sense them.

The Senses and Body Likened to a Lute, the Human Mind to a Musician

If "giving" and "receiving" are inconceivable apart from one another, if in the receiving what is given is made into something suitable, useful, and instructive, and if the "visual language," Berkeley's name for the order of natural phenomena, requires like all language to be understood, that is, inter-

[6] A. A. Luce in *Works,* Vol. I, 148.
[7] *Ibid.,* 247.

preted, then the relation givenness–interpretation is not confined to man. Berkeley never limits his general principle *esse* is *percipi* either to the actual perceiving of particular men or to human perceiving taken generally. In one direction he did not rule out the existence of an "other order of finite created spirits before man" (DHP 252)—spirits made to perceive in their specific way, different from our way, which is that of the senses because we have a body. In the other direction, that of animals, the following observation by Berkeley about man holds even more of their sensibility:

> Figure and extension are not patterns or resemblances of qualities existing in matter, because to the same eye at different stations, or eyes of a different texture at the same station, they appear various, and cannot therefore be the images of anything settled and determinate without the mind. (PHK § 14)

The "different texture" of the organs of sense (and of the other bodily organs) introduces a kind of relativity of the sensed and the sensing that has nothing to do with relativism as a philosophical theory, for this supposes in "things" something *in se*, wholly beyond the reach of our apprehensions (sensory and all other), which are relative to our individual structure, whereas in a theory for which the very "things" themselves have an *esse* inseparable from their *percipi* such things are regarded as coming into existence differently in perceivers differing in nature and in the condition in which they happen to be.

Although *Siris* abounds in confessed conjectures and therefore cannot be taken literally, when used with care it enables us to fill in important gaps in Berkeley's other works. For example, it emphasizes the morphological parallels between animal and plant organisms:

> Those who have examined the structure of trees and plants by microscopes have discovered an admirable variety of fine capillary tubes and vessels, fitted for several purposes, as the imbibing or attracting of proper nourishment, the distributing thereof through all parts of the vegetable, the discharge of superfluities, the secretion of particular juices. They are found to have ducts answering to the tracheae in animals, for the conveying of air; they have others answering to lacteals, arteries and veins. They feed, digest, respire, perspire, and generate their kind, and are provided with organs nicely fitted for all those uses. (SIR § 29)

He goes on to say:

> A plant or tree is a very nice and complicated machine, by the several parts and motions whereof the crude juices, admitted through the absorbent vessels, whether of the root, trunk, or branches, are variously mixed, separated, altered, digested, and exalted, in a very wonderful manner. The juice, as it passeth in and out, up and down, through tubes of different textures, shapes, and sizes, and is affected by the alternate compression and expansion of elastic vessels, by the vicissitudes of seasons, the changes of weather, and the various actions of the solar light, grows still more and more elaborate. (§ 35)

Now if animals and plants are "machines" (not, as will be evident in a moment, in the Cartesian sense), they must have been designed and constructed by an inventing mind, and need thereafter to be controlled and used by someone capable of doing this. As early as the first paragraph of *Siris,* the human body is likened to a lute and the mind to a musician who has to know how to play it. The lute, however, needs to be well tuned:

For if the lute be not well tuned, the musician fails of his harmony. And, in our present state, the operations of the mind so far depend on the right tone or good condition of its instrument that anything which greatly contributes to preserve or recover the health of the body is well worth the attention of the mind.

If in these words there is an echo, as Jessop notes *in loco,* of a well-known passage in Plotinus,[8] this passage is relevant in its remark that the musical instrument which the mind uses to accompany its song will no longer be at its disposal after death; but the mind will then be able to sing without accompaniment. The instrument is thus by no means necessary for the mind to sing. We shall be able to think without sensing.

This or that instrument need not have been invented, or a different one might have been devised instead. Also, once a particular instrument has been constructed, it may or may not be used; but if it is to be used it must be in good order. There is no question here of a necessary but only of a suitable and useful structure. When "the mind we depend on excites in us the ideas of sense" it does so not "at random . . . but in a regular train or series" that "gives a sort of foresight, which enables us to regulate our actions for the benefit of life, and without this we should be eternally at a loss." (PHK § 30 f.) By this provision the infinite Mind, out of compassion for us, keeps the instruments He has made in operation and well tuned and, so long as He deems them fit and useful, neither breaks them up nor ceases to use them. Thus through His compassion we find our way about the world and manage to conduct our lives.

The Activity of the Body and of the Corporeal Universe Not Their Own, But God's, Communicated As and When He Wills

In *Siris,* where Berkeley looks at the Neoplatonists with considerable sympathy, he takes over the idea of a "chain" or "ladder" of being (§§ 296, 303), in the sense not of an evolution from below, from simple to complex or lower to higher, but of action and influence from above.

8 *Enneads,* II, iii, 13. On this see my "Plotino maestro" in *Idealisti ed empiristi* (Florence: 1935), 57 f.

> It is the doctrine of the Platonic philosophers that Intellect is the very life of living things, the first principle and exemplar of all, from whence by different degrees are derived the inferior classes of life: first the rational, then the sensitive, after that the vegetal; but so as in the rational animal there is still somewhat intellectual, again in the sensitive there is somewhat rational, and in the vegetal somewhat sensitive, and lastly, in mixed bodies, as metals and minerals, somewhat of vegetation. By which means the whole is thought to be more perfectly connected. Which doctrine implies that all the faculties, instincts, and motions of inferior beings, in their several respective subordinations, are derived from and depend upon Mind and Intellect. (SIR § 275)

On the linkage of minerals and metals with plants Berkeley adduces Boyle:

> Air may also be said to be the seminary of minerals and metals, as it is of vegetables. Mr. Boyle informs us that the exhausted ores of tin and iron being exposed to the air become again impregnated with metal, and that ore of alum having lost its salt recovers it after the same manner. And numberless instances there are of salts produced by the air, that vast collection or treasury of active principles, from which all sublunary bodies seem to derive their forms, and on which animals depend for their life and breath. (SIR § 142)

When he was writing *Siris* it had not been discovered that the air contains a gas, oxygen, that is necessary for both combustion and life. He attributes these to air in the unanalyzed sense (§ 201). Neither supported nor restrained by the science of his day he soared on the wings of fantasy to write a new and lovely poem *Peri phuseos* (for this is what *Siris* is), in which the ancient themes reappear—air as the receptacle of everything, and the primordial fire that vivifies the air and actuates in it the processes that make up the life of the universe. The following are samples of his handling of these themes:

> The air or atmosphere that surrounds our earth contains a mixture of all the active volatile parts of the whole habitable world, that is, of all vegetables, minerals and animals. Whatever perspires, corrupts, or exhales impregnates the air which, being acted upon by the solar fire, produceth within itself all sorts of chemical operations, dispensing again those salts and spirits in new generations, which it had received from putrefactions. . . . (§ 137)
>
> The seeds of things seem to lie latent in the air, ready to appear and produce their kind whenever they light on a proper matrix. . . . The whole atmosphere seems alive. There is everywhere acid to corrode, and seed to engender. Iron will rust, and mould will grow in all places. Virgin earth becomes fertile, crops of new plants ever and anon shew themselves; all which demonstrates the air to be a common seminary and receptacle of all vivifying principles. . . . (§ 141)
>
> Air, the general menstruum and seminary, seemeth to be only an aggregate of the volatile parts of all natural beings, which variously combined and agitated produce many various effects. . . . Hence divers fermentations, and all the varieties of meteors, tempests, and concussions both of earth and firmament. Nor is the microcosm less affected thereby. Being pent up in the viscera, vessels, and

membranes of the body, by its salts, sulphurs and elastic power it engenders cholics, spasms, hysteric disorders, and other maladies. (§ 145)

Here is certainly a new and lovely poem *De rerum natura,* in the style of those ancients of whom Berkeley by his extensive reading of them had made himself a contemporary; and in it, also certainly, "one of our ablest and most learned minds is writing things which the most mediocre student of today knows to be wrong."[9] Nevertheless, however fantastic the "air" and "fire" he writes of may seem to us to be, *Siris* enables us to see that for Berkeleianism the cosmic show which God presents to human minds is not a film, visible yet flimsy, but a life in action, in which everything is real and in motion. Berkeley had, indeed, always been saying that, but we were not always attentive to this point, being obsessed and misled by his insistent dictum that the vast play of natural phenomena is "passive." It is now evident that it is called "passive" only because it is "given" to us; but it is given alive, forming and unrolling itself before our eyes, which "receive" it by grasping and understanding and interpreting it.

The course of nature is passive in another sense, which is the most important one. While for the Neoplatonists life, when it has been infused from higher sources into the sensible world, becomes the world's *own* natural life, for Berkeley it remains the life of the "spirit" that kindled it. The "spirit of the world" is as much a creature as our spirits are. Berkeley calls it by several names, "some active subtle substance—whether it be called fire, aether, light, or the vital spirit of the world." (§ 147) What Berkeley had always said, again and again, that there is nothing active except "spirit," thus still stands. For him the analogy between the microcosm (man) and the macrocosm (the universe) holds of all effects:

In the human body the mind orders and moves the limbs: but the animal spirit is supposed the immediate physical cause of their motion. So likewise in the mundane system, a mind presides: but the immediate, mechanical, or instrumental cause that moves or animates all its parts is the pure elementary fire or spirit of the world. The more fine or subtle part or spirit is supposed to receive the impressions of the First Mover and communicate them to the grosser sensible parts of this world. (§ 161)

In this way Berkeley does more than set himself against Descartes' doctrine that bodies are self-sufficing in their motions and are therefore to be called machines—Berkeley's "machines" being like musical instruments, which need a mind to design and build them and other minds able to tune and play them. He goes further by rejecting any sort of panpsychism that regards bodies severally and the great body of the world as animated in and through themselves. For him no body lives of itself: it is kept alive, as it was made alive, by God if and as long as He wills at each moment to do so. Life is not given once for all, but has to be continually received from moment to moment.

9 T. E. Jessop in *Works,* Vol. V, 8.

The Causal Relations between "Things," Being Neither Effectual nor Logically Necessary, to Be Understood as Providential

Due attention is not always paid to the use Berkeley made of Newton's *Optics* in his own thinking about the variety of production in the world of living things (we have already noted that he draws no rigid boundary between the organic and the inorganic). The relevant passage runs:

> As from Sir Isaac Newton's experiments it appears that all colours are virtually in the white light of the sun, and shew themselves when the rays are separated by the attracting and repelling powers of objects, even so the specific qualities of the elaborate juices of plants seem to be virtually or eminently contained in the solar light, and are actually exhibited upon the separation of the rays, by the peculiar powers of the capillary organs in vegetables, attracting and imbibing certain rays, which produce certain flavours and qualities, in like manner as certain rays, being reflected, produce certain colours. (SIR § 40)

This comparison of colors and odors is immediately followed by a comparison of the saps of plants and the glandular secretions of animals:

> It hath been observed by some curious anatomists that the secretory vessels in the glands of animal bodies are lined with a fine down, which in different glands is of different colours. And it is thought that each particular down, being originally imbued with its own proper juice, attracts none but that sort; by which means so many various juices are secreted in different parts of the body. And perhaps there may be something analogous to this in the fine absorbent vessels of plants, which may co-operate towards producing that endless variety of juices elaborated in plants from the same earth and air. (SIR § 41)

Now what precisely is the meaning of "produce" and "elaborate" and "co-operate" in a Berkeleian world, in which the only agent and cause is God? In what sense can bodies created by God, and by His will maintained in life and distinctive activity, be said to "co-operate" with their creator? They select from the common medium which they breathe that alone which suits their life. What is this selective power that alone enables them to "elaborate" their productions, which contribute to the life of the universe, so "co-operating" with the Author of the universe? If it is not intelligence—and only spirits are intelligent, while organisms and their organs are corporeal—what is the function of the organic "machines" in the unceasing action of God?

In Berkeley's phrase "that endless variety," the adjective is not a mere splash of rhetoric for "large." If everything that happens in the universe is the present volition of God, which is infinite because He is infinite, then infinite too in the strict sense are the results to which the natural processes, started by Him when, where, and in the manner He wills, can lead.

All this is contained in Berkeley's general critique of the concept of cause. In his *De Motu* of 1721, he had drawn a distinction between the real cause of motion, which is mind and falls for investigation to metaphysics, and what are called causes in physics:

> We say that a moving body is the cause of motion in another body, or impresses motion on it, and that it draws it or impels it. This is the sense in which we must understand second corporeal causes, leaving out of account the real seat of forces or active powers, or the real cause in which these reside. (§ 71)

In *Siris,* Berkeley proves that "there is a Mind that governs and actuates the mundane system, as the proper real agent and cause" (§ 154), and goes on to consider the other sense of cause:

> The principles whereof a thing is compounded, the instrument used in its production, and the end for which it was intended, are all in vulgar use termed causes, though none of them be, strictly speaking, agent or efficient. There is not any proof that an extended corporeal or mechanical cause doth really and properly act, even motion itself being in truth a passion. Therefore though we speak of this fiery substance as acting, yet it is to be understood only as a mean or instrument, which indeed is the case of all mechanical causes whatsoever. They are, nevertheless, sometimes termed agents and causes, although they are by no means active in a strict and proper signification. When therefore force, power, virtue, or action are mentioned as subsisting in an extended and corporeal or mechanical being, this is not to be taken in a true, genuine and real, but only in a gross and popular sense, which sticks in appearances and doth not analyse things to their first principles. (§ 155)

Here Berkeley gathers up and sharply clarifies the critique of "second causes" that he had been conducting all his life. Such causes are "means or instruments" of the real Cause, which when using them uses them freely (it is man, in his present state, that is forced to use the instrument allotted to him, his body). There is, however, a reason why the real Cause prefers to make use of instruments instead of dispensing with them.

> Without instrumental and second causes there could be no regular course of Nature. And without a regular course Nature could never be understood; mankind must always be at a loss, not knowing what to expect, or how to govern themselves, or direct their actions for the obtaining of any end. Therefore in the government of the world physical agents, improperly so called, or mechanical, or second causes, or natural causes, or instruments, are necessary to assist not the Governor but the governed. (§ 160)

There, then, we are told what "things" are—instruments, means, concauses,[10] with which God operates when and so long as He pleases and for the ends He pleases. Berkeley has expressed himself quite clearly—without ambiguity, reserve, or omission. If even greater precision is desired, turn to a

10 Plato in *Timaeus,* 46C and 68E, draws the distinction between cause and concause, *aitia* and *sunaitia.*

passage in which he brings under his criticism every sort of mechanism, evolutionism, and preformism:

> Nothing could be more vain and imaginary than to suppose with Descartes that merely from a circular motion's being impressed by the supreme Agent on the particles of extended substance, the whole world, with all its several parts, appurtenances, and phenomena, might be produced by a necessary consequence from the laws of motion. Others suppose that God did more at the beginning, having then made the seeds of all vegetables and animals, containing their solid organical parts in miniature, the gradual filling and evolution of which, by the influx of proper juices, doth constitute the generation and growth of a living body. So that the artificial structure of plants and animals daily generated requires no present exercise of art to produce it, having been already framed at the origin of the world, which with all its parts hath ever since subsisted, going like a clock or machine by itself, according to the laws of Nature, without the immediate hand of the artist. But how can this hypothesis explain the blended features of different species in mules or other mongrels? Or the parts added or changed, and sometimes whole limbs lost, by marking in the womb? Or how can it account for the resurrection of a tree from its stump, or the vegetative power in its cutting? In which cases we must necessarily conceive something more than the mere evolution of a seed. (§ 232 f.)

Clearly, it is the contingency, fully recognized, of the "endless" effects of natural structures that is the obstacle to a philosophy of necessitation. The forms of nature have been and are being invented by an artist, who also maintains them in life and specific functioning with a "present exercise of art," when and so long as he wills to do so. Berkeley the theologian thus explains Berkeley the philosopher: his philosophy seen in the light of his theology is no longer a pungent paradox but a recognition that things are made to be experienced and minds in order to experience them, and that a universe composed of these two orders of being was willed by a single Author who, having made them for one another, designed and willed connections between them.

From Berkeley's time until now, indeed now more than ever, there have been many attempts, increasingly subtle, to reduce Berkeleianism to that pure ideism which, while at one moment it did flash into Berkeley's mind, was decisively rejected and therefore was not *his* doctrine—but Hume's, for the latter somehow took it from him, and started a whole tradition of thought that is nowadays more combative and acrimonious than ever before. Everybody has undoubtedly the right to fashion and declare the philosophy he believes to be true, and to hang up his thoughts on the pegs of classical philosophers, of whom Berkeley is one. But nobody who has seen that Berkeley's occasional reserve, his not saying everything that was in his mind, was tactical[11] would accuse him of deceit: he seems only to have been trying

[11] "Berkeley was a tactician; he had a revolutionary creed to announce; he was afraid of being laughed out of court before the case was heard; and he had hopes that by a wise economy of truth the notion of immaterialism 'might steal unawares on the reader.' "

not to prejudice the reception of his basic position by startling and bewildering his readers with contentions too uncommon.[12] It is therefore permissible to inquire of the Doctor of Divinity the ultimate meaning of his writings on philosophy.

(Luce, *Works,* Vol. I, 150) His tactical reason regarding his immaterialism is not in the *Essay on Vision* only. In the *Principles,* and afterwards too, whenever he spoke of the givenness of the sense as "passivity," leaving in the background the activity of the sensing from which the sense is inseparable, he thought he was saying something so plain that the reader would accept it straightway, and see that perception did not require any "material support." Much trouble is needed to free Berkeley's thought from his excessively prudent simplifications of expression and to present it in its entirety.

12 "He was not a liar" when he was using metaphors, as he often did, writes C. M. Turbayne in "Berkeley's Two Concepts of Mind, Part II" (*Journal of Philosophy and Phenomenological Research,* 22 [1962], 578); and he was speaking metaphorically when he called mind a substance, for he had himself explained that ideas are "in" the mind only in a metaphorical sense, the strict sense being that they are perceived by it. Turbayne was countering "A Note on Berkeley's Conception of the Mind" by S. A. Grave (*Ibid.,* 574–576). The discussion sprang out of an article on the theme in 1959 by Turbayne (*Ibid.,* 20 [1959], 85–92), in which he argued that as in the *Essay on Vision* Berkeley had withheld his immaterialism, so in the *Principles* (intended as Part I only) he withheld his "secret" concept of mind as "to act, cause, will, operate" (PC # 829), and instead wrote of mind as substance out of ecclesiastical prudence.

Grave pursued the question further in an article "Some Problems in the Interpretation of Berkeley" (in *Australasian Journal of Philosophy,* 42[1964], 199–210), here accepting the thesis that Berkeley did have two concepts of mind, as substance and as will. Inserting the *Essay on Vision* into the *Principles* could be one way of moving towards that "unified Berkeley" of whom Grave speaks at the end of his article.

E. J. Furlong in his "An Ambiguity in Berkeley's *Principles"* (*Philosophical Quarterly* [St. Andrews], 14[1964], 334–344), examines the clause in PHK § 1, "or else such as are perceived by attending to the passions and operations of the mind," and contends that the syntax of the whole sentence requires us to supply "ideas" after "such" (Locke's "ideas of reflection"). But the development of Berkeley's thought precludes that insertion, since for him what the mind apprehends of itself is not an "idea" but a "notion." As I have tried to show, an "idea," that which is sensed, is independent of my will (though not of the perceptual act of apprehension as judgment)—not, however, as a distinct perceptible in the sense of being always there for someone to perceive it. The *divine* "perceiving," by the way, is different from this, for in the act of creating what we perceive, His awareness of the creating and of what is created precedes or accompanies the act, whereas in our perception we are aware first of the object and only then of our own activity of perceiving. We ought therefore to avoid the same term for God's awareness and our own.

VII

Substance in Berkeley*

HARRY M. BRACKEN

Great boldness and originality characterize the Cartesian theory of substance.[1] It is against this background that I shall explore Berkeley's doctrine of substance. In the Cartesian theory, made explicit by Malebranche, the usual talk about participation, inherence, exemplification, and so forth, is replaced with a new model of explanation. In accordance with this new model, the question of whether any given mode does or does not inhere in a certain substance is resolved by determining whether the ideas composing the mode are logically deducible from the ideas composing the substance. The murky metaphorical relation of participation or exemplification is replaced by the logical tie of deducibility. The resultant substance doctrine, however, is limited to the domain of essence. A doctrine of substance that fails to deal with questions in the existential order may strike us as perverse, but the Cartesians distinguished, more sharply than Hume, between "relations of ideas," and "matters of fact."

Ideas and Substances for Malebranche and Locke

Because Locke thought the Cartesian way of ideas was geared to the question of, for example, a piece of gold and its qualities, he (in good company)

* I wish to thank Professor David Norton, Department of Philosophy, University of California, San Diego, and Professor Richard A. Watson, Department of Philosophy, Washington University, St. Louis, for their many helpful comments on earlier drafts of this paper.

[1] An elaboration of this interpretation occurs in "Some Problems of Substance Among the Cartesians," *American Philosophical Quarterly,* 1 (1964), 129–137.

thought that he should be able, first, to find the idea of substance, and second, to discern the ties binding the qualities together. That he found no such things is reported frequently and with no little perplexity. Locke's discussion of the primary–secondary quality distinction is very different from what might appear to be its analogue on the Cartesian model. In Malebranche, for example, we have a purely mathematical conception of material objects. Two material objects do not constitute two material substances. Indeed, what we can properly be said to *know* of these two bodies is not whether there *are* two bodies, but rather, that *if* one (mode of body) is triangular then necessarily the sum of its interior angles equals two right angles. It is as if one took the axioms of geometry to comprehend all that is knowable about all possible material objects. But geometry does not tell us whether there are any bodies. What exists is a function of what God chooses to will in His role as Creator. One effect of this is to mark out two realms of "ideas": (1) eternal, immutable Ideas that constitute the realm of what Malebranche calls Intelligible Extension. And it is this realm that we may think of in mathematical terms. A mode of a substance is tied to the substance on the model of a theorem being deductively tied to the axioms from which it is derived. In our experience these Ideas are mixed with very different sorts of things: (2) the mental modes. These include our sensations, or what Malebranche calls Sentiments. Their being is in some way dependent on our mind. Just as mathematics comprehends the essence of material substance, so presumably there is available to God, although not to us, some variety of "mind-mathematics" whereby He can know the essence of mental substance—the formulae for an awareness contrasted with those for a willing. But while we may be aware that we have, say, a pain, we are unable to say what a pain is or to express the deductive ties between the idea of an awareness of pain and the idea of mental substance.

There is, then, a sharp ontological difference between these two sorts of "ideas."[2] The distinction is present in Descartes, although it is drawn much more sharply in Malebranche. The Cartesian "way of ideas" is intimately tied to the radical Cartesian doctrine of substance. Locke is insensitive to the ontological contrast built into the Cartesian way of ideas and accordingly is bewildered by the logical "tie" discussions. He finds no such glue, no such ties, no such necessary connections among the ideas in *his* experience. I think his bewilderment is a bit of evidence in favor of my interpretation of the Cartesian substance doctrine.

Berkeley appreciates the Cartesian version of the way of ideas as well as Locke's formulation of it. It is surely to Berkeley's credit that he was able to cut through Locke's muddling of the primary–secondary quality distinction and the attendant confusion over the nature of substance. Since Locke had

[2] Not all critics agreed. For a discussion of this and closely related questions see R. A. Watson, *The Downfall of Cartesianism, 1673–1712* (The Hague: 1965).

blurred the Cartesian primary–secondary quality distinction and the theory of substance that went with it, Berkeley started out accepting as a fact the collapse of the distinction. Where Locke had sought in vain for logical ties among ideas and necessary connections among things, Berkeley broke with the deductive model of the Cartesians. This feature of Cartesianism, providing as it did the explication of the tie between substance and mode, would have been difficult to rehabilitate given the collapse of the primary–secondary quality distinction on which it rested. I suggest that Berkeley (a) recognized the collapse of the distinction; (b) nevertheless understood the ease with which Cartesians could talk of *idea of substance;* (c) understood the logic behind both Locke's search for and failure to find such an idea.

Immortal Spiritual Substances

Deprived of the Cartesian solution, and keenly aware of the ramifications of Locke's account of substance, Berkeley returns to an apparent variant of the "old" inherence pattern. Long before Hume, indeed immediately after publication of the *Essay,* Locke's defense of spiritual substance was subjected to a most vigorous series of attacks.[3] The literature of the period is replete with discussions of minds, their existence, our knowledge of them, whether they are material, and so forth. The need to render intelligible our language about souls and their immortality is at the very core of this tradition. And it is out of this tradition, with its religious concern, that our concept of mind arises. It is all too easy to treat the account of mind in Descartes, for example, as a muddle if one assumes that Descartes is working only with our own concept. But the history of recent philosophy makes it evident that it is difficult to make much sense of this and related concepts after having excised all religious factors. Miss G. E. M. Anscombe[4] once argued to the effect that the concept of obligation has gradually become detached from the divine law-giver framework in which it originally derived its meaning. Nevertheless, relics of that framework, a framework that has long since been succeeded by a very different one, remain embedded in the language. This disparity provides the ground for the unsatisfactory character of contemporary discussions of the concept. I am inclined to believe that some present discussions of "mind" run into somewhat analogous difficulties.

How Ideas May Be "in" Minds

Berkeley, however, thought that the "way of ideas" not only need not produce Locke's disastrous conclusions but that it could actually provide a defense of spiritual substance. There is ample evidence that Berkeley wanted that

[3] See the accounts of these discussions in John W. Yolton, *John Locke and the Way of Ideas* (Oxford: 1956).

[4] "Modern Moral Philosophy," *Philosophy,* 33 (1958), 1–19.

defense for a variety of reasons—but primarily so that he would be able to talk sensibly about a spiritual thing which could be immortal.[5] He tells us that he chose *idea,* "because a necessary relation to the mind is understood to be implied by that term . . ." (DHP 235–236)

That ideas are necessarily related to the mind is a key Berkeleian axiom. Nothing could be clearer than this principle. Furthermore, it is common sense that attests to the necessity of the relation between *idea* and *mind.* Although presumably a philosophical account may be based on this axiom, it must be noted that Berkeley does not base the axiom on a philosophical account. And for good reason—commentators have often forgotten that many philosophers would have rejected Berkeley's axiom. Specifically, neither Malebranche nor Locke would have accepted it. For the domain of eternal Ideas, Malebranche would have declared the principle false, and for Sentiments he would have found it unjustified. Locke, whose talk of qualities "without" substances is itself puzzling, would also have rejected Berkeley's axiom. Nowhere, thanks to Stillingfleet, was Locke more conscious of his failure to find "necessary relations" than in discussing the relation of ideas to minds.

In the ontologies of the period, I think that at least four distinct "primitive" relations can be discerned. (a) *Inherence,* or the tie between substance and accident on the so-called Aristotelian pattern. Berkeley's axiom may appear to be based on this pattern, but not if, as I hold, the axiom derives its strength from common sense. (b) *Substance–mode,* the Cartesian, or at least Malebranchian, tie. As explained above, this is explicated on the deductive model and holds only among eternal entities. (c) *Part—whole,* or the collection pattern. For example, a physical object is construed as being a collection of ideas. To say that an object has a certain property is to say that a certain idea is a member of the collection that constitutes the object. This account is generally associated with phenomenalism. (d) The *intentional* tie, a unique relation on some scholastic models as well as the Cartesian, where it is disguised by occasionalism. Initially the term arises in the context of explicating the acts whereby immaterial minds know material objects, and thus the relations of *meaning* between concepts (and words) and things.

As I explained at the outset, in presenting (b) the Cartesians broke radically with the various forms of (a). Locke, for the reasons mentioned, sought to explain (b) in terms of (a) or something like it. Berkeley was aware of the problems that had been generated by (a) but was uneasy with a doctrine of substance that was limited to the nonexistential, as in (b). A certain aura of scientific attractiveness surrounds (c) and it has the backing of Locke. What Berkeley presents is often taken to be a mixture of (a) and (c). But I maintain that (d) provides an alternative which has both an inherent plausibility and textual basis.

[5] See my "Berkeley on the Immortality of the Soul," *The Modern Schoolman,* 37 (1960), 77–94; 197–212.

Berkeley's Account of the Substance–Accident Tie

It is my contention that knowing that a certain set of ideas is to be called a die is, for Berkeley, like knowing that a certain set of marks *means* something. This connection between marks or signs and their meaning is one half of the intentional account. The other half concerns the relations that hold *among* the meanings. Traditionally, the formation of concepts and the composition of propositions had been contrasted. One comes to know that a certain set of ideas is to be called a *die,* and one also comes to learn that *the die is hard.* Medieval accounts have a way of getting complicated at this juncture (relating the composition of the proposition itself to the composition of what it is "about"), even if their discussions of the intentionality of concepts have been fairly straightforward. Berkeley's account remains simple, and hence runs the risk of being overlooked.

Usually, Berkeley appeals to the language metaphor in contexts where we are, for example, learning the meaning of a "phrase." The question of the *tie* binding "die" and "hard" seldom arises. And when it does he says: "to say a die is hard, extended and square, is not to attribute those qualities to a subject distinct from and supporting them, but only an explication of the meaning of the word die." (PHK § 49)

It is this tie with which I am primarily concerned. I propose to call it "intentional," and I claim that Berkeley relies on it in presenting his account of, say, objects and their properties. I call it "intentional" primarily because it is the conceptual correlate of the linguistic predicative tie; secondarily, because I believe that Berkeley is well acquainted with medieval as well as seventeenth century accounts of meaning, concept formation, intentions, and notions. Berkeley wants to appeal to the radical contrast between seeing letters and reading their meaning.[6] *Then* he wants to talk of the ties among

[6] A terse statement of this contrast occurs in *Alciphron* IV, § 12, "It may be also worth while to observe that signs, being little considered in themselves, or for their own sake, but only in their relative capacity, and for the sake of those things whereof they are signs, it comes to pass that the mind often overlooks them, so as to carry its attention immediately on to the things signified. Thus, for example, in reading we run over the characters with the slightest regard, and pass on to the meaning." (ALC 156) But cf. *Principles,* §§ 108, 109. Also, "My aim is only to know what ideas are connected together; and the more a man knows of the connexion of ideas, the more he is said to know of the nature of things. What therefore if our ideas are variable . . ." (DHP 245) And in *Principles* § 65, "the reason why ideas are formed into machines, that is, artificial and regular combinations, is the same with that for combining letters into words. That a few original ideas may be made to signify a great number of effects and actions, it is necessary they be variously combined together: and to the end their use be permanent and universal, these combinations must be made by *rule,* and with *wise contrivance.*" (Italics in original.)

the concepts in terms of the predicative tie. Berkeley's whole attack on the redundancy of matter is evident here. Why, he may be seen to ask, should he struggle to reproduce among *material* things, the elements already found both in language and in thought? Given the history of the problem of relating mind to matter, what can possibly be the point in attempting to construct on the side of matter what is nothing more than an analogue of predication?

This point about the redundancy of matter in relation to the intentional tie becomes clearer if we compare Malebranche with Berkeley. Berkeley certainly does want to preserve an element from the Malebranchian tradition, that is, an object of knowledge worthy of the name.[7] For Malebranche, Ideas are eternal and ontologically independent of human minds; Sentiments are, we might say, mental. For Berkeley, the *meanings* of the sense signs function like Malebranchian Ideas. The sensory signs themselves function like Malebranchian Sentiments. The sharp ontological distinction Malebranche drew between Sentiments and Ideas now shows itself in Berkeley as the contrast between marks and their meanings. But there is also this difference: Malebranche and the Cartesians sought to offer an explication of the mystery shrouding the exemplification or *inherence* tie by appealing to the *substance–mode* deductive model, which amounts in the new metaphysics to an account of the predicative tie in terms of the deductive tie. Berkeley, however, converts Malebranchian Ideas into divine Meanings. But the predicative tie is just a predicative tie. And neither a materialist ontology nor the Malebranchian deductive tie will provide us with a clearer explanation of how our concepts may be related.

There is also another difference. Matter still "existed" in Malebranche's system, although it did no work. In Berkeley the process is complete. Initially, it had seemed to some scholastics reasonable to say that our concepts intended objects. But they said this knowing full well that the *matter* of substances had always been puzzling. Aristotle's own suggestions—for example, that matter is, in itself, unknowable, and that matter is only apprehended in sensation—hardly made the task of relating intentional entities to material substances any easier. But regardless of whether any given ontology contained many or few entities, bewhiskered or clean-shaven, these links between material objects, sensible species, and intentional entities nevertheless became progressively more problematic. By the time of the Cartesians what seem very much like intentional entities emerge as proper objects of knowledge. Malebranche tried to distinguish between Sentiments and Ideas because he was anxious to assure the status of Ideas as entities whose being was wholly independent of us. Material things no longer played an intelligible role in Malebranche's ontology and in Berkeley they are, of course, dismissed.

Berkeley's situation can perhaps be put this way: material objects are invented because we think that there must be *things* for our concepts to be

[7] See A. A. Luce, *Berkeley and Malebranche* (London: 1934). See also my "Berkeley and Malebranche on Ideas," *The Modern Schoolman*, 41 (1963), 1–15.

about. We apprehend the meaning of sensory signs and then proceed to introduce still another *thing* for the meaning to be about.[8] Part of the attraction to Berkeley of the language metaphor is that he hoped it would enable him to talk successfully about concepts. He knew the risk of talking about them: concepts turn up as intermediary entities. Thinking of the problem in terms of letters and their *meaning* minimized the risks of confusing these two very different kinds of things. But he could not see how *matter* helped matters. Material things are not only unnecessary to the completeness of our account of reality, they are confused and contradictory fictions. It is nonsense to think they can play roles either in our metaphysics of concepts or in our analyses of linguistic meaning. Since at best they are merely ontological spare gear and at worst logically absurd, we may dismiss them. However, unless Berkeley is prepared to forego his wish to "bring men back to common sense," we must, on his system, still be able to talk about things we normally talk about—physical objects, properties, and so forth.[9]

Berkeley's Rejection of the Inherence Model

My claim that Berkeley is offering us a new and different account of what many philosophers have taken to be the relation between a material substance and its accidents runs counter to a position Allaire has recently advanced.[10]

[8] In the *New Theory of Vision,* where the language metaphor is frequently employed (see especially §§ 51, 159), Berkeley had spoken of visual ideas as signs of *independently* existing data of touch. At *Principles* § 44, Berkeley rectifies this "vulgar error" by treating visual signs as signs of tactual signs: "visible ideas are the language whereby the governing spirit, on whom we depend, informs us what tangible ideas he is about to imprint upon us . . ." Archetypes are mentioned in the next section in the context of not existing without being perceived. See also *Theory of Vision Vindicated* § 40. In the *Third Dialogue,* reminiscent of *Principles* § 50, he says: "to explain the phenomena, is to show how we come to be affected with ideas, in that manner and order wherein they are imprinted on our senses." (DHP 242)

[9] I am not convinced that Berkeley's use of the language metaphor in the early works is significantly different from what he says in *Siris.* Berkeley does say, in *Siris,* such things as: "Strictly, the sense knows nothing." (§ 253) But he says them in the context of a discussion of God's language. "As the natural connexion of signs with the things signified is regular and constant, it forms a sort of rational discourse . . . and is therefore the immediate effect of an intelligent cause." (SIR § 254) The temptation to think of Berkeley as rejecting "empiricism" in favor of "Platonism" in his old age should be checked by the knowledge we now have of Berkeley's relationship to Malebranchianism. Berkeley was alert *both* to the need for an ontological account of epistemic objects and to the uselessness of matter before he set out to write the *Principles.*

[10] Edwin B. Allaire, "Berkeley's Idealism," *Theoria,* 29 (1963), 229–244. (I deal with only one segment of his paper.) For some discussions of other aspects of the inherence question, cf. R. A. Watson, "Berkeley in a Cartesian Context," *Revue Internationale de Philosophie,* 17 (1963), 381–394; and Phillip Cummins, "Perceptual Relativity and Ideas in the Mind," *Philosophy and Phenomenological Research,* 24 (1963), 202–214.

He sees Berkeley as wrongfully utilizing features both of the *inherence* tie and the *part–whole* (collection) pattern. He holds that Berkeley errs by saying that qualities must inhere in a substance while at the same time maintaining that such qualities must *not* be predicated of that substance. Put positively, Allaire argues that Berkeley *should* say that qualities are such only as relative to that of which they are predicated, inasmuch as Berkeley *does* claim that qualities must inhere in a substance. However when Berkeley turns to the analysis of "a die is hard" he (1) treats the sensible quality as mind-dependent *without* saying that the mind is hard, and he (2) considers hard both a quality of, and a predicate of, the die. Allaire views Berkeley's "idealist" conclusions as resulting from the illegitimate (that is, partial) use of the *inherence* pattern. Presumably Berkeley could reject the inherence pattern and treat "hard" simply as a quality (part) of the collection it is predicated of. But this would deprive Berkeley of what Allaire considers the key to his idealism: Berkeley's use of the inherence relation in order to guarantee binding ideas to minds.

Lying behind, and giving force to the inherence pattern, is what Allaire calls "Aristotle's dictum": a quality is a quality of that of which it is predicated, namely, a substance. But is Aristotle's "dictum" really so straightforward? Aristotle does distinguish between what is "predicable of," and what is "present in," in the sense of being incapable of existence apart from the subject. But in giving examples of the various combinatorial possibilities the distinction affords, Aristotle seems to say that while all accidents are present in a substance, some are predicable of it, as the color of a body; some are not, as a particular whiteness; and some—for example, knowledge—are present in one substance but only predicable of something else—in this case, *in* the mind but *predicable* of grammar.

I assume that Aristotle need not have used the mind in his last example in order to illustrate the possibility involved. And yet for a good portion of what is called the Aristotelian tradition it makes sense to speak of a range of entities which have *intentional being* in the mind. As such, they are *present in* the mind as accidents, but of course from the concept "white" being in the mind it does not follow that the mind *is* white. (Recall Berkeley: "it no more follows, that the soul or mind is extended because extension exists in it alone, than it does that it is red or blue, because those colours are on all hands acknowledged to exist in it, and no where else."[11] (PHK § 49) Medievals proceeded to work out a technical vocabulary in an attempt to avoid the confusions that talking about *signs* and *signification* has traditionally engendered. For better or worse, it is, I believe, in this portion of the Aristotelian tradition that the roots of Berkeley's account (including what I have called the *intentional* tie) are to be found.

Of course there is no lack of evidence that Berkeley made frequent use of

[11] Cf. *Third Dialogue*, "It is therefore evident there can be no *substratum* of these qualities but spirit, in which they exist, not by way of mode or property, but as a thing perceived in that which perceives it." (DHP 237)

some relation between idea and mind. And this connection certainly fits with the inherence pattern, even though this pattern itself has been notoriously lacking in precision. However, I have contended that in talking about *this* tie Berkeley relies on an "axiom" of common sense—all ideas are necessarily related to the mind—rather than the other way around, that is to say, he does not seek to support the "axiom" by an appeal to the inherence patern. Furthermore, I have tried to show that coupled with "ideas being necessarily related to the mind" is a wholly distinct account of the very different tie holding between a "thing" and its "properties"; the tie I have called "intentional."

Things as Collections or as Combinations

This takes us back to the question whether Berkeley offers us a "collection" theory of physical objects. When Berkeley turns to talk about physical objects and their properties does he explicate the link that holds between "die" and "hard" on the *part—whole* (collection) model? I realize that Berkeley has functioned historically as one of the seminal thinkers of the phenomenalist movement.[12] And it is obvious that part of what he says is compatible with the "collection" theory of objects. But it is important to note that although Berkeley does speak of *things* as *collections,*[13] his preference becomes *combinations,*[14] a term much more appropriate to the language metaphor.

Speaking of things as collections was apparently a well-established tradition, with its roots in Greek atomism, when Locke appealed to it. In the *Philosophical Commentaries* Berkeley says: "The substance wood a collection of simple ideas see Locke B.2.c.26.S.1." (PC # 179) Locke himself writes: "So also, finding that the substance, wood, which is a certain collection of simple *ideas* so called, by the application of fire is turned into another substance, called ashes, i.e. another complex *idea,* consisting of a collection of simple *ideas* . . ."[15]

My contention is that despite Berkeley's own occasional use of "collection," he does not think of physical objects as mere collections nor does he analyse the tie between *die* and *hard* as part–whole. Moreover his use of "combination" fits with what I have been calling the intentional tie. The sensory data function as signs. We learn what they mean. Learning what they mean is learning God's language. But the sensory data are *not* parts of which the meaning is the whole. It is true that it is in collections or combinations that

[12] In this connection, see John W. Davis, "Berkeley and Phenomenalism," *Dialogue,* 1 (1962), 67–80.

[13] Notably (PHK §§ 1 and 148), "Congeries" is used in reference to the cherry. (DHP 249)

[14] Thus letters are combined, not collected, into words and so forth. See, for example, PHK §§ 26, 38, 145; *First Dialogue,* the instance of the tulip (DHP 195), and also the famous challenge to Hylas 200; and in the *Third Dialogue* 245.

[15] John Locke, *An Essay Concerning Human Understanding,* ed. John W. Yolton (London: 1961), I, 271.

we find the interesting meanings, but the items (ideas) in a set of data stand in the same relation to their meaning as letters, suitably combined, do to theirs. Hence my use of the term "intentional" for this tie. To treat it as *part–whole* would involve a "category-mistake."

Since a dispositional element is obviously present in this discussion of combinations, meanings, learning the rules for the use of God's language, and especially in the question of the status of meanings "in" God, I wish briefly to discuss a position that Luce considers Berkeley to have rejected. In the *Dialectic of Immaterialism,* Luce argues that Berkeley initially opts for a *powers* theory of objects; that Berkeley was originally intrigued with Locke's account of things as collections of powers to affect our sensory organs, although the powers rested in God, not matter. Berkeley rejected this line because, Luce argues, he saw its panpsychist implications and because he realized it posed problems for an account of Creation.

What then *are* bodies for the Berkeley of the *Principles*? They are "the things the effects themselves," which we perceive by sense, which really exist and are still perceivable, even when not actually perceived by man. They are "still with relation to perception."[16]

In one important respect the combination of powers, sign-meaning, and archetype discussions all belong to the same general worry. There being obvious difficulties in taking variable ideas of sense as independent objects of knowledge, Berkeley wants something additional. Accordingly, these discussions all generate questions about the ontological nature of the relevant additional item[17] in contrast with ideas of sense. Luce points out that although there is one passage in the *Third Dialogue* (DHP 239–240) referring to divine powers, there is no "combination of powers" discussion in the *Principles.* And there is none, Luce maintains, because by that stage in his development Berkeley is appealing to God's powers only as sustaining causes and no longer suggesting that powers *are* body. Quite apart from the question whether Berkeley can distinguish two such accounts of powers in God,[18] the absence of a "combination of powers" doctrine does not establish the "collection of ideas" thesis. It does not because Berkeley's more general use of "combination" is in itself perfectly compatible with the language metaphor and intentional tie analysis. And as Berkeley's concerns for an independent object of knowledge and for an account of the nature of objects "in" God coalesce, the language metaphor takes on increased importance. Sometimes Berkeley's use of "combination" occurs in contexts where he is underscoring the contrast between a combination of letters and the meaning of the word; at other times

16 A. A. Luce, *The Dialectic of Immaterialism* (London: 1963), 154.

17 Impetus is thereby given to interpreting Berkeley as, for example, a realist, or as a defender of the act–object distinction.

18 See my "Berkeley's Realisms," *Philosophical Quarterly,* 8 (1958), 41–53. Reprinted in *The Early Reception of Berkeley's Immaterialism: 1710–1733* (Revised ed.; The Hague: 1965).

he seems to use it in the scholastic sense that combination and division are basic judgmental activities with regard to propositions. "Intentional" is used to cover both sorts of cases, although of course it is the latter sort that I have been contending is immediately at issue with reference to the question of *hard* being in a *die*.

The Ontological Status of Signs and Meanings

But even if we take Berkeley to be offering such a radically revised account of the substance–accident tie in his discussion of physical objects and their properties, certain questions still remain concerning that other tie that binds ideas to minds. Even if we grant that Berkeley is seeking to talk about the tie between "die" and "hard" as intentional, and even if we take that very different tie between an idea and a mind as resting on a common-sense "axiom," we still must see whether Berkeley falls prey to a new variant of Allaire's argument. In brief, can the intentional account do a better job of explaining how properties are related to physical objects while retaining the essential features of Berkeley's over-all account?

By way of an answer, it may again help to recall that for Malebranche, Sentiments, although ontologically "in" the mind, are not properly said to be known. Ideas, although known, are not "in" the mind—they are, however, somehow "in" God. Berkeley draws a somewhat similar contrast: "To know every thing knowable is certainly a perfection; but to endure, or suffer, or feel any thing by sense, is an imperfection." (DHP 241) Ideas of sense are "in" us; another sort of idea (?) is "in" God. The latter I take to be Meanings. Just as Berkeley often wishes to contrast what we feel with what we know, the sense signs with what they mean, so in God he also contrasts feeling and knowing—for the purpose of excluding the former. And as long as Berkeley retains a distinction between ideas as sense signs and as meanings he attenuates the connection between meanings and minds. The tidy "necessary relation," the self-evidence of which Berkeley grounds in common sense and common language, becomes blurred. With the suggestion that it is not the ideas but the meanings that count, Berkeley's argument loses a bit of its elegance—albeit in the interests of truth. However, it does not follow that immaterialism fails. Meanings, intentional things, and notions, are not material things.[19] Instead, what we find is the emergence in Berkeley of Male-

[19] In this paper I am not concerned with all the implications of the language metaphor for Berkeley's analysis of mind. But criticism, à la Ryle, of historical accounts of the mind as a "thing" should be tempered by our recognition that a major point to such accounts was quasi-theological, that is, personal immortality. As for notions, see I. T. Ramsey, "Notions and Ideas in Berkeley's Philosophy," *Proceedings of the XIth Int. Congress* (1953), Vol. 13, 66–71; John W. Davis, "Berkeley's Doctrine of the Notion," *Review of Metaphysics,* 12 (1959), 378–389; Reinhardt Grossman, "Digby and Berkeley on Notions," *Theoria,* 26 (1960), 17–30; and my "Berkeley and Mental Acts," *Theoria,* 26 (1960), 140–146.

branche's problem of relating Ideas both to the human and to the divine minds. When we read God's language, the sense signs God presents to us, we grasp what He means—but this meaning is not ontologically on a par with the sense signs. Like a Malebranchian Idea, it is what it is independently of us. Accordingly, I conclude that although this interpretation may generate new problems, they are not simply variations on the older ones.

Berkeley appealed to this language metaphor throughout his philosophical writings—from the *New Theory of Vision* to *Siris*. I have discussed elsewhere[20] some of the advantages he thought would accrue to him. But none is more important than the contrast it illustrates (but not elucidates) between marks and meanings. It is beyond the scope of this essay to do more than to mention, first, that Berkeley's use of the language metaphor fits with his doctrine of *notions* (notional knowledge is, of course, concerned primarily with substances) and second, that the doctrine of notions and the appeal to the language metaphor have sound roots not only in scholasticism but also in portions of late seventeenth century philosophy that Berkeley knew well.

Summary

In conclusion let me summarize: (1) I distinguished four accounts of relations between "things" and "properties": (a) *inherence,* on the so-called Aristotelian pattern; (b) *substance–mode,* the Cartesian, or at least Malebranchian, mathematical-deductive tie; (c) *part–whole,* the collection pattern; (d) the *intentional* tie on the language model. I sketched the uses to which one or more of these were put by Malebranche and Locke.

(2) Berkeley wants his *ideas* to inhere in *spirits* but he tells us that he chose the word *idea* "because a necessary relation to the mind is understood by that term." I have called this Berkeley's "axiom" because he grounds it not in the philosophical tie of inherence, but in its common-sense acceptance. For however clear it may be to common-sense, the necessity of the tie between ideas and minds is frequently denied by seventeenth century philosophers—including Malebranche and Locke.

(3) Coupled with the discussion of ideas in relation to minds is an account of the very different relation between "things" and "properties" in terms of the intentional tie and the language metaphor. The account was viewed (a) as an extension of Berkeley's appreciation of the redundancy of matter, in that traditional questions about inherence and participation were now construed as questions about predication, since there would no longer even be any possibility of trying to build on the side of matter a parallel to the predicative model; (b) as an alternative, by substituting Meanings for Ideas, to the Malebranchian account of the object of knowledge; (c) as an improvement on the Cartesian-Malebranchian *substance–mode* deductive tie, confined

[20] Cf. "Berkeley on the Immortality of the Soul," and "Berkeley and Malebranche on Ideas."

as the latter was to the domain of essence. And generally, I have been urging that this intentional tie, and the use of *combinations* of ideas that goes with it, are Berkeley's considered preference—and *not* the *part–whole* (collection) analysis usually associated with the phenomenalist tradition. Or as Berkeley put it: "to say a die is hard, extended and square, is not to attribute those qualities to a subject distinct from and supporting them, but only an explication of the meaning of the word *die*."

VIII

Berkeley as Religious Apologist

T. E. JESSOP

Apologetic Motive a Clue to His Philosophy

Berkeley's system, whatever may be the right textbook label to apply to it, was plainly a piece of religious apologetics, the outline of a constructive natural theology, of a theistic metaphysic. From the *Principles* onwards he was fashioning a reasoned case for the existence of God, of a certain kind of God with a certain kind of relation to the world. The intention was unconcealed; it is explicit in his texts, confessed in his prefaces, and flourished on his title pages. His "*esse* is *percipi*," his denial of the representative theory of perception and of material substance, his critique of natural science, and his theory of signs, all arise in the context of that intention.

To that extent he was arguing a prior personal conviction. On this ground it may be objected that he was not a philosopher at all, but only an advocate. The objection, if applicable, would apply to St. Thomas; and it would apply equally to those who have set themselves to prove that there is no rational room for religion. As Berkeley himself said, any objection that can be leveled against both sides of a dispute has no force when directed against one side only (DHP III), or, as he has also said, the charge that only the religious, not their critics, think with *praejudicia* is patently false. (ALC 81) After all, what makes a philosopher is not his being without prior controlling convictions but his use of certain techniques of argumentation, such as, the kind of problems he considers, the special relevance of the evidence he adduces, the degree of consistency of his theorizing, and the range of his critical and explanatory power. We may not like St. Thomas's technique, or Hobbes's or

Hume's or Hegel's, but the method of each, though different from that of the others, is recognizably a philosophical one, and each was a master of it. The same must be said of Berkeley; and it is an external fact that philosophers have treated him as one of themselves, as arguing—and to be argued with—in the field of reference, methods, and criteria generally acknowledged to be philosophical.

Although his religiously apologetic intention is thus irrelevant to the question whether or no his system is genuinely a philosophy, it is one illuminating guide to the understanding of the content and shape of his system. In this paper I shall expand this statement by sketching how with that intention he faced, judged, and brought an original contribution to the cultural situation of his day, and by eliciting from his contribution the special religious insights or emphases he was seeking to clarify and ground. I shall conclude with a brief account of the work in which he let himself go in extraphilosophical religious apologetics.

We may begin by observing that if the vindication of theism had been all that mattered to him, he could have been content to make himself a spokesman of one or other of the modern philosophical systems, the chief of which were openly theistic—that of Descartes, both epistemologically and metaphysically based on God, or the high and charming idealism of Father Malebranche, or the devout and erudite theism of the Cambridge Platonists, or the spiritualist metaphysics of Leibniz, or the sober religious reasoning of Locke. (I omit Spinoza because he was at that time a reputed atheist.) All these thinkers can be ranged with Berkeley as minds open to the new science[1] as well as to the old religion. Why, instead of following one or other of them, did he forge the outlines of a philosophy of his own? Through a vain love of novelty or an arrogant ambition to be original, as some of his contemporaries supposed? The true answer is, I think, that they failed to satisfy either his piety or his lucid intellect: his discontent with them was both religious and technically philosophical. This is what I have to explicate.

First in summary form. In Descartes the religious air was thin, and his philosophical procedure abstract, much too a priori for Berkeley's taste; and the scientific cosmology of vortices had been antiquated by Newton. Malebranche, whose *Recherche de la vérité* Berkeley had read closely and usefully (as Professor Luce has amply proved),[2] put even our own body beyond the reach of both our mental action and our clear and certain knowledge, a paradox that shocked the empiricist side of Berkeley; and he proclaimed that intellectually we see all things not in themselves but in their Ideas or archetypes in God, which Berkeley took to mean that we look directly into God's mind, a claim from which he shrank reverently. The Cambridge Platonists,

[1] Berkeley's tenacious criticism of the new physics was not of its strictly scientific findings but of its metaphysical assumptions and extrapolations.

[2] See A. A. Luce, *Berkeley and Malebranche: A Study in the Origins of Berkeley's Thought* (New York: 1934).

elevated, charitable, and by the standards of their time undogmatic, were so far congenial, but they retained the traditional habit of collecting and quoting from old books, and had little of Berkeley's interest in the everyday particulars of the physical world. Locke, as we shall see, left a door ajar for materialism; he also shared the new physicists' reduction of the corporeal world to the "primary" qualities (quantities), and by this impoverished view of the world precluded any a posteriori cosmological natural theology from concluding to anything but an impoverished God. On Leibniz I must say nothing, for Berkeley seems to have known him only through his articles in the *Acta Eruditorum,* where he appears as a mathematical physicist.

There was indeed another line that he could have chosen, the skeptical one, which was very much alive. Its well-thumbed text was Sextus Empiricus. Its home was France, with Montaigne as its first and Bayle its latest brilliant exponents. Skepticism regarding the existence and nature of the physical world is dismissed in the opening sections of the introduction to the *Principles,* though the arguments in the main body of the work are chiefly against a skepticism which Berkeley saw to be latent in the new science. We have to bear in mind, however, that skepticism was used not only to attack but also to support religion, priests arguing the impotence of reason in order to champion the articles of the Church's faith. Unlike these clerical skeptics, Berkeley was modernist enough to recoil from justifying the fundamentals of religious belief by forcing reason to commit suicide.

Against Newtonianism

The chief contemporary provocations to Berkeley's philosophical thinking appear to have come from Newton and Locke, whom we must look at with more than a fleeting glance. We shall have to think of the Newtonian and the Lockian conceptions of matter, and of the distinction, of which Locke was only the most recent exponent, between "primary" and "secondary" qualities. In the first two he detected a latent materialism, in the third a latent skepticism. That both Newton and Locke were avowedly and sincerely religious was irrelevant to his purpose; he was concerned not with their personal beliefs but with the logical consequences of some of their published teaching. His sharp exposure of those consequences, and his effort to provide a theory that would avoid them, were haunted by a sense of urgency that sprang from his alarm at the irreligion and immorality of his day. It was not enough to *preach* against these, for they were being encouraged by purveyors of second-hand knowledge who claimed to have been freed from superstition by the new currents of thought, and such men had to be countered not by declamation or exhortation but by reasoned argument. Berkeley's theorizing, while expressing his irrepressible intellectuality and published by him for intellectual testing, was spurred by the practical apologetic aim of depriving "free-thinking," and the "free-living" that invoked it, of any contemporary scientific and philosophical excuse.

Instead of speaking of the Newtonian conception of matter I ought to speak of the Newtonian vindication of Galileo's conception, but the first designation has the convenience of brevity. It was Galileo who consciously and effectively expelled "secondary" qualities from physics, reducing the observational data to measurements, and in these seeking universalizable mathematical regularities. Newton, born, curiously, in the year Galileo died, raised the fragments of new mathematicized theory into a general system, and showed that this was borne out by the expanding and improved observations and experiments. Here was an impressively presented elucidation of the material universe as a homogeneous and apparently closed or self-maintaining system, operating in all its parts in accordance with laws of mathematical precision and generality. Berkeley, though admiring the scientific achievement, fastened on its possible religious bearing: a world so self-explanatory could be regarded as providing no room for God, or at most as making His connection with it extremely remote, as the Power that once created it and then left it to work by its fixed, inherent nature. Both these inferences, the atheisic and the deistic, had in fact already been drawn and accepted in some circles. They made Berkeley keenly aware that in order to establish the reality of a God possessing the panoply of omnipotence and providential control he would have to find a doctrine of the physical world that would exhibit this as closely and constantly dependent on a divine source: matter must have no independence.

Further, Newton, in order to supply a constant frame of reference for the intricate criss-cross of relative motions in the vastly dispersed heavenly bodies, had postulated an absolute space and an absolute time, within which alone the idea of absolute motion can have meaning. Berkeley's direct attack on these postulates was to exhibit them as "abstract ideas" in his special sense of having an alleged sensory content yet being incapable of becoming realized in sensory experience. This was a technical epistemological point. More broadly, he was disturbed by Newton's characterization of absolute space and time as infinite and eternal respectively. These marks, he deeply believed, should be reserved to God alone. Some English thinkers had merged absolute space with the immensity, and absolute time with the eternity, of God. Here for Berkeley was a grave confusion of two quite different orders of concepts, the material and the mental, not, like Plato's dictum that time is a "moving image of eternity" (*Timaeus* 37d), a merely suggestive hint of a relation exceedingly hard to conceptualize. Newton and More were in effect making space and time *attributes* of God, and Samuel Clarke did so explicitly. At least the spatialization was abhorrent to Berkeley's unwaveringly spiritual notion of the divine nature.

Against Lockianism

The Lockian conception of substance was agnostic, but was susceptible of a materialistic interpretation. The division of all *things* into overt properties and concealed substance was retained by Locke in a new and undogmatic way. What had been predicated of substance by the Schools—essence and causal power—was jettisoned by him as unverifiable. He postulated substance as a merely formal concept, defined as that to which experienced qualities belong: qualities being always "of" something, we have to posit the "something" to complete the "of." But to that something we can ascribe no hidden nature or power, no content other than the overt properties. Substance means for us simply a rationally indispensable *x*, the bare logical correlate of quality. This holds of both material and spiritual substance, of a lump of wood and of a mind. A purgation of Scholastic doctrine, especially its assertion of occult properties, was thoroughly congenial to Berkeley. Nevertheless he could not subscribe to a concept of substance that made this not only unknown but unknowable. So far as corporeal things are concerned he believed it shocking to common sense to say that "something there is in every drop of water, every grain of sand, which it is beyond the power of human understanding to fathom or comprehend." (PHK § 101)

When Locke went further, admitting with typical candor that the unknowableness of material and spiritual substance leaves open the possibility that both sorts may really be one and the same, Berkeley scented a danger to a religious philosophy. It is, of course, easy to identify two *x*'s. The abstractly possible single kind of substance could indeed be interpreted in either of two ways, with a materialist or a spiritualist bias; but Berkeley feared that the former interpretation was the one more likely to be seized on in the fashionable circles of his day. (A third possibility, that substance is neither material nor mental, would have been rejected by Berkeley as utterly indeterminate, therefore empty, and thereby useless.) The upshot of his reaction to Locke's open alternatives was a doctrine of his own that claimed to refute the materialist one and to establish the spiritualist one. The hypothesis that the substance of mind is material is for him philosophically intolerable because what my mental states belong to and spring from, their unity of "locus" and source, I directly experience (here Locke being wrong), whereas material substance is not experienced at all (here Locke being right); and the hypothesis that the substance of corporeal qualities is mental is philosophically acceptable because it keeps to the analogy of experience, mind being the only owning, unifying, and productive kind of thing we *know*.

Locke on substance, then, was unhelpful: he was agnostic, and a line of conjectural materialism could be drawn from him.

There was also Locke's acceptance of the distinction of material qualities into primary and secondary, a vindication of sense-perception in respect of the former, a condemnation of it in respect of the latter. It was on the latter that Berkeley pounced, without putting all the blame for it on Locke as it was a doctrine distinctive of the new age, a commonplace of the modernist scientists (Galileo and his successors, including the Newtonians) and the modernist philosophers (the Cartesians and Hobbes as well as Locke), so that to question it was to risk the dreadful charge of being intellectually either out of date or boorish. Berkeley defied the risk. He was too well read in Newton to be obscurantist, and too acute to be naive. His cognitive simplicity and confidence were due to his remarkably lucid intellect and to his quick sense of philosophical and religious implications. He took his stand on the fact that secondary qualities are stubbornly and inexpugnably perceived as in or on the objects of sense, and contended that the denial of their objective reality is not a mere paradox, not a necessary scientific correction of common sense, but an arbitrary and drastic reduction of the reliability of the primary sources of our knowledge of the corporeal world. He also underlined an even worse implication of the position within which the denial was made. The position was that *all* sense-qualities are subjective, parts of the sensing mind's own nature, the corporeal world being *never* directly apprehended; and the implication he exposed, damning the whole theory of representative perception, was that the claim that *any* of our sensations are copies of a reality inaccessibly outside them is *necessarily* unverifiable since it precludes the very possibility of our ever being able to compare the former with the latter. In short, in the modern science and philosophy our knowledge of the material world is (a) whittled down to "primary" qualities, and (b) by implication dissolved into entire nescience. Berkeley put forward a philosophical way of escape from both these grades of what he attacked as "skepticism": drop the two-world assumption of a "real" world of stars and hills and trees never open to perception, and of a mental copy (whether wholly or in part) of that world locked up within the perceiving mind, and accept the stars and hills and trees we directly perceive as the real ones.

A Richer Basis for Natural Theology

Berkeley's sharp formulation of the problem and his way of dealing with it are clearly philosophical: he was competently attempting to clear up a muddle in the contemporary intellectual situation. But he was also taking the sting out of a threat to his theistic conviction. In his day, Natural Theology was still very largely an a posteriori argument from the physical world to God. Any loss of confidence in the sensory means by which we get our ideas of such a world would therefore lessen the chances of working towards certainty about the existence and nature of God. The doctrine that all our sensory objects are parts of the perceiver's own mental being—the *hereditas damnosa* of the revived Greek skepticism, given legality by the modern philosophers and scientists—logically makes the very existence of the physically world gravely problematic, and a "physico-theology" worthlessly precarious. This is one reason why Berkeley set himself against (not for, as many suppose) the subjectivization and mentalization of the immediate objects of perception. As for the dogma that the "primary" qualities of sensed objects, and they alone, do represent the nature of extra-mental reality, Berkeley turned away from it as the assertion of a mere ghost-world of mathematical abstractions, which was all that the physicists and philosophers were presenting for the practitioners of Natural Theology to infer God from, thereby leaving room for only a cosmic mathematician or "mechanic" (which is what Sir James Jeans has inferred to in our own day), an impoverished world impoverishing our idea of God. He himself was intent on keeping the world as it is perceived, splashed with color, ringing with sound, charged with odor. For this he had several reasons: because those qualities are in fact just as much given as the so-called primary ones, because they are inconceivable apart from these, because they provide constant and varied sources of delight, because many of them are guides ("signs" in Berkeley's terminology) to our biological survival and health, and finally because the range of sensed objects taken in their entirety supplies a ground for inferring the Creator's handsome providence for man. It is, then, from a richly caparisoned world, not from a mechanical skeleton, that we have in fact to start in our quest for the nature of God. This is an evidently operative motive, at times emerging into the open, of Berkeley's philosophizing. The note of wonder in his writings at the wealth and beneficence of the corporeal universe when taken concretely as it is experienced lifts him out of the Age of Newton and makes him a precursor of the Romantic period, as Whitehead, alone I think among philosophers, has noticed.

Immaterialism and Theism

So far, I have proceeded from the provocations to Berkeley's thinking and how he reacted. Some further clarification may be got by starting from his philosophical conclusions and then indicating the religious convictions he had been trying to safeguard. To state the conclusions more than summarily would take me beyond my theme, and to pepper them with documentation would take me beyond my share of the space in this book.

"Immaterialism" is Berkeley's name for his philosophy in its negative aspect. There is no matter in the sense of an inaccessible substratum of material qualities: to say that there is to postulate a useless *x*. And there is no matter in the sense of groups of material qualities beyond the reach of perception, as the realities of which our percepts are alleged to be subjective copies: to say that there is, is to postulate again something unverifiable and also to aver something self-contradictory, sensory qualities that *cannot* be sensed, and further to commit oneself to such plainly silly language as "when we see colors we are *really* seeing motions." The only matter we can clearly and verifiably think about is the immediate objects of sense perception—instances of color, hardness, shape, and so forth: these alone are given, and are to be taken as what they appear to be, namely, as corporeal realities. So much is comprehended in Berkeley's basic principle that the *esse* of "ideas" is their *percipi,* that is, expressed negatively, that the existence of corporeal qualities which are not and cannot in principle be perceived is meaningless. Color and shape are inseparable correlates of seeing, shape again and hardness and softness are inseparable correlates of touch, and so on. In other words, the corporeal can exist only as object of perception: it is tied to mind, yet just because it is extended and so on it is not mental. Again keeping to its apprehended nature, it is powerless. We never perceive one quality or group of qualities *producing* another, but merely accompanying, preceding, or following another, so that the laws of Nature established by science are not causal explanations but simply statements of uniform connections. Berkeley's immaterialism means, then, that the corporeal is mind-dependent and destitute of causal power.

Two problems are thereby thrust upon us. We have to account causally for (1) the connections among material objects, and (2) their appearance to us; since what makes the connections and what brings the objects to our minds are never *perceived*. The Cartesians and Locke had seen that (2) is a problem, on the assumption that the corporeal *exists* (however it may have originated) independently of mind. So had Hobbes, who puts it well: "Of all phenomena or appearances which are near to us the most admirable [surprising, evoking wonder] is apparition itself, namely that some natural bodies have in themselves the patterns of all things, and others of none at all."[3]

Now the only causal power, Berkeley insists, we are ever directly acquainted with (as the less extreme Occasionalists and Locke had pointed out) is that of our own minds: we can produce ideas and move our limbs. Instead of arbitrarily inventing the concept of corporeal power or force, we should keep to the one analogy of experience and maintain that the cause of both (1) and (2) is itself mental. Berkeley's explanation of (1) follows traditional lines: the corporeal world is a single world and therefore must be referred to a single mind; its vastness and order show this mind to be superlatively powerful and wise; and the beneficence of the order shows the ruling mind to be benevolently providential. Berkeley's explanation of (2) is original: the world we directly confront in perception, though unthinkable apart from mind, is obviously independent of the minds of individual human perceivers, and therefore its mode of existence is as object to a cosmic mind, who presents it to us. The Cartesian and Lockian enigma of how anything material could produce or evoke in our minds a copy of itself is thus not solved but, more deeply, shown not to arise at all in Berkeley's system. The second explanation is a brilliant intellectual intuitive step from "the *esse* of corporeal things is their *percipi*" to "the existence of the corporeal universe consists in its being the object of the divine awareness, and its occurrence to and impact on our awareness are the immediate consequence of the divine volition."

[3] Thomas Hobbes, *Concerning Body,* Part IV, Chap. 25.

His Kind of Theism

From this bare summary it should be easy to see the religious points which Berkeley in his philosophical system was trying to reach and safeguard. No arbitrary interpretation is required to state what they are, for here and there he himself in effect tells us. A mere proof of the *existence* of God was not enough. His interest was in the kind of God, and in the kind of relation He stands in to the corporeal universe and us humans, which his religious sensibility demanded. Quite clearly his most general antipathy was towards the conception of God as First Cause, who could leave the physical universe alone as soon as He had created it because He had built into it all that was necessary for its continuance and orderly working—the conception of the recent deists, some of whom could see no farther than the physicists' purely linear category of causality and purely mechanistic systematization of natural phenomena. The reason why Berkeley coupled deism with atheism, as though they were much the same, was that the deistic conception was too thin to ground anything that deserves to be called religion, too unrelated to man's circumstances and inner needs to supply any strong stimulus to worshipful and virtuous living. For religion, God must be close to His creation in the sense of being in direct and continual control of it, a control so complete that without it the physical universe would neither persist as an ordered whole nor collapse into chaos, but merely disappear into nothingness. Berkeley depicts that world not as a system of mechanical forces but as an instrument that cannot do anything (indeed, cannot even be) without the Mind that uses it. *Mens agitat molem,* he quotes, putting far more meaning into the assertion than Vergil did (*Aeneid* vi, 727).

That depiction has nothing distinctively Berkeleian in it until we see it under the far-reaching grasp of his principle "*esse* is *percipi.*" Everything except mind—and what is not mental is material—exists wholly as object to mind, to *God's* mind. Every element of it and every change in it are the direct result of His volition, which includes His presentation of it to our minds, so that everything we see, hear, smell, taste, and touch, every object that is *given* to us, is a witness of the present activity of God, and to that extent a theophany. When we survey the sensed world in gathered recollection and intelligent thought we can realize what an astonishingly rich world it is, and that its reliable regularities tell us where what promotes our life is to be found, and where what hinders or destroys it. Here is an hourly manifest providence, with God *immediately* behind it. Philosophically, the inference to God is not a trudge along a line of innumerable causes and effects, but simply a step or two. Religiously, we have no need to make the arduous ascent of the mystic; we have only to open our eyes (Berkeley thought largely with his eyes) to be confronted with the first-hand effects of divine power, wisdom and benevolence. Being the cause of every sensory object and of its appearing to us, God is far more evidenced than our minds are to each other, for we know one another by only a few sensory cues. That is Berkeley's distinctive reply to the atheists and deists, with the special point for the latter that awareness of that divine nearness had more religious and moral potency than the intellectual recognition of a temporally remote First Cause.

In this last sentence we have the most general mark of his theism. In all his philosophizing he could not forget that the term "God" belongs primarily and irremovably to religion. He would not contract it into the name for *anything* that philosophers might regard as the ultimate principle or power. The First Cause of the old Natural Theology contains no entitlement to worship, gives no sense to liturgy, and can neither receive nor respond to prayer. That was largely the consequence of the cosmological approach. The day of argument from the religious experience in which the notion of God originates had not come in Berkeley's time, yet he managed to retain the essentially religious reference in his bold theory of a Mind in communication with us (the "divine visual language") even in our perceptual experience. The theory suggests (and was, I think, intended to do so) that God is for everybody, not the rarefied entity discovered or invented by the intellectual elite.

What Berkeley's insight prods us to ask ourselves is whether any cosmologically orientated natural theology other than an idealism somewhat similar to his can yield anything more than a religiously feeble idea of God. Tennyson puts his finger on this limitation in two short lines of *In Memoriam,* the first pointing to the traditional cosmological arguments, the second to William Paley's attempt to improve them:

> I found Him not in stars or sun,
> Or eagle's wing or insect's eye.

His Nonphilosophical Apologetics

So much on the religious motives in Berkeley's philosophizing. The title of this paper requires me to bring in one of his writings, the longest of them, in which that motive loosens itself from the firm shackles of strictly philosophical procedure. His *Alciphron* is not a philosophical work (although the philosopher cannot help breaking through, with his *"esse* is *percipi,"* however much kept in the background), but in content and avowed intention a piece of outright and forthright religious apologetics, in which he strides beyond a general theism to a defense of religion in its Christian form. For this reason philosophers naturally say little about it. Christian apologists seem to ignore it, presumably because, as Berkeley was well aware, their task is to address themselves to the culture and temper of their own day. They are missing both a delight and a profitable example of their craft, adaptable to their needs, for there are many relevant similarities between the first half of the eighteenth century and the present time.

It is a delight because it is the literary masterpiece of one of the best writers of English prose. In seven dialogues his pen runs at ease through delicious portrayals of character, caricature, satire gentle and mordant, wit, repartee, mock declamation, earnest appeal, close argumentation, short sentences in which every word smites, and periods in which many clauses and phrases are knit into logical or picturable wholes. Literary versatility and excellence are not so common in religious apologetics as to warrant the neglect of the finest example we have of them. *Alciphron* even shows us how to bring fun into the subject; dialogues II and III, which are uproarious, deal with the "new morality," handled nowadays with nervous solemnity.

An outline of the scope and structure of the work may be of interest. It starts not from the physical world but from morality, conceived as that which makes for the general good of one's society and of mankind. Two current fashionable views are discussed: that our impulses, being natural, are entitled to full satisfaction; and that morality is an affair of taste, tact, and gracefulness. Both are dismissed as not making for the general good, and as heavily underestimating the practical function of reasoning, which also is a part of our nature, the part that makes us human. The pragmatic argument for religion is then introduced: to become moral we need all the motives we can get, and religion is a powerful one. Religion, then, is morally useful. But is belief in God *true?* Berkeley replies with a simplified statement of his philosophical argument: as each of us infers another mind from a limited set of percepts, so from all our percepts we can infer a divine mind.

The discussion now passes to the Christian religion. Again there is first the pragmatic contention–Christianity does conduce to virtue and happiness; and replies are given to such objections as that the same has to be said of other religions (for example, that there were Roman pagans better than any Christians), and that Christianity has sprouted wars and the nastiness of theological squabbles. Then comes the final question of the *truth* of Christianity, handled by countering one by one a number of contemporary criticisms (some of which are still heard) of the historical reliability and moral and religious worth of the Scriptures; and lastly by rebutting the two philosophical charges that Christian belief rests on terms for which no clear or tenable meaning can be adduced, such as "grace," and on assumptions that are absurd, such as freedom of the will, on which latter point Berkeley comments on the oddity of "freethinkers" mouthing determinism. One philosophical issue had been touched on in the fourth dialogue (ALC §§ 17–21), namely, that we cannot rightly apply to a supposed divine mind features drawn from our very restricted minds: surely, it was being said, "knowledge" and "goodness" cannot there have *anything like* their usual human meaning, and therefore express *nothing*. This is an ancient point, going back to the "negative theology" of Alexandria, and St. Thomas Aquinas took it up, ensuring its discussion ever since in the seminaries. Some of our linguistic analysts have repeated it, and it is troubling empiricist theologians. Berkeley's answer is that if we hold that as our goodness is to our finite nature so is God's to His infinite nature, we do not destroy, but only make a necessary modification in, the idea of goodness.

The learning skilfully carried in his deploying of the "evidences" of Christianity was up-to-date. Although much of it has been surpassed, the ways in which he used it could in many instances be suggestive to a modern apologist. One striking feature is the force with which he puts some of the objections, so rousing the reader's eagerness to see how he will manage to cope with them. His remarks on the tactics of objectors are acute and still relevant, for example, when by multiplication of objections, without care for their consistency, they force the apologist to be on the defensive:

> It seems as if a man should stand still in the same place while his adversary chooses and changes his situation, has full range and liberty to traverse the field and attack him on all sides and in all shapes, from a nearer or farther distance, on horseback or on foot, in light or heavy armour, in close fight or with massive weapons. (ALC 321)

The picture is well drawn. Berkeley devised the dialogues to leave the objectors ample room for such maneuvers, but often himself moves to the attack by exposing and examining the *presuppositions* of the objections and sometimes showing that whatever force one particular criticism may have destroys all the force of another. His sense of the logic of argumentation seems to me to be masterly. "The author hath not confined himself to write against books alone," he says in his preface, and it was his wider reference, together with his adoption of the dialogue form, that enabled him to depict the faults and twists of oral disputation.

IX

Berkeley's Objective Idealism: An Indian View

D. M. DATTA

Berkeley's Principles and Objective Idealism

Some of the leading contemporary realists have tried to refute idealism by exposing the practical and theoretical absurdities that follow from subjective idealism. But these realistic attempts are thought by some to be inconclusive, because they think that even if subjective idealism be refuted objective idealism may remain unaffected and consequently the case for idealism is not totally disproved. These thinkers can readily point to the philosophy of Berkeley as the most important and original system of modern idealism and can contend that his objective idealism is free from many of the charges which are brought against idealism of the subjective type. By admitting the existence of other spiritual realities—the finite spirits and God—besides his own, Berkeley tries in his *Principles of Human Knowledge* (1) to provide a real extrasubjective cause for our perception, (2) to explain Nature and the laws of Nature in a realistic way, and (3) to show that our daily life of practice is not materially affected by his idealism. As many of the arguments of Berkeley have still retained their force with those who are idealistically inclined, the refutations of idealism based primarily on the refutation of subjective idealism carry little or no conviction to them. In his classical paper on "The Refutation of Idealism," Professor Moore has laid the axe at the root of all kinds of idealism. The scope of the present paper is limited to the objective idealism of Berkeley, and its object is to show that this form of idealism is not consistent with his own fundamental principles and that subjective idealism is the only logical consequence which follows from them.

The most important and fundamental principle on which Berkeley bases his idealism is that of the "impossibility of abstract ideas." He dilates on this theory in his introduction to *The Principles of Human Knowledge,* and considers it indispensable to the understanding of his idealistic theory. He uses this theory in many different ways to refute the existence of matter. The conception of matter existing independently of the perception of it presupposes the possibility of abstracting in thought the existence of an object from its perception; but such abstraction is impossible; therefore the conception of matter is impossible. If matter is to exist as a substance outside of all minds, it must have some qualities; the secondary qualities are acknowledged to be subjective and the primary qualities are, therefore, ascribed to unperceived matter; but it is impossible to abstract and separate the primary qualities from the secondary ones in thought; hence we cannot think of the qualities of the unperceived material substance and such substance, therefore, becomes inconceivable. Again, the conception of matter is that of a general substance without any particular quality (size, shape, and so forth); but the conception of such a general substance involves an impossible abstraction; therefore the general conception of matter also is untenable.

Another principle of great importance which Berkeley admits, is that an idea is *passive* and consequently it cannot represent a spirit which is *essentially active.* He uses this principle to show the great difference between a spirit and an object and also the difference between the knowledge of these two. The knowledge of a spirit is called a notion, as distinguished from an idea.

We shall show that these very fundamental principles stand in the way of believing (1) that the other finite spirits are different from God, (2) that God is different from the self, and (3) that the notion of a spirit, as desired by Berkeley, is possible. If these points are satisfactorily proved, it will follow that the objective idealism of Berkeley is wholly untenable and also that even as subjective idealism his theory should have been very different. Let us deal with these points one by one.

Difficulties in His View of Other Selves

The chief reason why Berkeley admits the existence of realities other than his own spirit is that he has certain ideas (the ideas actually perceived by sense), which, he feels, are not dependent on his will; and that he has, therefore, to explain these ideas by some other cause or causes. The reason why these causes are admitted to be spiritual and not material is that matter is inert and inactive and therefore unfit for any causation; activity belongs only to a spiritual substance and therefore nothing but a spirit can cause the ideas received in perception. We shall not raise here any objection against the assumption that a spirit is the only kind of active substance, but granting, for a moment, that this is true we shall try to see whether Berkeley has any sound reason to hold that these extrasubjective spirits are of two different kinds, namely, finite spirits and the Infinite Spirit.

The grounds for believing in these two kinds of spirits have been clearly stated by him in the following passages of the *Principles of Human Knowledge:*

> From what has been said, it is plain that we cannot know the existence of other spirits otherwise than by *their operations, or the ideas by them excited in us.* I perceive several motions, changes and combinations of ideas, that inform me there are certain particular agents, like myself, which accompany them and concur in their production. Hence, the knowledge I have of other spirits is not immediate, as is the knowledge of my ideas; but depending on the intervention of ideas, by me referred to agents or *spirits* distinct from myself, as effects or concomitant signs.[1]
>
> But, though there be some things which convince us, human agents are concerned in producing them; yet it is evident to every one that those things which are called the *works of Nature,* that is, the far greater part of the ideas or sensations perceived by us, are not produced by, or dependent on, the wills of men. There is therefore, some other spirit that causes them; since it is repugnant that they should subsist by themselves. . . . But, if we attentively consider the constant regularity, order and concatenation of natural things, the surprising magnificence, beauty, and perfection of the larger, and the exquisite contrivance of the smaller parts of creation, together with the exact harmony and correspondence of the whole, but above all the never enough admired laws of pain and pleasure, and the instincts or natural *inclinations, appetites,* and *passions* of *animals;* I say if we consider all these things, and at the same time attend to the meaning and import of the attributes one, eternal, infinitely wise, good, and perfect, we shall clearly perceive that they belong to the aforesaid spirit, *who works all in all* and *by whom all things consist.*[2]

The gist of the whole argument may be put thus: I observe first in my own case, certain kinds of ideas of motion, change, and so forth, which are caused by my own volition. I then receive, through sense, similar ideas, which, I feel, are not caused by me. Hence, by analogy, I refer these ideas to causes that are outside me, but like my spirit. Thus I come to believe in other finite spirits like myself. There are again other ideas received through sense, namely those of what are ordinarily called "works of nature," and as I find that I cannot produce such kinds of effects, I cannot think that these ideas are caused by spirits like myself. The magnificence, perfection and other exquisite qualities of the "works of nature" make me refer them to a

[1] PHK § 145, italics added.
[2] PHK § 146, italics added, except in last two lines.

perfect and magnificent cause. This cause must be a spirit, because a spirit alone can be active. Hence I come to believe in a Perfect Spirit or God.

But it will be found that this argument for supposing two kinds of spirits glosses over a very great difficulty which arises out of the very theory of the impossibility of abstraction which Berkeley uses for the refutation of materialism. The difficulty consists in the impossibility of abstracting divine (natural) effects from human effects. To take a concrete example; when I perceive a human figure moving its hand, I receive many ideas, such as the idea of the color of the hand, the idea of its size, and the idea of its shape, together with the idea of its motion. Of these various ideas it is only the idea of motion that can be credited to a spirit like my own self. The ideas of color, size, and shape cannot be ascribed to such a spirit because in my own case I find that these ideas are not dependent on my will. If I am to infer, therefore, the existence of any finite spirit, I have to do so from the residual idea of motion. But according to the nominalistic theory regarding abstraction, which Berkeley makes the corner stone of his idealism, I *cannot abstract the idea of motion, from that of extension, color, and so forth.* But how can I then think of the motion of the hand, apart from the color, extension, and so on, of the hand? And if this is impossible, how can I suppose that there is a separate cause of the motion, namely a spirit like myself, unless I can think of its effect separately? It will follow, therefore, that the evidence for the existence of other finite spirits, distinct from the Perfect, Infinite spirit, is inconclusive.

Though the force of this argument should be sufficiently conclusive, there can be some arguments to defend Berkeley's position against this attack.

It may be argued that in all natural causation we find that phenomena are complex and consist of various factors, still by applying the inductive methods we can successfully isolate the cause and the effect and thereby establish a relation. In this case, the effect phenomenon is, of course, a complex of many factors, say, CEM (C = color, E = extension, and M = motion). Starting initially with my own experience, I observe first that there are C and E (of my hand) even when there is no will of mine (to move my hand). But as soon as there is the will (W), there is M. By this method of difference I can establish in my own case a causal relation between W and M. By multiplying instances and applying other tests this relation is confirmed. Then when I perceive M (motion of a hand) outside myself and not dependent on my will, I ascribe it to W (a will of another spirit like myself).

But it is easy to show that such a defense, rigid and logical as it may outwardly appear to be, forgets the depth of Berkeley's objection to abstract ideas. Such a defense would be effective if Berkeley simply held that M cannot exist anywhere apart from C and E. But, as already stated, Berkeley goes farther to assert that M cannot be thought at all apart from C and E. Consequently M cannot be isolated from CE even in thought, and we fail, therefore, even to think of M alone in order to be able to relate it with a cause W, distinct from, say, G (God), the cause of CE. It means that we can think neither of M, apart from the effect-complex CEM, nor of W apart from the causal complex GW. But this conclusion only shows that we have no right to believe in other spirits apart from that of God. The effects of the so-called other spirits are inseparable, even in thought, from those of God, and therefore there can be the supposition of only one cause, God, as responsible for all effects that are not dependent on my will. The existence of other human spirits, therefore, remains unproved. And even apart from these reasons, if Berkeley ascribes the actions of animals—the "instincts or natural inclinations, appetites and passions" (PHK § 146)—to the Divine Will, it is only a short step that he has to take to ascribe human actions also to the same cause.

His Belief in God Not Consistent

But the logical implications of Berkeley's principles do not stop with the denial of the other human spirits alone; they reach still further, to subvert Berkeley's belief in the existence of the Divine Spirit as distinct from that of the self. This conclusion can be reached in various ways.

It is clearly stated by Berkeley that he is immediately aware of his own self in its operations. These operations can be threefold, as he says: "For, by the word *spirit* we mean only that which thinks, wills, and perceives; this and this alone, constitutes the signification of that term." (PHK § 138) The existence of the Divine Spirit is known by inference from His effects, the works of nature. Now, though it is true that there are operations of the self which are doubtlessly its own, the so-called effects of the Divine Will, which are revealed in sense-perception, cannot always be shown to be so beyond all doubts. To take the example already used, when I move my hand I have the perception of the color and the extension of the hand along with its motion. Now, in such a case Berkeley would hold that the motion is due to *my* will, whereas the color and the extension, which are not dependent on my will, are due to *God's* will. But as shown in the previous section this supposition is against Berkeley's nominalism. Consequently here also we cannot but think of one cause as responsible for the effect-complex, color–extension–motion, which cannot be analyzed even in thought.[3]

Other difficulties apart, this one cause is either the self or God. If it be God then the consequence is suicidal. For it then means that God is the cause of even the motion of the hand, which I clearly feel to be my own operation; and this further suggests that in the other cases also, where I am clearly

[3] The legitimate question, namely, if the factors cannot be separated in thought, how can we use separate terms for them? need not be answered. It may prove fatal to nominalism, the only defense for which is that these are mere *words*. But this does not affect our reasoning, which grants the truth of Berkeley's nominalism and only shows that his objective idealism is not consistent with it.

aware that I am acting, I may be suffering from a similar illusion and God may be the cause of what I feel to be my own activity. The very rock of immediate awareness of activity on which the belief in my own self stands, according to Berkeley, gives way to doubt. But however God-intoxicated the Bishop might have been, his philosophy *starts with the self,* as a fact of immediate awareness, and comes only *next* to God by mediate thinking. And if the fact of immediate awareness is liable to error, that of mediate thinking, which is dependent on it, becomes more so. For it has been shown already that the belief in God rests ultimately on my immediate awareness that certain effects are not dependent on my will. The existence of God, therefore, becomes doubtful.

If, on the other hand, the self is thought to be the cause of the whole effect-complex, the plain consequence is that even the ideas of sense, namely color and extension, are due to the causality of the self; and then the necessity for admitting the existence of God as the cause of these will vanish. Subjective idealism, therefore, will take the place of Berkeley's objective idealism.

This dilemma, then, makes the position of Berkeley very precarious. The first alternative involves this idealism in contradiction; for the subjective certainty is the very basis on which idealism founds the existence of God and other realities, if any, and if the existence of the self is uncertain, the existence of other realities tumbles down. The second alternative presents the lesser of the two evils. It can at least enable Berkeley to retain the existence of the self and also idealism, relieved of its unproved burdens of God and other spirits. Subjective idealism, therefore, is the only reasonable conclusion of Berkeley's position.

An attempt, however, may be made to avoid this conclusion by showing that the two alternatives mentioned above are not exhaustive and that the dilemma may be rebutted by showing that a third alternative is possible. It may be pointed out that the complex-effect, color–extension–motion, may be said to be due to the cooperation of both God and self, and not to either one of them singly. But such a defense is not at all effective. For, as already pointed out, such a supposition will require us to think that God is the cause of color–extension and the self is the cause of motion; and this will involve an impossible abstraction. If, however, it is said that we can think of the complex *as a whole,* without any analysis, to be a joint effect of two conditions, namely God and the self, which together constitute the cause, the assertion will require further proof. For Berkeley states that color and extension are the effects of the Divine Will, and motion, change, and so forth in such a case are the effects of the human will. If we are to proceed on this statement the known elements of the effect-complex should be explained by the known causes. The supposition of the joint production of the indivisible effect-complex, color–extension–motion, will require us to suppose, however, that the self is the condition of color and extension in addition to motion, and God is the condition of motion in addition to color and extension. This subverts the statement of Berkeley and cannot be easily set aside. The existence of God remains doubtful.

But an objection to this conclusion can be raised from another direction. It can be said that this subjective idealism has been deduced from the consideration of only the cases of mixed effects of God and the self. Even if the conclusion be guaranteed by these cases, there are the cases of effects that are not at all dependent on the will of the self, and that, therefore, require to be explained by some spirit other than the self. The ideas of the so-called objects of nature, unaffected in any way by the self, are such cases. If the self is the only reality, how can I explain the ideas of the color and the extension of a mountain, for example, which I perceive and also find to be independent of my will?

In reply to this it should be said that if any conclusion is deduced from any one principle or theory advocated by Berkeley, and if the deduction is not fallacious, then the conclusion is irresistible and must be admitted as a legitimate one. But still, it will be to our advantage to consider the cases pointed out above and stated by Berkeley to be purely divine effects.

Now, according to Berkeley, the mountain is nothing more than a collection of ideas. These ideas are in my mind, *which* perceives the ideas. This follows from the two clear assertions of Berkeley, namely, (1) that an idea can exist only in a mind, and (2) that the existence of an idea (an object, according to Berkeley) consists in its being perceived. But though Berkeley admits that while I perceive the mountain it is nothing but a collection of ideas in *my* mind, he *wants* to hold that the *cause* of these ideas is not my self (which cannot change them at will), but God. This is, however, an unjustifiable position. If Berkeley's dictum *esse* is *percipi* means, as we have reason to believe it does, that the existence of an idea *consists* in its being perceived, it follows that the entire reality of an idea is determined by its being perceived and consequently that in the very act of perception my self causes its existence. There is no reason, therefore, for supporting the existence of an extrasubjective cause of the idea. God therefore, is redundant.

Though this should have been the natural interpretation and conclusion of his dictum *esse* is *percipi,* Berkeley swerves aside. For in spite of his idealism Berkeley cannot ignore the fact that the ideas of color, size, extension, and the like, are not dependent on my will. The recognition of this fact compels him to admit the existence of God only by sacrificing the reasonable sense of the dictum. If the dictum does not mean that the existence of an idea is wholly determined by the perceiving activity, then it may mean either (1) that it is partly determined by itself and partly by some other cause or (2) that it is wholly determined by some cause other than the self. But neither of these senses is compatible with the proof that Berkeley advances in support of this dictum. We quote the relevant lines of the proof:

It is indeed an opinion strangely prevailing amongst men, that houses, mountains, rivers and in a word all *sensible* objects, have an existence, natural or real, distinct from their being perceived by the understanding. But, with how great an assurance and acquiescence soever this principle may be entertained in the world; yet whoever shall find in his heart to call it in question may, if I mistake not, perceive it to involve a manifest contradiction. For, what are the forementioned objects but the things we perceive by sense and what do we perceive besides our *own* ideas or sensations? And is it not plainly repugnant that any one of these, or any combination of them, *should exist unperceived?*[4]

Again, showing the impossibility of abstracting the existence of a sensible object from the perception of it, he observes:

Hence, as it is impossible for me to see or feel anything without an actual sensation of that thing, so is it impossible for me to conceive in my thoughts any sensible thing or object distinct from the sensation or perception of it. (PHK § 5)

In the first edition of this work, the last statement is even more clear. "In truth, *the object and the sensation are the same thing,* and cannot, therefore, be abstracted from each other."

It will clearly appear from these quotations that as I cannot at all conceive, according to Berkeley, the existence of a sensible object as distinct from my idea of it, and as *my* idea, according to his dictum, is caused by *my* perception, the existence of the idea cannot be due, either partly or wholly, to any other cause than my self. It will follow, therefore, that *esse* is *percipi,* as explained and proved by Berkeley, does not *require* the existence of God, as the cause of any sensible object.

But it is possible for Berkeley still to hold that though the *immediate* all-sufficient condition of a sensible object of my perception is my perceiving activity, yet my perceiving activity in such a case is caused by the Divine Will, so that without this will the perception will not exist in my mind. God, therefore, is the *mediate* condition of the existence of sensible objects, though my perception is their *immediate* cause. Such a defense, however, only raises fresh difficulties. If the perceiving activity of my self is constrained and determined by another will, when I perceive a sensible object, it means that my self is *acted upon* by another will. The plain consequence of this would be to admit that the self is *passive,* at least partly, and is insofar acted on. But this militates against a fundamental theory of Berkeley, namely, that a *spirit is active.* The activity of a spirit is for Berkeley the essential attribute of it—a spirit is distinguished by him from an object, on the basis of this attribute. (PHK § 27) If, then, the self is somehow acted upon by any foreign will, as will be the case if God is the cause of the *perception* of the colors and shape of a mountain, it will so far cease to be a spirit. The admission of God, therefore, is suicidal to Berkeley's position. Subjective idealism is the logical outcome of the very principles on which his refutation of matter and his theory

[4] PHK § 4, italics added.

of spirit are based. As a subjective idealist he may believe in God only if he *identifies* God with the self, and can explain the independent character of sensible objects only by creating, like Fichte, a division within the self between the self as the knower and the self as the cause of sensations. Whatever may be the logical reconstruction of his theory, our interest here is to show that Berkeley's attempt at foisting a sort of objective idealism on fundamentally subjective principles is unsuccessful and that the belief in God as different from the self is untenable.

Self as Substance Inconsistent with Nominalism

So far we have tried to show that Berkeley's theory of other finite spirits and the Divine spirit is inconsistent with his basic principles. We shall show now that, even as subjective idealism, his theory should be different from what he wants it to be. As before, so here also, his theory of abstraction proves a fatal rock.

One of the chief grounds on which Berkeley dismisses the belief in matter is that the conception of matter involves an impossible abstraction.

> If we enquire into what the most accurate philosophers declare themselves to mean by *material substance,* we shall find them acknowledge, they have no other meaning annexed to those sounds but the idea of Being in general, together with the relative notion of its supporting accidents. The general idea of being appeareth to me the most *abstract and incomprehensible* of all other. (PHK § 17. Final italics added.)

In other words, the conception of a material substance cannot be identified with the sensation of the particular qualities perceived at different moments. The series of qualities so perceived are not always compatible. Taking even a so-called particular material substance, a ball, we find that sometimes it is in motion, and sometimes at rest; its size and color also vary from moment to moment according to the distance from which it is perceived. But how can we think of the ball as both in motion and also at rest, and as having more than one color and size? It is an impossible abstraction to think of it as something general that subsumes all the particular states and qualities. But the abstraction becomes all the more impossible when we are asked to think of matter in general, being neither solid nor liquid nor gaseous; neither in motion nor at rest; neither small nor big, and so forth. The impossibility of the formation of an abstract general idea therefore prevents the very conception of matter, either particular or general.

But do not the same difficulties arise when we are asked to think of a spiritual substance?* As a thoroughgoing nominalist Berkeley may not admit that he has any conception of spirits in general. But does not the notion of even a so-called particular spirit require a good deal of abstraction? A spirit

* [For a different view see Professor Tipton's chapter, pp. 66 f.—Ed.]

is said to have the activities of perceiving, thinking, and willing. Now, according to Berkeley's own statement, we cannot abstract an object of perception from the act of perception, because they are inseparable, even in thought. If this is so, when we think of a spirit we have to think of it as perceiving some particular object. But a spirit is not a momentary substance; it is said to be indestructible. It perceives, therefore, sometimes motion, sometimes rest, sometimes black, sometimes not black. But if motion and rest, black and not-black, are incompatible (and, therefore, cannot be ascribed to the same material substance), the perceptions of these incompatibles, which are inseparable from their objects, must be equally incompatible, and they cannot be ascribed to the same spirit. If, therefore, we want to have any notion of a spirit at all, we shall have to attribute to it not any particular perception, but perception in general. Similarly we must attribute to it thinking in general and volition in general. But though this appears to be what Berkeley means when he says, "for, by the word spirit we mean only that which thinks, wills and perceives," it is not consistent with his nominalism. Perception in general and thinking in general are impossible abstractions.

But what is more embarrassing, a spirit does not always perceive or think or will; though it must at every moment possess some one of these activities. It is necessary, therefore, to have the general notion of activity, common to the three particular forms of it, in order to have the notion of a spirit. Berkeley actually speaks of the spirit in a such general way, when he describes it simply as an active substance. But this takes him only one step forward along the forbidden path of abstraction.

The notion of God will require far greater abstraction, as His activities are varied in nature and infinite in number. But it is not necessary to discuss it any longer, as the belief in God has already been shown to be inconsistent on other grounds.

We find, then, that the ground on which Berkeley rejects the existence of a material substance should force him to reject the notion of a spiritual substance as well. The concept of substance, insofar as it connotes a general substratum in which diverse qualities or activities of a mutually incompatible character exist, is inconsistent with the nominalistic view of abstraction, whether that substance is material or spiritual. Deprived of the notion of a substance, Berkeley's idealism will be reduced to an unsubstantial shadow of what he desired it to be. It will be a subjective idealism which can speak at most of the consciousness of passing ideas and acts and cannot even ascribe them to the self, unless it conceives the self as the mere changing totality of an increasing series of acts and ideas.*

* The first four sections of this paper appeared in substantially the same form in *The Monist,* 43 (1933–1934), 220–235, and are reprinted here by permission of the Open Court Publishing Co., La Salle, Illinois.

Modern Western and Indian Analogues

It would be interesting to review briefly the position of Berkeley in the light of more recent Western thought[5] and Indian thought. His versatile insights still carry fruitful suggestions for scientists and for philosophers of different trends. One can trace in his writings the germinal elements of modern phenomenalism, and even of the "therapeutic analysis" of ordinary language. Subjectivism, for which Berkeley used to be criticized, has reappeared now in diverse new forms, such as the "endocephalic" subjectivism of epistemologists (Russell and Neurath, for example, for whom percepts are in the brain),[6] the linguistic subjectivism of some positivists, for whom philosophic knowledge is confined to sentences they analyze, and the existential subjectivism of Kierkegaard and his recent followers.

The reality of physical substances, which Berkeley denied, has also been undermined by the scientific conception of the world as energy-field, which is closer now to mind—also conceived as energy. This has paved the way even for *panpsychism* in scientific philosophers such as Eddington. The realistic reaction that started against the esse–percipi idealism of Berkeley in British thinkers (Moore and young Russell, for example) culminated in a full antithesis in the American new realists, in what has been named by Lovejoy "panobjectivism,"[7] since it tried to reduce even consciousness to objects. But this led later to a reasonable synthesis in American critical realists, such as Pratt, who admit without denying consciousness or mind that the object as perceived is a content of the mind, but that it is not identical with the object as existing. They admit, moreover, that the epistemological critical realist can quite consistently be "a panpsychist, a metaphysical dualist, a Platonist, or an ontological idealist of some other type."[8] Even G. E. Moore, who initiated the modern realistic refutation of *esse* is *percipi*, comes to realize later that in cases like a toothache, existence *does* consist in being perceived, and that there are some real objections to common-sense realism.

We have elsewhere shown[9] that if it is true, as Perry complains, that idealism suffers from the fallacy of the "egocentric predicament," it is equally true that the American new realism suffers from the opposite fallacy of the "object-centric predicament." Anything known must be related to the ego or knower, and be also an object. But this neither implies that nothing can remain unknown and unrelated to any mind, as Berkeley would hold, nor

5 The author's *The Chief Currents of Contemporary Philosophy* (Calcutta; 1961) may be referred to, under relevant topics, for fuller discussion of recent idealistic and realistic trends noted on the following discussion.

6 *Ibid.,* 381, 479–480.

7 *Ibid.,* 331, 342 f.

8 *Ibid.,* 354.

9 *Ibid.,* 338 f.

implies that everything must be an object, as the panobjectivist neorealist would assert.

Though Berkeley has come down in history as an idealist, it is important to know in which sense or context—epistemological, ontological, or axiological—he is so, if he is at all.* In epistemology an idealist holds that the object perceived is an idea of, or dependent on the knower, whereas the realist holds that the object is real or independent of the knower. Professor T. E. Jessop thinks that Berkeley is epistemologically a realist,[10] since he holds that what we perceive is not dependent on our mind but on God, who wills to excite the perceptual ideas in us. Even admitting this we must remember that the object, as perceived by us with all its sensuous qualities, depends largely on us also, on our senses and our finite perspectives through which our mind receives the effects of the divine will. So Berkeley is perhaps to a larger extent an epistemological idealist as well. If the perceiver's knowing apparatus is also thought to be God's, he is engulfed in God, and the epistemological situation presupposing the existence of the knower disappears. But even the faint streak of realism (which makes the object known dependent on God's will) would be untenable if the belief in God is not consistent with Berkeley's basic arguments (as shown by us in the preceding sections).

In ontology an idealist (as distinguished from a materialist, a dualist, and a neutralist) is one who holds that ultimate reality is spiritual. Berkeley is an ontological idealist since he rejects material substances, accepting only spiritual ones. He is an objective idealist insofar as he believes in other selves, and does not believe like a subjective idealist in his own self only. We have shown that his desired objective idealism is inconsistent with his arguments, which should rather logically warrant a kind of subjective idealism much against his cherished faith.

In axiological perspective idealism is *ideal*-ism, or devotion to higher values or ideals in practical life. Berkeley, whose life is exclusively devoted to high ideals and the service of God, is a practical idealist. But axiological idealism may also mean the *theory* that values are subjective, rather than objectively real. For Berkeley truth and good are not subjective, but universal ideals for all men. He is thus a realist rather than an idealist in this sense.

Turning to Indian philosophy we find in Buddhist idealism (*vijnana-vada*) the example of a consistent epistemological and ontological position that rejects all substances, universals, and permanent things and accepts only successive, changing, unique and momentary mental states forming a causal series composing an individual. Such an idealism would be nearer to the subjective idealism logically deduced by us from Berkeley's premises and arguments. But the objective, theistic idealism that he intended to establish has also its

* [Cf. Professor Leroy's essay, "Was Berkeley an Idealist?", this volume, Chapter XI.—Ed.]

[10] Luce and Jessop, *Works,* II, 10.

analogues in the many schools of theistic Vedanta, all of whom reject the Buddhist idealism just mentioned and accept epistemological realism. This is also true of the great nondualist (*advaitin*), Shankara, for whom, however, theistic worship and self-surrender may only pave the way to self-transcendence and identity with the Absolute Self (*Brahman*), the only ultimate and changeless Reality that underlies the self and the world and yet transcends both. So Shankara is not a pantheist as ordinarily supposed. For him the self is essentially self-manifest consciousness, other than all objects (inner and outer). Objects alone undergo change. The self reveals itself and all objects, and cannot itself be an object, nor does it change.[11]

[11] For a fuller discussion, see S. C. Chatterjee and D. M. Datta, *Introduction to Indian Philosophy* (Calcutta: 1960), chapters on Buddhism and Vedanta.

X

Berkeley's Ontology and Islamic Mysticism

WAHEED ALI FAROOQI

There is a misconception prevalent in some philosophical circles that the idealism of Berkeley is something entirely different from the idealism of Plato and that while Plato's idealism has an ontological reference, Berkeley's idealism is only subjective in nature, born out of the exigencies of Locke's epistemological investigations. Berkeley is therefore sometimes ranked only as a link between Locke and Hume. On the contrary, we find that while Plato's idealism first took its birth in the epistemological considerations of the Sophists, Berkeley's idealism propounds the objective nature of the "ideas." The Sophists anticipated Berkeley and Hume when they declared that all we know are our own perceptions. What they failed to see, however, was the universal element in these perceptions that Socrates pointed out, thereby restoring the objectivity of human knowledge.

It is, however, unfortunate that Plato started with a noumenal world (or the world of ideas) as the ultimate reality and could not give a satisfactory explanation of the world of sense. In order to explain the multiplicity of phenomena he had to posit another multitude of things—the ideas—and thus doubled the number of things to be explained. The ideas fail to explain the existence of phenomena and his philosophy ends in an apparent dualism of ideas on the one hand and matter on the other. Matter, says Plato, is only a potentiality or a possibility, but if the ideas are the only realities, how can this potentiality or possibility come into existence? The ideas and matter stand face to face in Plato's system as equally ultimate and absolute realities, neither derived from the other.

Aristotle made an advance on the philosophy of Plato by assuming that the universal or the idea lies in the particular thing itself, but ultimately he too was led to believe that the particular is not the idea or form alone but a combination of matter and form.

Among modern philosophers Descartes considered the existence of his own consciousness as the basic reality, but he found the extended world so diametrically opposed to the unextended substance of mind that intercourse between the two seemed impossible to him. The two substances were mutually exclusive. That is why Malebranche went to the extreme in asserting that things of the physical world, because extended, could not become an immediate object of our perception, and being in themselves powerless and unintelligent, they could not be the active cause of our perception of their existence.

The greatest contribution of Berkeley to human thought, therefore, lies in his drawing attention to the fact that throughout our whole experience of the physical world we never apprehend anything besides our own ideas. We are never aware of any material substratum whatsoever. Ideas are the only reality we know and need to know. "It is a very extraordinary instance of the force of prejudice, and much to be lamented," says Berkeley, "that the mind of man retains so great a fondness against all the evidence of reason, for a stupid thoughtless *somewhat,* by the interposition whereof it would, as it were, screen itself from the providence of God, and remove him farther off from the affairs of the world." (PHK § 75) Descartes, we know, had even invoked the goodness of God to guarantee existence to the material world.

Thus Berkeley for the first time in modern philosophy bridged the Cartesian dualism of mind and matter and once and for all resolved the great Cartesian difficulty—how were consciousness and extended beings, living thought and dead matter, to be reconciled in a coherent philosophy. He melted the external world of Descartes into psychical entities and brought them within the pale of the *cogito.* But we should not think for a moment that in so treating the phenomenal world, Berkeley considered the physical world an illusion or a dream. Such interpretations of his philosophy are not lacking. Accordingly, at one place, Berkeley asserts:

> I am not for changing things into ideas, but rather ideas into things; since those immediate objects of perception, which according to you, [Hylas] are only appearances of things, I take to be the real things themselves. (DHP 244)

Berkeley emphasizes this spiritual existence of the external things when he admits to one of his critics that it sounds very harsh to say we eat and drink ideas, and are clothed with ideas.

Now, so far Berkeley's idealism is irrefutable. The full-blooded matter of

Descartes, who had exclaimed "give me matter and motion and I will give you a world," crumbles down at his hand. Our ideas are not merely the only objects of knowledge but the only existing things.

Can Phenomena Be Mind Dependent?

Certain mystics agree with Berkeley that the objects of the external world are ideas and that we never apprehend in the physical world more than what we can perceive. His great error, they would say, lies in the false conclusion that therefore the *essence* of the external world is to be perceived—"that it is fully mind dependent in the sense that it only exists in and by being perceived."[1] For it is one thing to say that things are only ideal entities susceptible to mental operation, and quite another to say that they are therefore dependent upon the mind. Berkeley had been led to this hasty inference in consequence of having taken too limited a view of the great problem that he could only partially solve. Mystics affirm Berkeley's thesis that the phenomena, alike severally and in aggregate, are a hierarchy of spirits and ideas, but how has Berkeley proved that these ideas, like spiritual stuffs, are not things existing independently of being perceived?

The consequence of this questionable inference was that Berkeley unintentionally involved himself in a number of difficulties. Having started with a so-called phenomenal world (the ideas of sensation) he could not give a proper explanation of the world of noumena (the archetypal ideas). His account of the relation of the human ego to the rest of the cosmos remains obscure. The coherence and mutual interdependence that subsists in phenomena Berkeley cannot explain. The divine ideas that serve as objective conditions for the ideas of finite minds, we are told, are "archetypal" ideas, and the ideas that are presented to finite minds are referred to as "ectypal" ideas. (DHP 254) But what the relationship is that exists between these archetypal and ectypal ideas, Berkeley nowhere elucidates. It is no more than a translation into philosophical terminology of the popular belief that the cause of all our ideas lies in some external object. But unless we have a proper explanation of this causal relation, from a metaphysical point of view, it is hardly of any avail whether we say that the cause is some divine agency or whether it lies in some object lying without. Such expressions even fail to explain the proper significance of "coming from without" for a being conscious only of its own ideas. Nor do we find any reason why the concept "without" occurred at all to such a being. It would perhaps not be wrong to say that had Berkeley himself made a critical analysis of the implications of such a mechanical theory of finite and infinite minds, and archetypal and ectypal ideas, he might have rejected this somewhat grotesque explanation about the nature of reality.

[1] C. R. Morris, *Locke, Berkeley, Hume* (London: 1931), 76.

In the *Principles,* Berkeley asserts: "It were easy to dilate on this subject and show how the arguments urged by *sceptics* in all ages, depend on the *supposition of external objects.*" (PHK § 87)[2] Sentences such as these seem tantamount to a denial of the objective world, and Berkeley was accused of solipsism. When he expresses the fear that things may evaporate as soon as he ceases to be conscious of them and when he feels a sort of compulsion to introduce God to guarantee the continued existence of things, one feels that Berkeley is preaching an extreme type of subjectivism. Just as Plato, finding himself unable to give an explanation of phenomena, covers up the gaps in his system by having recourse to the use of myths, so Berkeley, it is sometimes said, having failed to give a rational explanation of existence, calls in theology for help in bestowing continued existence to things of the phenomenal world.

Berkeley doubtless still believed in a sort of phenomenal world; he never denied the existence of a *rerum natura.* We do not produce these ideas, he says, ourselves; they plainly come to us from some independent source. "When in broad daylight I open my eyes, it is not in my power to choose whether I shall see or no, or to determine what particular objects shall present themselves to my view." (PHK § 29) Again, if the external world is denied, what becomes of physics? Berkeley considered it impossible to dismiss the discoveries of Newton and his followers as mere chimeras. What is there for the laws of physics to hold true of, if there is really no objective world to deal with? In the *De Motu,* Berkeley tried to resolve this difficulty, but due to the over-all subjectivity of ideas, no systematic doctrine of physics could be derived from them. It was the *reductio ad absurdum* of the empiricism of Locke. In order to account for the remarkable regularity in the succession of sense data, and also for the remarkable similarity between the sense data perceived by different observers, we are bound to postulate the existence of external objects. The reason why a thing is almost exactly the same to so many individual minds proves that things, though ideas, exist all the time objectively in the external world. The phenomena are present to us as one identical world of homogeneous objects. All our social and ethical relations are based on this supposition.

The Anthropomorphic Fallacy

Where then can we discover the fundamental difficulty of Berkeleian idealism? The root cause of Berkeley's problems can be attributed to the anthropomorphic fallacy, when Berkeley treats ultimate divine reality on the same level as that of human spirits.* Having once destroyed the material substance of Locke he was in search of a mind in which his "ideas" could inhere. But

[2] Second italics added.

* [Note the recognition of this problem by Professor Ramsey in this volume, p. 25. –Ed.]

was he justified in passing from human perceptions to divine perception in advancing his proof for the continued existence of the external world?

Berkeley's greatest failing from the point of view of a mystic philosophy, however, consists in his thoroughgoing division between the perceived data and the perceiving mind. This led him to believe that the ideas of sense were inert and powerless. By so perceiving reality he once more created an artificial chasm which it was his life's avowed mission to bridge. Surprisingly enough, Berkeley makes no such mistake in his youthful *Philosophical Commentaries* (or *Commonplace Book*), where he asserts that experience constitutes a whole, of which both will and understanding, subject and object, are nothing but abstract aspects, neither of which can be without the other.[3] What considerations led him subsequently to abandon this position it is difficult to ascertain. For in the *Principles* he informs us that "*Spirits* and *ideas* are things so wholly different, that when we say *they exist, they are known,* or the like, these words must not be thought to signify anything common to both natures." (PHK § 142)

Moreover, in *Siris,* as we shall see later, Berkeley once more asserts his earlier thesis (as contemplated in his *Philosophical Commentaries*). And if a complete reconciliation is effected between the "ideas" of the *Principles* and the "phenomena" of *Siris,* Berkeley's system culminates in a consistent spiritualism much akin to the thought of the Eastern mystics and the post-Kantian German idealists, who considered the dichotomy of the subject and the object a negation of all reality. I would therefore first give a brief exposition of the nature and ontological status of the "ideas" as understood by some Western philosophers and certain mystics in Islamic thought, and then show that once a reconciliation is brought about between Berkeley's epistemology and ontology as respectively represented in the *Principles* and *Siris,* the logical outcome of his "ideas" is fundamentally in agreement with the ideas of these mystics. As a matter of fact, this was the program of work that Berkeley himself had but dimly visualized when in his *Philosophical Commentaries* he jotted down such notes as the following: "Consciousness, perception, existence of ideas, seem to be all one" (PC # 578), and "Nothing properly, but Persons, i.e. conscious things, do exist." (PC # 24) There was perhaps something prophetic in Berkeley's remark when he declared: "My speculations have the same effect as visiting foreign countries: in the end I return where I was before, but my heart at ease, and enjoying life with new satisfaction."[4]

A historical survey of such systems of thought, where thought and its content are fused together in one organic unity, is neither desirable nor possible within the scope of this essay. I will, however, give a very brief resumé of the views of those philosophers who grappled with this problem and whose views have a direct bearing on the points I wish to make.

[3] See *Philosophical Commentaries* ## 609, 614, and 614a.

[4] A. C. Fraser, *Works of George Berkeley,* Vol. I (London: 1901), 92.

Some Historical Attempts toward Unity of Mind and Things

Plotinus was the first person in the history of philosophy to make a systematic attempt to bridge this dualism of Being—spirit and spiritual knowledge—between the known and the faculty that knows. The spiritual world and the spirit that beholds, says Plotinus, are correlatives neither of which has any meaning without the other. Plotinus emphasized the identification of the seer and the seen, the seeker and the sought. (*Enneads* III, 8)

A magnificent attempt to bridge the Cartesian dualism of mind and matter was made by Leibniz in modern times. Descartes had drawn a sharp line between consciousness and unconsciousness on the one side and self-consciousness on the other. For Leibniz, mind could not be regarded as identical with self-consciousness alone; self-consciousness must not be taken as entirely exclusive of mere consciousness or unconsciousness. The difference between mind and body becomes a difference not of kind but of degree. A true doctrine of substance, Leibniz maintains, makes matter by itself an abstraction; for matter is really confused perception, which is potentially clear and distinct perception—apperception or mind. There is only one reality that pervades the Universe. Body is confused soul; soul is clear and distinct body. Thus the absoluteness of the distinction between matter and mind that Descartes had insisted upon is removed. If the essence of matter is extension then it has no point of contact with the mental life. Spinoza tried to avoid this dualism by referring both thought and extension to a single substance, God. But this involves self-contradiction. It means asserting that the same substance is extended and unextended. But when instead, we characterize matter as force, which is synonymous with our own conscious life, a means of connection will appear, and Malebranche's fundamental difficulty—how the unextended soul is capable of cognizing the extended body—has been resolved. It is then in this sense only that the understanding prescribes its laws on nature.

The Persian mystic-poet, Jalaluddin Rumi, has expressed similar views in his *Mathnawi:*

جمله ذرات عالم در نهان   با تو می گویند روزان و شبان

ما سمیعیم و بصیریم و خوشیم   با شما نامحرمان ما خامشیم

"Day and night all particles of the Universe declare, 'We hear, see and are intoxicated. To the unushered we appear as mute.' "

And again:

باد و خاک و آب و آتش بنده اند   با من و تو مرده با حق زنده اند

"Air, earth, water and fire are busy in worship. To us they are dead but to God they are all alive."[5]

Similar views were also held by Fichte and Schelling in modern times. Consciousness (that is, ourselves), says Fichte, is the *Dasein* (Divine Existence) itself. "All is the Beloved, the lover is but a veil," says Rumi. In the following lines, Rumi gives us a positive aspect of this cosmic reality:

> If there be any lover in the world, O faithful,
> it is I.
> If there be any believer, non-believer, or Christian
> hermit, it is I.
> The wine-dregs, the cup-bearer, the minstrel, the
> harp, and the music,
> The beloved, the candle, the drink and the joy of
> the drunken,—it is I.[6]

Again, from the *Mathnawi:*

سر پنهان است اندر زیر و بم   فاش گر گویم جهان برهم زنم

"There is a secret in the melody of the flute which if divulged would upset the scheme of things."

Thus the essence of the starry heavens above and the moral law within is interpreted as one and the same. In the *Risalah fil Ishq* (Treatise on Love), Avicenna[7] tells us that God himself is the Lovable, Lover, and the Beloved, and thus the origin and the end of the Cosmos. This Love traverses the whole universe, manifesting itself in different ways at each stage of the ontological hierarchy. There is no existence save His existence. Tradition says that

[5] Maulana Jalaluddin Rumi (1207–1273), greatest Sufi philosopher and mystic poet of the thirteenth century, was born at Balkh in the northern Persian province of Khorasan and later settled at Qonia, an old Roman province, whence he acquired his name Rumi, or the Roman. For forty-three years he was engaged in writing his world-renowned *Mathnawi,* which deals with the deep problems of life and existence and still survives in its pristine glory. Hardly any Persian poetry can match the *Mathnawi* in its power of expression, ardor, exaltation, originality, and profundity. (All translations are by the author except as noted.)

[6] From E. H. Whinfield's translation (London: 1898). See R. A. Nicholson, *The Mystics of Islam* (London: 1961), 161.

[7] Or Ibn Sina (980–1037). His fame chiefly rests on his two voluminous works, the *Kitab al-Shifa* and the *Qanun fil' Tibb*. The first is an eighteen-volume encyclopedia of natural sciences, mathematics, and metaphysics, and the second contains remarkable contributions in the fields of medicine and surgery which earned him the title of second Galen. Though usually known as a Persian philosopher, he is equally claimed by the Turks and the Arabs.

Prophet Mohammed taught: "Revile not the World and Time, for God is the World and God is the Time."[8] And it is related that the Prophet declared that God said to Moses: "Oh my servant, I was sick and thou didst not visit me: I asked help of thee and thou didst not give it to Me." This means that the existence of the needy is His existence and the existence of the sick is His existence.

In the *Cartesian Meditations,* Husserl expresses the same insight by saying that the essence of the Cartesian *cogito* absorbs the *cogitatum.* Husserl wanted to emphasize that in all acts of consciousness the object of consciousness is contained. And, as he elucidates in his *Ideas* (Part I, Chap. 5, § 50), subject and object are only two aspects of the same cosmic reality. Husserl held out the ideal of bridging the dualism of the subjective and the objective, and though it is true that he could not make a thoroughgoing resolution of this duality in his own system, he was nonetheless conscious that in any true system of philosophy this distinction had to be overcome.

Berkeley Upholds the Mystic Thesis

Nor can we say that Berkeley was completely unmindful of this profound metaphysical insight, for a close study of the *Siris,* written in the concluding years of his life, reveals that it is a treatise writen on entirely novel lines, where one can discern Berkeley in a more sober mood.* Here the "ideas" are not those of Locke or like the sensuous ideas of the *Principles* and *Dialogues,* inert, inactive objects of perception. They rather breathe the spirit of Plato and extract a Platonic spirit from a thing of sense so commonplace as tar. We are transported from Locke to Plato and find revived the ancient conceptions of Active Intelligence, gradation in existence, and the constant animation of the Universe. Had Berkeley been a subjective idealist to the last, and had he not been once more aroused from his dogmatic slumbers, he would not have taken such great pains to show that behind the ideas (which form his phenomenal world) there is a spirit that moves, and a mind or providence that presides, and that Intelligence is the only summary explanation of the Universe. The ideas had been for all practical purposes psychical entities subjectively present in the human mind and implanted by God in our consciousness. What would be the point therefore in further asserting in *Siris* the spiritual nature of these ideas? But it was too late for him to effect a thoroughgoing reconciliation between the ideas of the *Principles* and the ideas of the *Siris.* In the latter we find an effort to obliterate this distinction between souls and spirits and the so-called passive and inert ideas of sensation. Berkeley comes quite close to Schelling's conception of the Absolute when he declares that

* [For a different view, note the comment by Prof. Jessop regarding *Siris:* "neither Professor Luce nor I can see in it any change of basic doctrine." *Works* I, 7.—Ed.]

8 From the *Hadith,* or Sayings of the Prophet Mohammed.

there is a mind that governs this mundane world, suggesting that "there is no chasm in nature, but a Chain or Scale of beings rising by gentle uninterrupted gradations from the lowest to the highest, each nature being informed and perfected by the participation of a higher." (SIR § 274) Thus in *Siris* Berkeley is in sympathy with the conception of the immanence of the Deity in nature, favored by the neo-Platonists and by the Alexandrian theologians with whom he became familiar in his later years. The "ideas" or passive objects of which Berkeley talks so much in his Dublin life have assumed an entirely different character. The objects presented in sense are in *Siris* called *phenomena* instead of ideas or sensations. They are metamorphosed into objective spiritual entities. Nevertheless, in spite of all that he says in *Siris,* Berkeley could not fully bridge the old partition of reality, between mind and things. The distinction between subjective and objective, though to a large extent blurred, was by no means completely obliterated. *For it is one thing to say that things possess consciousness and quite another to say that they are consciousness, or ideas.* And it is here that the mystics take leave from the positions held even by Leibniz, Fichte, and Schelling that things are ensouled or possess consciousness. For if we adhere consistently to the original Berkeleian thesis, the so-called things of the external world do not simply possess consciousness, but *are* consciousness, spirits and ideas. However, Berkeley's search for a mind wherein these ideas may inhere was a vain search based on an anthropomorphic delusion. There is no parallel between what is essential for human minds and what is essential in God.

Now, what do the mystics say of the relationship prevailing among these "ideas"? The ideas, as Berkeley tells us in the *Principles* and the *Dialogues,* are isolated atoms—minima—possessing no system of inherent relationship among them. But Reality, as mystics understand it, is a hierarchy of spirits, where the monads instead of being windowless are all windows. For even a superficial examination of any one of these ideas will reveal the inescapable fact that it cannot be isolated from the rest of the ideas but belongs to the totality of all ideas and is conditioned by the Universal Consciousness. There is a relationship of mutual interdependence prevailing among these spirits and ideas analogous to the relationship of the various members of a college community.

This mystic conception of Reality should not, however, be construed as a night in which all cows are black. For the nature of these spirits and ideas is many and varied. They are things and thoughts, imaginations, dreams, and hallucinations; they include persons, events, truths, beauties, goodnesses, artistic visions, moral laws as well as tragedies. There are innumerable realms of ideas and spirits, and there can be no obliteration of the distinctions of their rank and value. In *Siris,* Berkeley affirms: "As all parts in an animal are not eyes: and in a city, comedy, or picture, all ranks, characters, and colours are not equal or alike; even so excesses, defects, and contrary qualities conspire to the beauty and harmony of the world." (SIR § 262) Thus our sunset-hues, the starry heavens, the thoughts of the philosopher, the songs of the nightingale, the desires of the lover, the pangs, sufferings and sorrows of mankind are all various realms of this Universal Reality.

What then is the relationship that obtains between God and these ideas and Spirit, and all their various realms of being? Berkeley holds that man's knowledge of God is neither innate nor an integral part of the metaphysical structure of the mind. Since existence means to be perceived, and since nobody perceives God, there can be no such thing as an idea of God discoverable by any mind, though he may be known inferentially. The consequence was that in spite of his highest regard for religion, some have argued that Berkeley introduced God simply as a *deus ex machina* to perceive objects of the physical world.[9] As Wild points out, this solipsistic argument, even if valid, would not lead to God at all, but to a heightened man.[10]

The whole difficulty found in all such considerations, says Plotinus, is that we first take for granted the existence of things and the phenomenal order, and then when we have made them all secure, bring God into it. And then when we have brought Him in, we begin to ask whence and how He came—as if He were a new arrival; we have been wondering how He got there, and what He is, as if He had suddenly emerged from some abyss or dropped down from the clouds. (*Enneads* VI, 8, 11)

For the mystics, God exists because He is, as Avicenna puts it, a Necessary Being.[11] And as it is impossible to think of a contradiction, so it is unthinkable that a Necessary Being should not exist. He is not a terminus of a process of ratiocination and is not postulated to avoid an infinite regress of cause and effect. All beings, ideas, and spirits including all realms of their existence are only possible beings. They may or may not exist. But these ideas do in fact exist, and they are true and real. However, the ground of their reality cannot reside in themselves, for they are only possible. Hence their reality is due to the Necessary Being. Spirit and ideas along with all their realms are only possible when considered in themselves; they are, however, necessarily existent when considered in relation to the Necessary Being. Our world is, therefore, not only the best of all possible worlds, but the only possible world.

Now, is there a possibility of knowledge of these universal ideas and spirits, their various realms and their relationship to God? In his *Philosophical Commentaries,* Berkeley says: "certainly I cannot err in matter of simple perception. so far as we can in reasoning go without the help of signs, there we have certain knowledge." (PC # 693) But in *Siris,* Berkeley rejects this position

[9] This is suggested, for example, in the *Second Dialogue*. Philonous says: "Men commonly believe that all things are known or perceived by God, because they believe the being of God, whereas I on the other side, immediately and necessarily conclude the being of a God because all sensible things must be perceivd by him." (DHP 212)

[10] John Wild, *George Berkeley* (Cambridge, Mass.: 1936), 175.

[11] See J. L. Teicher's "Avicenna's Place in Arabic Philosophy" in G. M. Wickens (ed.), *Avicenna: Scientist and Philosopher* (London, 1952).

and makes a clear distinction between the ideas of sensation and the ideas of the intellect. (SIR § 253) It had now become evident to him that the so-called simple ideas of Locke were in fact nothing more than "simple." He therefore departs here from the empiricism asserted in his criticism of the doctrine of abstract ideas and describes the ideas as purely intellectual constructs, differing essentially from the contents of sensory experience. There is a clear distinction between the archetypal ideas and the ectypal ideas. Here Berkeley is laying down the propositions that the principles of science are neither objects of sense nor of imagination, and that intellect alone is the sure guide to truth.

As a matter of fact the error of earlier Berkeleian epistemology was its thoroughgoing separation of perception from conception, of notions from the ideas of sensation. For the mystics, sensations, spirits, mental operations and their relations have a common root in our nature. The sense and understanding are fused into one activity and are the manifestations of one Universal Spirit. The fountain-spring of sensibility being the same Universal Spirit, sensibility, too, gives us more than the contingent and the ephemeral. In sensation are concealed the deepest and the highest truths. The old absolute philosophy placed the senses in the sphere of phenomena of finite things as if they were something contrary to the divine, the absolute. Though when we are thinking of the most sublime and apparently the most supersensible objects, the sense centers of the brain are in essential cooperation. But perceptions without conceptions are blind. Mystics would rather add that not even the joint efforts of sensibility and understanding can lead us to the source of ultimate Truth. For, as Goethe remarks, existence divided by human reason leaves a remainder. In *Siris,* Berkeley himself admitted that "it cannot be denied that, with respect to the universe of things, we in this mortal state are like men educated in Plato's cave, looking on shadows with our backs turned to the light." (SIR § 263) Thus, as the Phoenix cannot be contained in the sparrow's nest, so mere sense and understanding cannot exhaust reality. The pure intuition of reason is considered by the mystics the sole organ and medium by which we can achieve this ideal. We shall have to increase our conceptual dimensions and evolve a new science fitted to the forms and categories of higher intuition in order to penetrate into the nature of things. Berkeley makes a right beginning but does not carry the process to its fruition.

XI

Was Berkeley an Idealist?

ANDRÉ-LOUIS LEROY

The Problem

It is worthwhile to consider a problem often discussed through the years in spite of Berkeley's own assertions regarding the nature of his philosophy. He thought he was an immaterialist and not at all an "ideist" as his contemporaries claimed. Nor was he an "idealist" as many of his followers have held up to the present. The persistence of an interpretation which is apparently contrary to the opinion of the philosopher himself suggests that we look at the philosophical situation in Berkeley's time. We shall try to understand the meaning of the word "idea," for it seems strange not to call a philosopher an "ideist" or "idealist" who apparently views the world as a mere spectacle of sensible ideas without a substance to sustain them. Berkeley himself admits that on first appearance, it is odd to call things ideas. (DHP 235) Yet he thought of himself as a realist, perhaps even more of a realist than other philosophers. (See PC # 517a) He declares himself the direct opponent of Descartes, Locke, and the other subjectivists, who distinguished primary qualities from secondary ones and viewed the latter as mere appearances, always deceitful. Now Berkeley followed the example of Locke and claimed he was a philosopher of practical concerns, able to discover the real meaning of ordinary daily knowledge. He appears to be suspicious of those excessive intellectual adventures that abandon real ideas of the senses, which are the works of God, for new scientific hypotheses, which are the works of men.

Now we must point out that Berkeley did not always give the same meaning to the word "idea," and this may be a source of some ambiguity for his readers. Sometimes he used that word in a common-sense manner, as when someone says "I have an idea," meaning that he has a design, a plan or pattern as yet unrealized. It might be the idea of a novel, or an outline of a program, a mere sketch that must be brought to maturity by further reflection and verbal formulation. This is a very common use and a very ambiguous one. But "idea" may mean one of the different significations suggested by Locke in the introduction to his *Essay Concerning Human Understanding:* "whatsoever is meant by phantasm, notion, species, or whatever it is which the mind can be employed about in thinking."[1] Now the former meaning is more ambiguous. Looking at the use of human language and considering the nature of the ideas perceived, imagined, or thought by human beings, we must distinguish different kinds of ideas, either particular and concrete ideas, or abstract and general ones, those used by scholars, mathematicians, and scientists —perhaps admired but not ordinarily understood by the common man and wrongly used by many philosophers.

To avoid these mistakes, Berkeley thinks we must look at the early conduct of children in their use of language. Young children in their chatterings do not use abstract words like triangle, proposition, or substance. (PHK Intro., § 14) But children often use abstract words from the common language of adults, such as "father," as if they were particular and not generic names—at least at the beginning. Berkeley is quite right in his introduction to the *Principles,* when he distinguishes sensible ideas—for example, ideas of colors that are particular—and general ideas, or abstract notions. A sensible idea is an object of the mind; it is outside the mind and not within it, as the disciples of Galileo had said. We must be careful not to make the common mistake of believing that a sensible idea is a mode of our mind. So we must reject the Galilean doctrine and not accept the distinction between primary and secondary qualities—the doctrine of Descartes and Locke. (The latter thought he was a practical philosopher and yet unwittingly engaged in an intellectual adventure towards skepticism.)

General ideas are quite different from particular sensible ideas. Human beings arrive at them when they have noticed some similarity between several particular ideas. Then they use the same word to point out this similarity. In its first years, a child does not think there is a similar relation between another child and another man as there is between himself and his own father. But "similarity" is not a sensible idea; it is never perceived by the senses; it is known by an operation of the mind, by a comparison between two or more sensible ideas. Moreover, this knowledge is strengthened by the permanence of a word and the act of the mind takes on a greater consistency; it appears as an object. But the stability of such a relation in every case is not easy for a young child to discover.

But a new phase of the mental process occurs and we get an abstract notion

[1] Locke, *Essay Concerning Human Understanding,* Introduction, § 8.

that may also be called a general abstract idea. The Scholastics and modern philosophers have often preferred to use the word "Essence" to translate the pseudo-reality of the abstract notion. Mathematicians were also fond of these kinds of reality. But Berkeley warns us that general ideas are works of the human mind, difficult to use and to understand. "The general idea of a triangle . . . is . . . neither oblique nor rectangle, neither equilateral, equicrural, nor scalenon, but *all and none* of these at once." (PHK Intro., § 13) It may be added that "triangle" is not the only example of a general idea; "matter," "substance," "extension," are also important instances of this type and there is an infinity of other examples, as many as there are common names and words. Accordingly, we must acknowledge that every abstract general idea is really a particular idea, backed up by the notion of a relation to many similar ideas. In this case, the perception of a sensible idea is combined with that act of the mind, a relation of similarity. Unfortunately, philosophers then speak of abstract notions and use words to give some consistency to these notions and to different signs. A geometrical figure, a number, an algebraic letter, all signs or symbols are fallacious realities; they suggest sensible realities, whereas they symbolize acts of minds.

Just as immediately as we perceive ideas—perhaps even more immediately—we perceive acts of the mind when we reflect on them. We must not think that those acts are of the same nature as the ideas composed by memory and imagination. The ideas we are discussing now show us the activities of our mind; they are the fruits of our efforts; they evidence the power of our mind. That power, immaterial and strong, creates new pictures, pictures never finished, and never complete, but always aims at a more complete realization; at first it is a manner of feeling, quite vague but always consistent. Such acts are known with great certitude, but they are so rapid that one cannot remember the process of their realization.

Thus we may readily understand that the second edition of the *Principles of Human Knowledge* uses different words for sensible qualities and for acts of the mind, *ideas* and *notions,* respectively. This explicitly contradicts the assertion of Locke, quoted above, in which that philosopher used the word "idea" to mean everything the mind could be concerned with in thinking, and rejected all other terms used by philosophers previous to him. The use of only one word to designate all the things the mind is busy about must not make us overlook differences between the modes of knowledge. We must not yield to the prestige of words and view as similar two different objects of thought and two different actions of thought. It is important to distinguish the character of those two types of immediate knowledge for Berkeley. Our *ideas* are always passive; our *notions,* on the contrary, are always active.

Did Berkeley think there was much more of immediacy in notions because they were the mind's knowledge of itself? It is possible to put a kind of spatial distance between an object I perceive and my own body; but actually, between my idea and my thought, there is only a difference of quality; the first is passive, the second is active.

So it seems that for Berkeley there are two worlds, the world of ideas perceived by our senses and the world of our mind; this last is mental activity, not only imagination, thought, and will, but also memory, which is like a medium for recalling past feelings and perceptions. Now, these two worlds are tightly related to one another. The mind is the cause; the sensible ideas are the effects, partly of human actions but more often of divine acts. There are no material causes; what we call "matter" is a general abstract idea, a mere word. We can say that we have a notion of matter and no sensible idea of it. The notion is always a consequence of the activity of our mind, which puts a fictitious reality behind this word.

Therefore Berkeley is an adversary of that doctrine called materialism, famous in ancient times with Democritus, Epicurus, and Lucretius, and present again in the modern period with Hobbes and the deists, John Toland and Anthony Collins. Just before the deists, Descartes had professed a mechanism, and Locke a rationalism, but they did not think of themselves as atheists. Moreover, in the Middle Ages, the Schoolmen discussed the three famous doctrines of realism, nominalism, and conceptualism, which upset the theologians because of their bearing on the difficult problem of the Trinity. The close relation between theology and philosophy prompted Berkeley to look carefully at the real meaning of such terms as idea, notion, abstract idea, and general idea, for these terms made up the vocabulary of philosophers writing at different times and in different languages. And they were often used with differing meanings.

Ideas and Notions: A Change in Berkeley's Vocabulary

Let us look more intently at the views of Berkeley on the nature of reality. The two worlds, the spiritual and active one and the one consisting of passive ideas, are different but complement each other. Sensible ideas cannot be modes of the mind. The modern theory of two kinds of qualities, the primary and the secondary, must be considered an unfortunate mistake. First, it marks the condemnation of the sensible by regarding the secondary ones as only qualitative and this is contrary to our perception. "The Trees are in the park, that is, whether I will or no whether I imagine any thing about them or no, let me but go thither & open my Eyes by day & I shall not avoid seeing them." (PC # 98) And we read: "I may say the pain is in my finger, etc according to my Doctrine." (PC # 444) Again, "the horse is in the stable, the Books are in the study as before." (PC # 429) The secondary qualities are on the side of things; the secondary qualities are more real than the primary ones because "extension, figure, and motion, abstracted from all other qualities are inconceivable." (PHK § 10) In the *Second Dialogue between Hylas and Philonous,* Berkeley extols nature and "its noble and delightful scenes of all reality," and God is blessed for His creation. (DHP 210 ff.)

But we must insist more on the opposing traits of the two kinds of qualities. First I must point out a mistake Berkeley did not correct in his works. In several passages, Berkeley uses the word "quality," which is taken from Descartes and Locke and seems to be contrary to his immaterialism. Yet Berkeley struggles against these philosophers; when he uses his own term he makes use of the word "idea."

> In common talk, the objects of our senses are not termed *ideas* but *things*. Call them so still: provided you do not attribute to them any absolute external existence, and I shall never quarrel with you for a word. The Creation therefore I allow to have been a creation of things, of *real* things. (DHP 251)

You must translate real things into real ideas, that is, sensible ideas. The primary qualities are expressed by general words or signs; they are extension, matter, time. But all those words cannot designate real things; all the abstract general ideas are similar to signs and numbers. In the *Siris,* commenting on the ancient philosophers, he writes: "That matter is actually nothing, but potentially all things, is the doctrine of Aristotle, Theophrastus and all the ancient Peripatetics." (SIR § 317) And later:

> If any one should think to infer the reality or actual being of matter from the modern tenet that gravity is always proportionable to the quantity of matter, let him but narrowly scan the modern demonstration of that tenet, and he will find it to be a vain circle, concluding in truth no more than this:—that gravity is proportionable to weight, that is, to itself. Since matter is conceived only as a defect and mere possibility; and since God is absolute perfection and act, it follows there is the greatest distance and opposition imaginable between God and matter. (SIR § 319)

Siris, like Berkeley's earlier works, lays stress on the fact that the reality of nature results from the complementary character of the acts of spirits and the passivity of ideas. We must admit that there are media, passive ideas combined with acts of the mind, in the same way that we form our remembrances or images. But they are not really original, as we have said. Our knowledge, then, consists of sensible ideas and of notions; the former are perceived by our senses; they are not in the mind, but we can say that they are apprehended by our senses; the latter are not things, but acts of the mind intuitively known. The first are passive, the second active.

Perhaps Berkeley did not modify his thought but changed his words. Or, rather, he changed his hypothesis to test it and see its relation to reality. For example, in the *Philosophical Commentaries* we read: "N.B. according to my Doctrine all thing are entia rationis i.e. solum habent esse in Intellectu.—according to my Doctrine, all [things] are not entia rationis, the distinction between *ens rationis* & *ens reale* is kept up by it as well as any other Doctrine." (PC ## 474, 474a) For if all things were *entia rationis,* abstract ideas would have existed, as well as scholastic essences. Now Berkeley rejected them, because his general abstract ideas were born from acts of the mind, upheld by words. Thus we may think there is a first phase which is conceptualism and a second which is nominalism.

In the *Third Dialogue,* willing to state his opinion more accurately, Berkeley writes: "You mistake me. I am not for changing things into ideas, but rather ideas into things; since those immediate objects of perception, which according to you, are only appearances of things, I take to be the real things themselves." (DHP 244)[2] But that apparent modification does not change his opinion; the realities of nature, the mysterious substances which should support ideas and qualities, are mere nothingness, or rather, they are mere interpretations of the appearances of ideas. This problem is more difficult to solve. The characteristics of ideas are expressed by interpretations in signs and symbols, signs of distances, shadows of qualities, ghosts of matter. It is a mistake, but we can easily correct it if we discount the modern doctrines of philosophers and scientists. We ought to deny that there is more reality to primary qualities than to secondary ones. "Lengths abstract from breadths are the work of the mind, such do intersect in a point at all angles, after the same way colour is abstract from extension. every position alters the line." (PC # 85) What we perceive has both color and extension, not extension without volume, or a line without breadth. Even less can we say that there is only one space or extension. There are two extensions or spaces; one is visible, the other is tangible. There is no perception without idea, no idea without perception. (PC # 572) Such is the complexity of reality. We must go further: a sensible idea is neither in the mind nor outside the mind. We can only say that an idea is presented to the mind and simultaneously the mind perceives the idea. Thus may we describe real experience.[3]

Such is the meaning of the famous word "Immaterialism." There is no unperceivable matter nor unperceivable extension; every extension is sensible, tangible, or visible, and so is every material object. What is more, there is no part of an extension we could perceive if it were as small as an infinitesimal. When a man says there are twelve inches in a foot, a young child cannot understand the meaning of such a remark unless he has seen the measuring operation. No related idea really exists if beforehand there is no sensible complex perception and no act of the mind. Now if we scrutinize Berkeley's assertion that no perception can exist without an idea, we shall see the reason why he did not want to accept Descartes' universal doubt or his doubts on the full reality of sensible ideas which would be the results of sensible ideas.

[2] Cf. *Philosophical Commentaries* # 517: "I take not away substances. I ought not to be accus'd of discarding Substance out of the reasonable World. I onely reject the Philosophic sense (which in effect is no sense) of the word substance."

[3] Cf. PC ## 359, 878; PHK §§ 33, 90; DHP 250, 262.

We cannot deny some reality to these illusions, although various perspectives and changing aspects are present. All philosophers have acknowledged these changes. Berkeley does so too, but he explains them differently from the rationalists. The latter thought that the identity of the thing of which the aspect was changing was preserved by an unvarying substance, an essence never perceived—and always imagined—only an abstract name and definition. As previously brought out, Berkeley denied reality to all substances and to matter. He thought that the unknown substance was more properly replaced by the notion of succession related to the notion of an active cause, namely of a spirit, since only spirits can be the real cause of acts or volitions or of the presence of sensible ideas to other spirits. (PHK § 150)

Thus we can suggest, quite in accordance with the thought of Berkeley, that we perceive steady relations between our various sensible ideas. This steadiness prompts us to apply the same name to that unity and the constant use of this name gives further strength to the relation as it occurs in common general practice. And here Berkeley has in mind a similar process that explains the apparent reality of infinitesimals for many mathematicians.

We may still perceive the line that represents a mile on a map. But we cannot perceive one ten-thousandth of that "paper-line." When we think of it, we may actually think of the process ad infinitum. (PC # 341) Berkeley writes:

> Three faults occur in the arguments of the Mathematicians for *divisibility ad infinitum*. 1. they suppose extension to exist without the mind or not perceiv'd. 2. they suppose that we have an idea of length without breadth—or rather that invisible length does exist—or that length without breadth does exist. 3. that unite is divisible ad infinitum. (PC # 342. Italics added.)

This criticism directed upon infinitesimals is made again in *The Analyst*. I will quote only some general questions from the list of the Queries in that book.

> *Qu.* 1. Whether the object of geometry be not the proportions of assignable extensions? And whether there be any need of considering quantities either infinitely great or infinitely small? *Qu.* 2. Whether the end of geometry be not to measure assignable finite extension? And whether this practical view did not first put men on the study of geometry? . . . *Qu.* 4. Whether men may properly be said to proceed in a scientific method, without clearly conceiving the object they are conversant about, the end proposed, and the method by which it is pursued? . . . *Qu.* 6. Whether the diagrams in a geometrical demonstration are not to be considered as signs, of all possible finite figures, of all sensible and imaginable extensions or magnitudes of the same kind? *Qu.* 7. Whether it is possible to free geometry from insuperable difficulties and absurdities, so long as either the abstract general idea of extension, or absolute external extension be supposed its true object? *Qu.* 8. Whether the notions of absolute time, absolute place, and absolute motion be not most abstractedly metaphysical? Whether it is possible for us to measure, compute, or know them? (*Analyst* § 50)

We find here the same main notions: the necessity of always considering sensible ideas, the danger of looking at signs and symbols as if they were images of realities, and the mistake of those metaphysicians who regard general abstract ideas as realities.

Understanding and Faith

We must now return and go more deeply into an important problem, namely, how there can be a dualism of spirits and ideas in an immaterialistic philosophy. Certainly it is a legacy of common sense as well as of early Christianity. The common man appears satisfied by that dualism which simplifies the complexity of our world. After some meditation, he perceives the truth of the word of Paul that we are debtors both to the wise and to the unwise. At first we are spirit and flesh. Later, as Berkeley said on the day of his death, it is the victory of the law of God.[4]

The victory of the spirit over the flesh, of the wise over the unwise, is highly desirable, but in human nature the struggle between the good and the evil continues. Even amongst Christians we find different patterns of behavior. Their conduct is too variable and weak to overcome materialism completely—which is itself so simplistic. Moreover, Berkeley attempted to perform a twofold task. He wanted to discard equally two opposite doctrines, materialism and idealistic subjectivism. And he wanted to give the victory to Christianity over these two doctrines. Now everywhere we meet diversity and antagonism in reality.

At the end of the *Principles of Human Knowledge,* Berkeley replies to the freethinkers who assert that we cannot see and meet God in the same manner in which we see and meet human beings. (PHK § 148) He observes that we cannot see and perceive immediately the minds of other human beings. We can only surmise their feelings and their thoughts by interpreting their gestures and physiognomies. And it might be more comformable to the dignity of God that we cannot understand his nature as fully as we know the nature of men. We may look at the world as at something almost analogous to the body of God, but the analogy is not so obvious as to satisfy the atheist. The main reason for that distrust might be that the body of God would be the only body of that kind, too difficult to apprehend, whereas the body of man is easily perceived in various ways and in the same manner as the bodies of various animals. Besides, the bodies of living beings are parts of our sensible experience and we perceive their gestures and discover that they express aims. The body of God would be directly imperceptible and even indirectly His body cannot be discerned through the features of Nature.[5]

[4] A. A. Luce, *Life of George Berkeley, Bishop of Cloyne* (Edinburgh: 1949), 221.

[5] See PHK § 150. However, § 151 cites the sentence of Isaiah: "Verily . . . thou art a God that hides thy self," and it adds: "yet to an unbiassed and attentive mind, nothing can be more plainly legible."

In *Alciphron,* Berkeley changes his pattern of argumentation. Not only does he find some help from passages in the Bible, where God is described as really different from man, but also from the Book of Cajetan on the *Analogy*. (Cf. ALC 169) Reasoning by analogy gives only probabilities and the persuasive power of such reasoning fluctuates from metaphorical analogy to proper analogy. A conclusion by analogy is only a probable conjecture, an incomplete similarity between two figures, two functions, two structures quite distinct from one another. Such a conclusion always needs another factor, another reason to become a practical certainty. That additional reason, when we consider the existence of God, is faith. Men who have no faith have no certainty, no assurance. At first, men sought a completely understandable knowledge by using erudite reasoning similar to scientific arguments. But that use of reason alone gives only a new, higher degree of probability and we cannot thereby reach a true intuition. We readily understand that we might arrive at a better kind of knowledge, but we can never establish our intellectual view at the level of God. Berkeley lives and breathes in a spiritual atmosphere. He does it because he is moved by a religious faith.[6]

Reasoning and Intuition

We come now to the last question of this Berkeleian problem. What are the meanings of the words "subjectivism," "idealism," "materialism," and "immaterialism"? This brings us back to the historical situation that attracted our attention at the beginning of this inquiry.

We may consider Descartes and Locke as subjectivists, for both of them followed the way opened by Galileo. They are mechanists and distinguish the primary qualities from the secondary ones. Descartes was a mathematician, Locke a physician and an educator. Both of them were partisans of a quantitative science. Descartes was a Roman Catholic, a serious enough one to vow, after his famous dream of November 19, 1619, to go as a pilgrim to Loreto. He waited six years before accomplishing his pilgrimage but he did achieve it. And if he carefully distinguished the human spirit from the body, it was because he hoped that the Catholic doctors of the Sorbonne would not be too averse to his mechanical physics. But his Catholicism was adjusted to his philosophical doctrine. It was exactly the same in the case of Locke, who

[6] The *Alciphron* propounds a progressive argumentation which the *Siris* extends further. It frees the Christian of some feeble arguments and places him in the core of an argument admitted by the freethinkers. Berkeley states that we must start from the concrete experience of everyone, which progresses by inference and analogy. A visual language is the word of God, but men must manifest their personality by bringing to the work of God their individual assistance. It is an act of faith which has to proceed by collecting information and by analogy. Cf. PHK §§ 72, 148; DHP 171, 215, 223; and the seventh book of *Alciphron*.

was a rationalist and did not want to become an Anglican clergyman. But in his *Essay Concerning Human Understanding* Locke attempts to reconcile Faith and Reason. He writes:

> Reason . . . as contradistinguished to faith I take to be the discovery of the certainty or probability of such propositions or truths, which the mind arrives at by deduction made from such ideas, which it has got by the use of its natural faculties, viz. by sensation or reflection. . . . Faith, on the other side, is the assent to any proposition, not thus made out by the deductions of reason, but upon the credit of the proposer, as coming from God, in some extraodinary way of communication. This way of discovering truths to men we call revelation.[7]

However, Locke soon withdraws this approval given to revelation, at least in part, when he distinguishes traditional from original revelation, and adds that "the same truths may be discovered, and conveyed down from revelation, which are discoverable to us by reason, and by those ideas we naturally may have."[8] In the following chapter, Locke is more reserved: "God, when he makes the prophet, does not unmake the man. He leaves all his faculties in the natural state, to enable him to judge of his inspirations, whether they be of divine original or no . . . Reason must be our last judge and guide in everything."[9]

Thus the two philosophers are equally mechanists and equally rationalists, but what is the exact meaning of the word "reason" here? Metaphysical, demonstrative, or even probable reasoning—either strict demonstration or a probable working hypothesis. Two opposing philosophical doctrines have issued from these different uses of reason. Descartes and Malebranche thought that the human understanding could intuit some of the ideas of the divine intellect. Thus human minds might grasp the meaning of the ideas of the divine intellect, and the science of man might be, in such cases, at the level of God's intellect. Now, when the spirit of mechanism prevails in human understanding, modern science is regarded as so perfect that it is thought to be at the level of the divine intellect. The materialists consider the God of the theists as at the same level of reality as Nature and matter.

John Toland (1670–1722) was one of the freethinkers of this period who struggled against the creed of the church. He used historical criticism to show that Christianity is without mystery. Then he tried to prove that Nature is a large organism completely animated. He taught mechanistic materialism and his books were read by many people in spite of the opposition of the clergy. Anthony Collins (1676–1729) was another important materialist who believed he had discovered the meaning of a statement by pondering the evidence of the reasons that support or resist it.[10] He gives a list of atheists

[7] Locke, *Essay Concerning Human Understanding,* Bk IV, Chap. XVIII, § 2.

[8] *Ibid.,* Bk IV, Chap. XVIII, § 4.

[9] *Ibid.,* Bk IV, Chap. XIX, § 14.

[10] Anthony Collins, *A Discourse of Free-Thinking,* VI. I mention only six of the forty so-called freethinkers from Socrates to Locke.

that is amazing, since, among the forty so-called freethinkers, it includes the names of Plato, Solomon, Archbishop Tillotson, and Richard Hooker (the author of the *Laws of Ecclesiastical Polity*), and he cites as a Lockian thesis the impossibility of distinguishing the reasonable and the rational.

In his adolescence, Julien LaMettrie (1709–1751) went first to Coutances and Caen, then to Saint-Malo and Paris to become a Catholic priest by studying in the famous College d'Harcourt. At that time, the college supported the Cartesian thesis of the animal-machine. LaMettrie's stay at Harcourt might have had some influence on his thought. During this period, the materialism of the English freethinkers was widely influential in France. Spokesmen for the churches had good intentions but very poor arguments to defend their dogmas. Two clerical protagonists, the Rector William Derham (1657–1735) in England ,and Abbé Noel Pluche (1688–1761) in France, proposed such feeble arguments that they rather favored the materialists. Pluche criticized Locke because he dared to establish reason as supreme arbiter of the mysteries of faith. LaMettrie maintained that the soul followed the gradual development of the body. Other philosophers had spoken about the various parts of spirit, but all these parts could be reduced to the imagination alone, which had formed all of them. The imagination alone perceives, he held, and it can examine intently its own sensations. It judges so quickly and it may be educated so swiftly that it is astonishing and its ways are diverse. LaMettrie adds that, in all the animal world, the same ends are reached by an infinity of various means, all of them really geometrical. A few pages before the end of his *Man a Machine,* LaMettrie condemned simultaneously the attacks of the atheists and the Christians against Descartes:

> It is true that this famous philosopher has made mistakes and nobody denies them. But he has known the animal nature and he was the first to demonstrate completely that animals were mere machines. Now after a discovery of such importance which supposes so much sagacity, how might it be imaginable not to forgive his errors![11]

> Let us conclude boldly that man is a machine and that in all the universe there is only one substance variously modified; it is not the work of prejudice, nor of my reason alone; I would have disdained a guide which I believe so unsafe, if my sense were not bearing the flaming torch, so to speak, and would not have engaged me to follow it, by its light. Experience has spoken to me in behalf of reason; so I have joined them together.[12]

Such was materialism at this time in Great Britain and France. It opposed the old social and religious doctrines, while libertinism was growing and

[11] *LaMettrie's L'Homme Machine,* critical edition by Aram Vartanian (Princeton, N.J.: 1960), 191.

[12] *Ibid.,* 197.

trying to free itself from the rules of the past to obtain more freedom for daily life.

It was natural then, that Bishop Berkeley wanted to refute the principles of materialism. He thought they resulted from a conflict between science and religion. The seventeenth and eighteenth centuries were periods of very important transformations in the sciences. New perspectives brought new views. Not all the scientists were really opposed to the various churches and not all the clergymen were intolerant and hostile to scientific novelties. Some men were inquisitive; others thought they alone had the truth, but, generally, good men were circumspect. Berkeley was distrustful of philosophical novelties and the new mathematics. He was committed to sensible ideas and the world of common sense. His solution was to condemn matter as an abstraction and to give full reality to sensible qualities, the work of God.

Must we say that Berkeley was an "ideist"—as Christopher-Matthew Pfaff (1686–1760) wrote in his *Discourse on Egoism*[13]—because he believed in the reality of the spectacle of nature? As Berkeley declares through the mouth of Crito:

> There is not need of much inquiry to be convinced of two points than which none are more evident, more obvious, and more universally admitted by men of all sorts, learned and unlearned, in all times and places, to wit, that man acts, and is accountable for his actions. (ALC 318)

A little earlier, Euphranor had said:

> In the next place, I observe that you very nicely abstract and distinguish the actions of the mind, judgment and will: that you make use of such terms as power, faculty, act, determination, indifference, freedom, necessity, and the like, as if they stood for distinct abstract ideas: and that this supposition seems to ensnare the mind into the same perplexities and errors, which, in all other instances, are observed to attend the doctrine of abstraction. (ALC 314)

That use of abstraction has the same bad consequence when it is applied to the acts of the mind as when it was employed for sensible ideas. Living reality is changed into signs, general and fixed. All life disappears, all reality hardens and withers. In actuality, excitations result from the activity of other human spirits, and, for a large part, from the acts of God, "*who works all in all* and *by* whom all things consist." (PHK § 146) The ideas are not merely creatures of a human subject; they result from the common activity of spirits.

Soon afterwards, the word "ideist" was supplanted by "idealist." But that new word is more ambiguous. "Idea" is a metaphysical word proposed by Plato; it also means a standard of perfection. Not always completely realized, it is a scheme, an intention that not only is achieved through its own exertion, but also reflects the act of God on the acts of human spirits. At this

[13] Tübingen, 1722.

time, Pere Buffier, Diderot, and d'Holbach spoke of the extravagances of Berkeley. Turgot spoke of his chimerical illusion. M. de Crouzas thought that Berkeley had the brain overturned and he mocked: "This author has not published a book in print; he has only an idea of this book and it is this idea we are reading. The bookseller from whom we believe we purchase the book has existence only as an idea, exactly as the money we give him.[14] Charles Bonnet (1720–1793), in his *Mémoires Autobiographiques,* considers Berkeley's immaterialism as ingenious. Unfortunately "idealism does too much violence to our natural way of seeing and judging . . . The subtle and profound Berkeley was not consistent enough: he was preaching *idealism* and he had to admit mere egoism."[15]

But these two terms are misleading. The first one takes away matter because it is an empty category, a mere abstraction—or, as Maupertuis wrote, an unknown cause,[16] like the thing-in-itself of Kant—so that we should have to dress its ghost with the apparel of the various sensible qualities. The qualitative spectacle is indeed real, but to understand it as the "substance" of common sense, we should have to give it firmness and consistency. The mistake here comes from our ordinary confusion between sensible matter easily perceived in practical life and merely intellectual physical matter, which is imagined on the pattern of abstract space and matter. Now the second word, "egoism," did not mean then what it means today, an excessive concern for our personal interest. Bonnet certainly knew that men are very often too concerned with themselves, but he wanted to indicate the philosophical doctrine that all the elements of our knowledge are in the ego and its relations. There is the common opinion, according to which we know and perceive not only the acts and feelings of our mind, but also sensible ideas. Our view of nature is composed of various ideas and notions and is felt in the course of our changes of place. But there is another kind of erudite presentation, which delights in the more recent scientific hypotheses, schemes, and symbols. It is not always easily understood even by scientists, for these hypotheses are often temporary and we must be cautious about their truth.

Berkeley preferred sensible experience to the rational imagination, which for him was merely formal speech or signs. "I am more for reality than any other Philosophers, they make a thousand doubts & know not certainly but we may be deceiv'd. I assert the direct contrary." (PC # 517a) His guide was the Holy Scriptures. "All things in the Scripture which side with the Vulgar against the learned side with me also. I side in all things with the Mob." (PC # 405)

The practical success of modern science has given it a great prestige; it

[14] *Examen du Pyrrhonisme ancien et moderne* I, § 146.

[15] *Mémoires Autobiographiques* (1948 edition). Translation by author.

[16] *Maupertuis, Oeuvres,* Tome I, § XXIX, 282–283. Translation by author.

has also distorted our conception of nature. But perhaps we should return to something not far from common sense. As Berkeley says:

> [We must endeavor to] place in a clearer light that truth, which was before shared between the vulgar and the philosophers: the former being of opinion, that *those things they immediately perceive, are the real things;* and the latter, that *the things immediately perceived, are ideas which exist only in the mind.* Which two notions put together, do in effect constitute the substance of what I advance. (DHP 262)

That conclusion agrees with a warning in the *Philosophical Commentaries* earlier: "Whoever shall pretend to censure any part—I desire He would read out the Whole, else he may perhaps not understand me." (PC # 680)

XII

Berkeley and His Modern Critics

WARREN E. STEINKRAUS

Critics of Berkeley have been at work for over two hundred and twenty-five years and the end is not yet. Whether any of them could qualify for the prize of £100 offered by T. Collyns Simon in 1847 for a refutation of the good bishop's philosophy remains doubtful.[1] Berkeley predicted that there would be many criticisms of his view and consequently, beginning with section 34 of his *Principles of Human Knowledge,* considered some sixteen possible objections. When one studies certain modern attacks on Berkeley, he sometimes wonders whether their originators have ever read beyond section 33.

That many of the conventional criticisms are based on misconceptions of Berkeley's thought is doubtless true. There are still the stone-kickers. But A. C. Fraser was surely overstating his case when he wrote: "The history of objections is very much a history of misconceptions."[2] There are careful and searching criticisms of Berkeley's views, but misconceptions do persist, partly because some critics cannot wait to hear his whole philosophy before attacking his initial statements. For example, E. G. Spaulding and J. Loewen-

[1] In his *Universal Immaterialism* (London: [1847] 1862). It was raised to £500 in 1850 but never collected.

[2] A. C. Fraser, *The Works of George Berkeley,* Vol. I (Oxford: 1901), 363. A. A. Luce suggests that the *Principles of Human Knowledge* has "never been answered except by misrepresentation and ridicule" (*The Life of George Berkeley* [London: 1949], page 49).

berg[3] rebuke Berkeley for not following consistently the formula *esse* is *percipi* for every kind of being, even though Berkeley repeatedly says it applies only to physical things.

Some critics have noted ambiguities or verbal inconsistencies.[4] Others have nibbled at details, suggesting that his view would make God too busy or that it implies strange things about animals and plants.[5] Occasionally, they raise a dust of artificial quibbles and complain that they cannot see.[6] Again, some have challenged his motives, arguing that he philosophizes purely for the sake of supporting traditional religious faith, adjusting his theory to fit his wishes.[7] But they fail to recognize that Berkeley could have adopted any number of positions which supported Christianity if his interests had been solely apologetic. Even psychoanalysis has been attempted—two hundred years after the fact—with, it must be said, some ingenious if not outlandish claims about his metaphysics being a "fantasy."[8] Still others attack the very fundamentals of his philosophy and charge it with being unempirical or inconsistent, hence basically wrong.[9] It is with several of these negative criticisms that this essay will be primarily concerned, though, of course, there are favorable critics of Berkeley like Bowne, Royce, or Ward, who adopt portions of his view and build upon it.

[3] E. G. Spaulding, *The New Rationalism* (New York: 1918), 240, and J. Loewenberg, *Reason and the Nature of Things* (La Salle: 1959), 45. Cf. *infra,* note 36. A similar slip occurs in M. Bunge's "New Dialogues Between Hylas and Philonous," (*Philosophy and Phenomenological Research,* 15 (1954), 193 f.

[4] Cf. E. J. Furlong, "An Ambiguity in Berkeley's *Principles,*" *Philosophical Quarterly* (St. Andrews), 14 (1964), 334–344, and W. T. Stace, *Theory of Knowledge and Existence* (Oxford: 1932), 91.

[5] For the "busy" God, see J. B. Pratt, *Personal Realism* (New York: 1937), 169; for the other, see R. F. A. Hoernlé, *Idealism as a Philosophy* (New York: 1927), 119.

[6] See, for example, F. Ueberweg, a generation ago, who charged that for Berkeley we know only our own notions of spirits and not spirits themselves (in Krauth edition of Berkeley's *Principles* [Philadelphia: 1874], p. 356); and J. E. Passmore, who says Berkeley has no way of knowing how we know notions and perceptions (*Philosophical Reasoning* [New York: 1961], p. 42). It seems absurd to ask that one provide an epistemological basis for his theory of knowledge!

[7] Cf. Morris Cohen, *Reason and Nature* (New York: 1931), 311. See also the remark by Warnock, *infra,* note 20. C. R .Morris pejoratively characterizes Berkeley's philosophy as "at any rate a confession of faith, if not a philosophical system" (*Locke, Berkeley, Hume* [London: 1931], p. 66).

[8] Cf. John Oulton Wisdom, *The Unconscious Origins of Berkeley's Philosophy* (London: 1953). Wisdom claims his findings are "rooted in clinical practice." (229)

[9] Thus R. W. Sellars, though not directly attacking Berkeley, wrote a positive essay entitled "Referential Transcendence" which has as its intent "to show Berkeley can be refuted by means of an adequate analysis of perceiving and not simply in the Samuel Johnson manner or by confrontation with our language habits" (*Philosophy and Phenomenological Research,* 22 [1961], 1–15). For a significant commentary on other modern criticisms of Berkeley, see Errol Harris, *Nature, Mind and Modern Sci-*

Berkeley once wrote: "There is nothing that I desire more than to know thoroughly all that can be said against what I take for truth."[10] With this posthumous sanction, I shall consider four fundamental objections to Berkeley's position, which, if sound, virtually annul his philosophy. None were directly foreseen by him, and none seem at first to be based on misconception. Nor are they fully exclusive of each other. They have become almost traditional, even routine—part of the lore of Berkeley criticism. Some recur about every decade, with the most recent critic often not aware of his predecessors' work. I do not say there are no other serious modern objections, but these are at once the most persistent and the most pervasive.

The Charge of Inconsistency

The first objection is that which claims Berkeley is fundamentally inconsistent when on the one hand he rejects material substance as a meaningless abstraction and on the other accepts spiritual substance as real. As early as 1756, Eschenbach[11] argued that the reasons produced against the independent reality of matter are equally conclusive against the independent reality of spirit. More recently, John Wild has written: "Just as his opponents, the materialists, abstracted the objective pole of spirit and 'froze' it into a self-subsistent carrier for the rest of the world, so now Berkeley takes the opposite, subjective pole and 'freezes' it into a self-subsistent soul."[12] Frans Bender observes that "After material causality has been rejected, spiritual causality is admitted."[13] And R. Frondizi speaks of the "incompatibility of the criteria by which Berkeley judges corporeal and spiritual substances" adding that if Berkeley "had applied to the *res cogitans* his theory concerning abstract ideas . . . he would have been obliged to adopt an attitude similar to that of Hume."[14] A. J. Ayer, C. D. Broad, P. Coffey, and others have made similar criticisms.[15]

---

ence (New York: 1954), Chapter VII. An earlier systematic account occurs in R. F. A. Hoernlé's *Idealism as a Philosophy* (New York: 1927), Chapter IV.

[10] In a letter to Sir John Percival dated January 19, 1711, and printed as # 16 in *Works,* Vol. VIII (Luce-Jessop edition), 44. In a letter to the American Samuel Johnson, November 25, 1729, Berkeley similarly wrote: "The objections of a candid thinking man to what I have written will always be welcome and I shall not fail to give all satisfaction I am able, not without hopes of convincing or being convinced." (*Works* II, 279)

[11] Pointed out by A. C. Fraser in *Works,* Vol. I, 369. See also H. M. Bracken, *The Early Reception of Berkeley's Immaterialism, 1710–1733* (The Hague: [1959], 1965)

[12] John Wild, *George Berkeley* (Cambridge, Mass.: 1936), 117.

[13] Frans Bender, *George Berkeley's Philosophy Re-examined* (Amsterdam: 1946), 70.

[14] Risieri Frondizi, *The Nature of the Self* (New Haven: 1953), 69. [For a similar treatment see Professor Datta's chapter, pp. 118 f.]

[15] A. J. Ayer says that Berkeley must be criticized for failing to see "that the argument which he uses to dispose of Locke's analysis of a material thing is fatal to his own conception of the nature of the self." (*Language, Truth and Logic* [New York: n.d.], 54. Peter Coffey remarks that like material substance, spiritual substance is "only

Now, a number of observations need to be made about this criticism. Did Berkeley actually hold to the spiritual substance view? There are those, such as Wild and B. Russell,[16] who do not doubt for a moment that he did. Aschenbrenner believes that Berkeley defended a substance theory but "only after thinking very seriously at one point that the mind might be no substance at all apart from a congeries of perceptions, in a manner that reminds one of Hume."[17] Luce seems to waver in his interpretation in saying first that mind "is a centre of experience . . . an *actus* which is not its states," and then in the next sentence: "It is a substance which supports its accidents; it is a subject which *has* its objects."[18] Ayer remarks that Berkeley should have given "a phenomenalist account of the self" but he did not see the consequences of his logic regarding matter.[19]

We must note here that we do not have any clear doctrine of mind because it was to be discussed in Berkeley's projected Part II of the *Principles,* the manuscript of which was lost. Warnock is surely wrong in guessing that the delay and subsequent loss of this manuscript "was due in part to his inability to harmonize the outlook of his early work with his theological and metaphysical beliefs."[20] Berkeley simply says that he never felt inclined to rewrite the manuscript.[21] This does not mean that we know nothing about his view but it keeps us from rushing into criticism when we recognize that he did not intend Part I to be a full expression of his philosophy of mind. One cannot charge him with inconsistency merely because his view is undeveloped and incomplete.

What the critics of Berkeley persistently overlook is a point Berkeley regularly makes, stating it forcefully in the *Third Dialogue.* "There is therefore, upon the whole, no parity of case between spirit and matter." (DHP 234) Whatever his view, we do have his clear argument that there is a marked

---

an unreal figment of thought inasmuch as it also is not an 'idea' or 'object' of direct awareness, and therefore, having no *percipi,* it has no *esse* or reality." (*Epistemology,* Vol. II [London: 1917], p. 11) See also C. D. Broad's "Berkeley's Denial of Material Substance," *Philosophical Review,* 63 (1954), 155–181.

[16] In his *History of Western Philosophy* (New York: 1945), he remarks: "Since he believed the ego to be a substance." (655) See also C. W. Morris, *Six Theories of Mind* (Chicago: 1932), 36.

[17] Karl Aschenbrenner, "Berkeley on Existence in the Mind" in *George Berkeley* (Berkeley, Calif.; 1957), 58. A questionable point about the temporal relationship between the *Philosophical Commentaries* and the *Principles* is presupposed in this remark.

[18] A. A. Luce, *Berkeley's Immaterialism* (London: 1945), 50.

[19] A. J. Ayer, *op. cit.,* 126. Cf. G. Boas, who asks: "How explain except psychologically Berkeley's failure to push his reasoning to the point attained by Hume?" in Krikorian (ed.) *Naturalism and the Human Spirit* (New York: 1944), 145.

[20] G. J. Warnock, *Berkeley* (Baltimore: 1953), 206.

[21] See his letter to Johnson of November 25, 1729. "The fact is that I had made a considerable progress in it; but the manuscript was lost about fourteen years ago during my travels in Italy, and I never had the leisure since to do so disagreeable a thing as writing twice on the same subject." (*Works* II, 282)

difference in the case between matter and spirit. Although he can find no reason whatsoever for believing in material substance, he does find evidence of the self.

> I have no reason for believing the existence of matter . . . . whereas the being of my self, that is, my own soul, mind or thinking principle, I evidently know by reflexion. . . . In the very notion or definition of material substance, there is in cluded a manifest repugnance and inconsistency. But this cannot be said of the notion of spirit. (DHP 233)

The whole argument here is a virtual anticipation of the criticisms of the moderns cited above.

We may ask whether a substantialist view is unequivocally *implied* in Berkeley's writings or whether some other, say an empirical or phenomenalist view, is intended. One can gather quotations that support a substantival view and others that suggest an empirical view. There is no distinctly *early* or *later* group of citations. Some of the earliest jottings suggest an empirical view and some of the later writings a substantival view and vice versa. In his *Philosophical Commentaries,* he remarks that he only rejects "the Philosophic sense" of substance (PC # 517).[22] Again: "Take away Perceptions and you take away the Mind." (PC # 580) He thinks Locke is mistaken "when he says thought is not essential to the mind" (PC # 650), and "to say the mind exists' without thinking is a Contradiction, nonsense, nothing." (PC # 652)[23] But he also suggests that the identity of a person consists "not in actual consciousness" (PC # 200), and in significant passages in his *Principles* as well as his *Dialogues* he uses substantialist language: "an active, simple, uncompounded substance . . . that is to say, *the soul of man is naturally immortal*" (PHK § 141), and, "The mind, spirit or soul, is that indivisible unextended thing, which thinks, acts, and perceives" (DHP 231); or "There is no substance wherein ideas can exist beside spirit." (DHP 237) At the same time, the *Principles* and *Dialogues* contain many passages clearly implying an empirical view: "For by the word *spirit* we mean only that which thinks, wills, and perceives; this, and *this alone,* constitutes the signification of that term." (PHK § 138. Italics added.) In the *Third Dialogue:* "But will and understanding constitute *in the strictest sense* a mind or spirit." (DHP 240. Italics added.)

The careful reader of Berkeley must admit that whatever view of the self Berkeley holds, it is not an obvious, self-evident one. The evidence is not clearly persuasive on either side and it may be that C. M. Turbayne is right

[22] Note also: "I must not give the Soul or Mind the Scholastique Name pure act, but rather pure Spirit or active Being." (PC # 870).

[23] Compare this with: "And in truth whoever shall go about to divide his thoughts or abstract the *existence* of a spirit from its *cogitation,* will, I believe find it no easy task." (PHK § 98)

when he speaks of "Berkeley's Two Concepts of Mind."[24] It is difficult to argue what he might have said had he rewritten Part II of the *Principles,* but it is probably also wrong to insist on holding Berkeley strictly to his words when his thought is so obviously struggling to break the bonds of traditional vocabulary. It is true that he uses substantialist language but he uses empirical, even phenomenalist, language as well. We can ask which view seems required by his general position. The weight of evidence, I find, is against a strict substantialist interpretation and on the side of an empirical view. What is more, such a view would be consistent with his total philosophy—a point which certain of the critics we have cited readily admit. To argue backwards, as Frondizi and Warnock have,[25] suggesting that if Berkeley did not hold to a substantialist view he would have had difficulty justifying his desiderated immortality, is quite unwarranted. The doctrine of immortality does not presuppose a substantival view and it is incorrect to say, therefore, that Berkeley avoided a nonsubstantialist position. Even Buddhists believe in the persistence after death of a nonsubstantial stream of consciousness. Moreover, it is not at all obvious that an empirical view would preclude immortality in Christian thought. Jessop's remark regarding the Johnson–Berkeley correspondence, which dealt in part with this problem, is especially apt, and I think correct.

> We lack his doctrine of mind . . . but remarks here and there indicate that for him its unity is a datum of introspection, not a postulated occult substance of which perceiving and willing are the manifest modes.[26]

The Priority of the Cognitive Consciousness

A second criticism holds that Berkeley is not justified in starting with the knowing self and is consequently unjustified in the conclusions he draws from that starting point. Because he assumes the priority of the cognitive consciousness, R. B. Perry and others argue, he is led into two serious difficulties that are sufficient to discredit his view. Accordingly, he is charged with (a) committing the "fallacy of initial predication," and (b) wrongfully exploiting "the egocentric predicament."[27]

[24] Turbayne comments that to say mind is a substance is to speak in metaphors, in *Philosophy and Phenomenological Research,* 20 (1959–1960), 85–92. See also the discussion by S. A. Grave, *ibid.,* 22 (1961–1962), 574–576, and Turbayne's rejoinder, 22 (1962), 577–580. See further S. A. Grave, "The Mind and its Ideas: Some Problems in the Interpretation of Berkeley," *Australasian Journal of Philosophy,* 42 (1964), esp. 205–210.

[25] R. Frondizi, *op. cit.,* 69; and G. J. Warnock, *op. cit.,* 206.

[26] In *Works,* Vol. II, 269. [Professor Tipton's essay in the present volume constitutes a convincing, perhaps decisive, demonstration of this interpretation.]

[27] R. B. Perry, *Present Philosophical Tendencies* (New York: 1912), Chapter VI. Parenthesized numbers following Perry's name refer to pages in this book. J. B. Pratt adopts this criticism approvingly (*Personal Realism,* 155 f.) as does A. S. Pringle-Pattison in his *The Idea of God* (New York: 1920), p. 192.

The first aspect of this twofold criticism claims that Berkeley's error lies in inferring that because something is seen, its being seen is therefore its essential and exclusive status. For instance, in talking about the tulip, Berkeley says: "but that any immediate objects of the senses—that is, any idea, or combination of ideas—should exist in an unthinking substance, or exterior to all minds, is in itself an evident contradiction." (DHP 195) Something may well belong to an order of ideas, but why not also to another and independent order? The letter "a" for example, possesses a multiple and not an exclusive particularity, for it occurs in many different positions in many different words. How can Berkeley say that sense qualities exist in only one context, the mental? He does say this, Perry argues, and thus commits the fallacy of initial predication. This fallacy "consists in regarding some early, familiar, or otherwise accidental characterization of a thing as definitive . . . [but] it does not follow that to be thought of, or otherwise known, is either necessary or important for things." (128)

Others have made the same criticism. Russell says: "If something is an object of the senses, some mind is concerned with it: but it does not follow that the same thing could not have existed without being an object of the senses."[28] And Coffey asserts: "It is at least not *prima facie* impossible that sense qualities may exist extramentally in an extra mental substance whether I perceive the qualities or know the subject or not."[29]

The egocentric predicament, which Berkeley is charged with illegitimately exploiting, is simply the recognition that whenever anyone considers something, that something becomes an object of consciousness. Whether it thereby becomes mental is a point of dispute in interpreting Berkeley.[30] As Perry puts it:

> No one can report on the nature of things without being on hand himself. It follows that whatever thing he reports does as a matter of fact stand in relation to him, as his idea, object of knowledge, or experience. (129)

On the surface, it proves nothing at all. Yet, Berkeley, we are told, uses this methodological peculiarity as an argument for his position. He concludes that one cannot "conceive it possible, the objects of . . . thought may exist without the mind: to make out this, it is necessary that you conceive them existing unconceived or unthought of, which is a manifest repugnancy." (PHK § 23) Berkeley's error is his failure to see that there may well be something which is not in consciousness despite the fact that all our ideas are

28 B. Russell, *op. cit.*, 652. For a careful analysis of Russell's arguments against Berkeley, see Errol Harris, *op. cit.*, 143–149.

29 P. Coffey, *op. cit.*, 113 f. See also A. C. Ewing, *Idealism: A Critical Survey* (New York: 1933), 15, and A. J. Ayer, *op. cit.*, "Berkeley made the mistake of supposing that what was immediately given in sensation was necessarily mental." (p. 53)

30 See A. A. Luce, "The Berkeleian Idea of Sense," *Proceedings of the Aristotelian Society*, Suppl. Vol. 27 (1953), 1–20; and K. Aschenbrenner, *op. cit.*, 37–64.

in consciousness. To recognize that "every mentioned thing is an idea" is a truth but says nothing. "The assertion that an idea is an idea conveys no knowledge even about ideas." (131) Nor is the egocentric predicament an inductive proof of the thesis that all things are ideas, for by its very nature it "prevents the observation of negative cases." (131) In short, nothing about reality follows from the fact of the cognitive relationship.

Now, both aspects of this criticism, so widely seconded, rest on a presupposition about the nature of philosophic truth which Berkeley does not seem to share, namely, that epistemological and metaphysical conclusions must follow with strict logical necessity. Berkeley would not say that the egocentric predicament is "the axiomatic foundation" of his system, as Montague claims,[31] though he might admit with H. Feigl, that "properly interpreted the egocentric predicament constitutes no more than a natural limitation of direct verifiability."[32] Nor would he claim that we have final proof that reality cannot exist outside of the cognitive relation merely because we cannot experience reality apart from its relation to our knowing selves. He even goes so far as to grant the bare possibility of the existence of extra-mental bodies. "But though it were possible that solid, figured, moveable substances may exist without the mind, corresponding to the idea we have of bodies, yet how is it possible for us to know this?" (PHK § 18. See also §§ 19, 53, 66.) It does not follow that there absolutely cannot be such bodies, but the question is what evidence or what reasons can be offered in their behalf? We surely cannot accept them on "animal faith" or because we are prejudiced against spiritual reality. (Berkeley says, "when reason forsakes us, we endeavor to support our opinion on the bare possibility of the thing." [PHK § 75]) That there are no known instances of things existing out of the cognitive relationship, though it proves nothing conclusively, is a significant fact. Can it really be, asks Hoernlé, "that such a fact justifies no inference about the nature and existence of the world?"[33] It may be merely circumstantial evidence but we do not even have that for matter and we must try to make the best of the evidence. Though reality "without the mind" is always a logical possibility, it is not, on Berkeley's view, a reasonable probability. "Though we should allow it possible, [it] must yet be a very unaccountable and extravagant supposition." (PHK § 53) Or as a friend, F. G. Ensley, once said: "The fact that all the books we have ever known have had authors could hardly be adduced as evidence that there are authorless books."

It must be remembered that Berkeley is not so much seeking to demonstrate a theorem as to solve a problem. His conclusions do not follow with perfect logical certainty, nor are they beyond all possible doubt. It is unlikely

31 W. P. Montague, *The Ways of Knowing* (London: 1925), 331.

32 H. Feigl, "The Power of Positivistic Thinking" in *Proceedings of the American Philosophical Association,* 36 (1963), 39. See also W. T. Stace's comment in his "Refutation of Realism," *Mind,* 43 (1934), 150.

33 In his *Idealism as a Philosophy,* 114.

that *any* metaphysical conclusions do but that does not mean we are lost in agnosticism or skepticism.

The allegation that Berkeley commits the fallacy of initial predication assumes that his view depends solely on the facts of the cognitive relationship and the knowing process, but it is evident that Berkeley draws upon other data as well, especially the order and regularity of nature. (Cf. PHK, §§ 30, 60–66) And, at best, recognition of the egocentric predicament indicates that Berkeley's view is as problematic as others. It does not result in its refutation. It does suggest the need for careful study of Berkeley's theory of explanation.

Alleged Solipsism

One of the persistent reprovals of Berkeley has been that his philosophy inevitably leads to solipsism because it is basically subjective idealism. Hence it is considered an absurd, impossible view. Some critics, relying in part on the previous objection, allege that Berkeley interprets all knowledge and thereby all reality as consisting of ideas. Since this is so, it is hard to see how there can be an independent objective order or a community of selves. Lenin, though remarking about the "consistent standpoint of Berkeley" nevertheless regards him as a solipsist.[34] A. E. Taylor thinks the "logical outcome" of *esse* is *percipi* is solipsism or skepticism.[35] And J. Loewenberg writes:

> The truth of the *esse est percipi* is obviously a subjective truth and he who accepts it is a solipsist *malgré lui;* other minds being imperceptible do not come within range of the ontology of the formula.[36]

Now Berkeley not only writes as though there are other conscious beings beside himself—"Besides spirits all that we know or conceive are our own ideas" (DHP 209)—he proposes a theory to account for them. Critics too regularly conclude that the substance of Berkeley's philosophy is contained in *esse* is *percipi;* then, noting that other minds cannot be perceived directly, come to the conclusion that he is a solipsist. But he has two ways of knowing, one regarding things, the other regarding persons.

> We cannot know the existence of other spirits otherwise than by their operations, or the ideas by them excited in us . . . Hence, the knowledge I have of other spirits is not immediate, as is the knowledge of my ideas; but depending on the intervention of ideas, by me referred to agents or spirits distinct from myself, as effects or concomitant signs. (PHK § 145)

[34] N. Lenin, *Materialism and Empirio-Criticism* (Moscow: 1920), 40. See 60.

[35] A. E. Taylor, *Elements of Metaphysics* (London: 1903), 202. See also Denis Grey, "The Solipsism of Bishop Berkeley," *Philosophical Quarterly* (St. Andrews), 2 (1952), 338–349.

[36] J. Lowenberg, *Reason and the Nature of Things* (La Salle: 1959), 45.

Other selves are known inferentially by analogy from evidence. One does not deduce their existence as logically necessary nor does one confront them in intuition. He knows them by reason or "notions."[37]

It is granted that we have neither an immediate evidence nor a demonstrative knowledge of the existence of other finite spirits . . . I have a notion of spirit, though I have not, strictly speaking, an idea of it. I do not perceive it as an idea or by means of an idea but know it by reflexion. (DHP 233)

And earlier he writes: "We may not I think strictly be said to have an idea of active being, or of an action, although we may be said to have a notion of them." (PHK § 142)

There are those who maintain that Berkeley's explication of how other selves are known is inadequate. Warnock regards "notions" as "scarcely an answer to the question" and as "a perfunctory introduction,"[38] and Luce remarks that Berkeley's inferential theory "does seem artificial,"[39] while Grey suggests it is not Berkeley's "official view"[40]—whatever that means. On the other hand, I. T. Ramsey has suggested that Berkeley's view of notions is of basic significance for his epistemology and has "permanent relevance for the possibility of an empirical metaphysics."[41] Indeed, it seems to be the case, as H. Bracken has pointed out in connection with Berkeley's earliest critic, Baxter, that the "vast majority of Berkeley criticism, stands only by ignoring the doctrine of notions."[42]

Though the presence of other selves known by notions manifestly saves Berkeley from the charge of solipsism, we must still ask whether he is a pure subjectivist regarding the existence of the physical world, as some aver. Can Berkeley properly account for an objective order of nature or does that world exist only as sights, sounds, odors, and colors in his own subjective consciousness? His *language* never gives that impression. "I assert as well as you, that since we are affected from without we must allow powers to be without in a being distinct from ourselves." (DHP 240) We similarly read: "Wherever bodies are said to have no existence without the mind, I would

[37] Cf. PHK § 89 and ALC, 145, 147) For a more comprehensive treatment, see my "Berkeley's Wisdom on Other Minds," *Philosophical Forum,* 10 (1957–1958), 3–24; and J. W. Davis, "Berkeley's Doctrine of the Notion," *Review of Metaphysics,* 12 (1959), 378–389.

[38] Warnock, *op. cit.,* 205.

[39] A. A. Luce, *Berkeley's Immaterialism,* 149.

[40] D. Grey, *op. cit.,* 348.

[41] I. T. Ramsey, "Notions and Ideas in Berkeley's Philosophy" in *Proceedings of 11th International Congress of Philosophy,* 1953, 66–71. [See also Chapter 2 of the present volume where Professor Ramsey develops this idea.] G. Boas remarks that once "the way is open for notions to be accepted as knowledge, the way to verification is closed." (*Dominant Themes of Modern Philosophy* [New York: 1957], p. 269). One wonders what kind of verification Professor Boas has in mind.

[42] H. M. Bracken, "Andrew Baxter, Critic of Berkeley," *Journal of the History of Ideas,* 18 (1957), 201.

not be understood to mean this or that particular mind, but all minds whatsoever." (PHK § 48) But it may rightly be asked whether his epistemological theory implies an ontology of pure subjectivism. Some critics, following the point about the egocentric predicament, think that Berkeley is caught in a hopeless subjectivism even though he tried to forestall such a criticism in his answer to the fourth anticipated objection in his *Principles.*

For though we hold indeed the objects of sense to be nothing else but ideas which cannot exist unperceived; yet we may not hence conclude they have no existence except only while they are perceived by us, since there may be some other spirit that perceives them, though we do not. (PHK § 48)

Of course Berkeley holds that the other spirit is God. Accordingly, though the sense data are subjective, the source of those data is objective and is, in some way, akin to the human mind. It is quite illogical to postulate matter as their objective source. Yet this supreme mind cannot be perceived or known immediately. Like human spirits it is known inferentially. "I do by an act of reason, necessarily infer the existence of a God and of all created things in the mind of God." (DHP 232)

The persistence and dependability of the objective order is not based on "discovering any necessary connexion between our ideas, but only by the observation of the settled laws of Nature, without which we should all be in uncertainty and confusion." (PHK § 31) It is the will of the "governing spirit" that "constitutes the Laws of Nature," Berkeley claims. (PHK § 31) It must be remembered that Berkeley considers only two hypotheses to account for these ideas not produced by his own imagination—Matter and God. There is no evidence and less reason to believe in matter as the objective source for nature,[43] but very good evidence to reason by analogy to the existence of God as such a source. It is not a "senseless conclusion" as Ayer egregiously asserts.[44] God is not introduced as a *deus ex machina* nor as an afterthought but is integral, even central, to the Berkeleian system. This has led certain sympathetic critics, in direct opposition to the subjectivistic interpretation, to call Berkeley's system "objective idealism."[45]

[43] In the *Third Dialogue,* Philonous says: "If you can prove that any philosopher hath explained the production of any one idea in our minds by the help of *matter,* I shall forever acquiesce . . . That a being endowed with knowledge and will, should produce or exhibit ideas, is easily understood." (DHP 242)

[44] A. J. Ayer, *Foundations of Empirical Knowledge* (New York: 1940), 225. Cf. A. A. Luce's remark that Berkeley's conception of God "was no pious ornament of the system, but its very ground and foundation." (*The Dialectic of Immaterialism* [London: 1963], p. 189)

[45] See G. Dawes Hicks: "Thus by employing what may perhaps be called a metaphysical method, the subjective idealism reached by a more or less psychological method of approach becomes transformed later into a species of objective or theological idealism," (*Berkeley* [London: 1932], p. 128) Also, G. W. Kaveeshwar, *The Metaphysics of Berkeley Critically Examined* (Khandwa: 1933), 291. Even the *quite* unsympathetic critic N. Lenin says: "Deriving 'ideas' from the action of a deity upon the human mind, Berkeley thus approaches objective idealism." (*op. cit.,* 24)

I do not intend to suggest that this interpretation frees Berkeley from all difficulties, for though there is an objective ground for the world of nature, namely God, Berkeley never expatiates on the relation of passive ideas to God's mind. Critics such as E. E. Harris have alleged that this deficiency really results in a subjectivism in which "there are no valid principles of order and so no means of deciding what is produced in us by God and what is purely fortuitous."[46] However, one can cite passages where Berkeley distinguishes between imagined ideas and the ideas of nature (PHK §§ 34, 36) and there is even the interesting proposal of archetypes (DHP 248 ff.), but much more could and should have been said. Nevertheless, the burden of proof is still on the one who charges Berkeley with pure subjectivism.

Presumed Confusion of Sensations with Sense "Objects"

Undoubtedly the most famous criticism of Berkeley's general view was introduced by G. E. Moore in his essay, "The Refutation of Idealism," in 1903. This virtually "classic" objection holds that Berkeley confounds perceptions of sense qualities with the sense qualities themselves and that because he does, he comes to the false conclusion that sense qualities are in the mind only, whereas they might just as well exist elsewhere.

The statement *esse* is *percipi,* Moore claims, is ambiguous because it led Berkeley and certain idealists after him to maintain that subject and object are necessarily connected, "that 'being' and 'being experienced' are necessarily connected: that whatever *is* is *also* experienced."[47] But *esse* and *percipi,* argues Moore, are as distinct as "green" and "sweet." To establish his point, he maintains that in every sensation there are two elements, consciousness and the object of consciousness. Now, Moore asks, when one has the sensation of blue, is it the consciousness that exists or the blue that exists or both? These three alternatives are "all different from one another," and anyone who regards them as the same "makes a mistake and a self-contradictory mistake." (18)

Accordingly, to identify either "blue" or any other of what I have called *"objects"* of sensation, with the corresponding sensation is in every case, a self-

[46] E. Harris, *op. cit.,* 163. W. P. Montague agrees that "the real problem for a Berkeleian now becomes the problem as to the true nature of objects in a divine mind." (*Great Visions of Philosophy* [La Salle: 1950], p. 310)

[47] G. E. Moore, *Philosophical Studies* (London: 1922), 16. Parenthesized numbers following in this paragraph indicate pages in this volume. W. Kaufmann calls attention to remarks of Collingwood and McKeon, who jointly think that Moore was criticizing a position which was not Berkeley's. (*Critique of Religion and Philosophy* [New York: 1958], p. 17) But that is definitely a minority report which has not been adequately substantiated.

contradictory error. It is to identify a part either with the whole of which it is a part or else with the other part of the same whole. (18)

Moore concludes that we "can and must conceive that blue might exist and yet the sensation of blue not exist" (19), and he points out that this confusion rests on a difficulty in language for philosophers have "always used the same name for these two different 'things' . . . and hence . . . have supposed these 'things' *not* to be two." (19 f.) Berkeley fails to see this and this constitutes the fundamental error of his thought.

This selfsame criticism, with slight variations, has been repeated or independently thought of by several other thinkers who oppose the Berkeleian position.[48] If it is sound, of course, it is a real knockout blow to Berkeley, for it justifies the view that reality exists apart from all knowing minds, the very point which Berkeley sets out vigorously to confute. It is not hard to see why Moore's objection has been so enthusiastically endorsed. Can it be countered?

In 1942, in an article published in the Schilpp volume on G. E. Moore,[49] C. J. Ducasse undertook to show, against Moore, that there is a certain class of cases in which *percipi* does follow from *esse*. He thinks that Moore's argument does not prove "or even render more probable than not,—that *esse* is *percipi* is false." (225) Towards the end of the same volume, in the section entitled "A Reply to My Critics," Moore made a striking but not widely noticed concession, saying, "And I may say at once that, on this point, I now agree with Mr. Ducasse and Berkeley, and hold that that early paper of mine was wrong." (653) Later he vacillatingly remarks that he is "very much inclined to think Mr. Ducasse is right and that I in that paper was wrong," though he claims to be puzzled and does not think Ducasse has "proved that his view is the true one." (658 f.)

The fullest statement of Ducasse's argument occurs in his Carus Lectures entitled *Nature, Mind and Death,* Chapter XIII.[50] Here Ducasse comments upon Moore's "reply" (cf. 282), and expands upon the earlier treatment, seeking to show that Moore's argument "does not prove what it claims to prove, viz. that the blue can exist independently of the sensing of blue." (259) The gist of his contention is that "blue," "bitter," "sweet," and so forth

[48] For example, see the following: B. Russell, *Problems of Philosophy* (London: [1912] 1959), 42; P. Coffey, *op. cit.,* says: "Sense qualities, however are not *acts* of perception but *objects* of perception." 114 f.; Warnock's extended treatment, *op. cit.,* 151–162; A. E. Taylor, *op. cit.,* 200*n;* W. P. Montague's treatment of the "Berkeleian Fallacy" in *The New Realism* (New York: 1912), 258 f. S. Chatterjee and D. M. Datta interestingly point out that the Sautrantika School of Buddhism anticipated long ago "the most important arguments which modern Western realists like Moore use to refute the subjective idealism of Berkeley." (*An Introduction to Indian Philosophy* [Calcutta: 1950], p. 154).

[49] C. J. Ducasse, "Moore's 'The Refutation of Idealism' " in P. A. Schilpp (ed.) *The Philosophy of G. E. Moore* (New York: [1942] 1952), 225–251.

[50] La Salle: 1951. Parenthesized numbers following refer to pages in Ducasse's book.

"are names not of objects of experience, nor of species of objects of experience, but of *species of experience itself*." (259) Accordingly, when one senses blue he is really, so to say, sensing bluely, "just as to dance the waltz is to dance 'waltzily' " (259). Sensing blue would thus be a mode or modulation of sensing. Ducasse adds:

. . . the noun 'blue' is the word we use to mention merely a certain *kind* of process . . . whereas the verb 'to sense blue' is the linguistic form we use when we wish not only to mention that same kind of process but also to mention at the same time some *case,* i.e., some *occurrence* of that kind of process. (260)

Or, to state it somewhat differently, "a sense-datum is not an *object* of consciousness but a *content* of consciousness,—a determinate modulation of consciousness itself; and more specifically, a determinate modulation of the species of consciousness called 'sensing.' " (287)[51]

This position is defended skillfully by Ducasse by an appeal to a language distinction first suggested by S. Alexander, who noted a difference between the cognate (or "connate") and the objective (or "alien") accusative. As an illustration, "in what is expressed by the phrase 'jumping a jump,' the jump is a connate accusative of the process called 'jumping'; whereas in what is expressed by jumping a ditch,' the ditch is alien accusative of the jumping." (254) Thus, with regard to experiencing or cognizing, connate accusatives exist only in the occurrence of the process. But "blue," "bitter," "sweet," and so on are connate with the type of experience called "sensing" rather than alien to it. Hence, "sensing blue . . . is . . . a species or modulation of sensing,—a specific variety of the sort of process generically called 'sensing.' " (259)

The full elaboration of this thesis, together with a consideration of possible counter-objections by Moore, Broad, and Chisholm, constitutes a meticulous and brilliant piece of philosophical writing that has not been given attention commensurate with its significance. If it is sound, and I think it is, the validity of Berkeley's philosophical position is not thereby finally established but one of the most formidable objections to it is decisively vacated, and, a fortiori, the similar charges of other critics.

Another consideration of Moore's "refutation" was undertaken by E. E. Harris, who reasons that Moore's analysis of sensation is abstract and "bogus," for "a little attention reveals that the 'being perceived' in one case and the 'object' in the other is really the whole of the experience with which we are dealing."[52] Moreover, Harris argues that Moore is implicitly trying to reinstate Locke's position, that entities exist independent of our perception and

[51] R. F. A. Hoernlé, in commenting on Moore's argument, makes this same point but does not develop it fully. "As act, a mind apprehends an object, but just because a mind is such acts of apprehending, these acts are not themselves apprehended as objects." (*op. cit.,* 104).

[52] E. E. Harris, *op. cit.,* 152.

we come to know them only when they enter into external causal relation with us.

Interestingly enough, Berkeley did not unknowingly commit the supposed confusion between sensing and sense qualities that Moore educes. He raises the problem in the *First Dialogue* when Hylas says: "One great oversight I take to be this: that I did not sufficiently distinguish the *object* from the *sensation.* Now though this latter may not exist without the mind, yet it will not thence follow that the former cannot." (DHP 194) Of course, Berkeley regards the distinction as untenable, though in our day we should have wished for more detailed clarification. In the *Principles* he wonders whether there can be "a nicer strain of abstraction than to distinguish the existence of sensible objects from their being perceived, so as to conceive them existing unperceived?" (PHK § 5)

To say, with Ducasse, that a sense-datum is not an *object* but a *mode* of sensing is not to say that it is consequently a mode of mind, though that might be casually inferred if one is not careful to distinguish epistemic from ontological issues, as Berkeley and some of his critics sometimes fail to do. It is Malebranche who holds that sensations are modifications of the mind, but Berkeley insists that,

> qualities are in the mind only as they are perceived by it, that is, not by way of *mode* or *attribute,* but only by way of *idea;* and it no more follows, that the soul or mind is extended because extension exists in it alone, than it does that it is red or blue, because those colours . . . exist in it, and no where else. (PHK § 49)

One could raise other objections, particularly about the passivity of ideas, or could point out other weak spots in Berkeley's philosophy, just as one might with Plato's views. And no doubt there are those who will do so for many years to come. But it is doubtful if there will ever be a summary refutation of Berkeley which would some day effectively bury his ideas in the philosophical graveyard. For in spite of his failings and even errors, all the way from vacillating linguistic usage to his facile acceptance of traditional theodicy, his thought raises the kind of perennial problems that are the lifeblood of philosophy. Like Plato whom he greatly admired, he does not really give us a finished, systematic theory, flawless in detail. Instead we are given a direction and emphasis that help us attain a perspective on reality, ridding our thought of crass materialism and stimulating it to wider spiritual horizons.

XIII

Notes to an Interpretation of Berkeley

W. H. WERKMEISTER

Kant, Berkeley, and James Beattie

In a letter addressed to Herder and dated April 20, 1782, Hamann wrote: "This much is certain: without Berkeley there would have been no Kant." This judgment finds ready support when we examine closely the historical development of the ideas involved. What is not so clear, however, is Kant's own relation to Berkeley.

There are passages in the *Critique of Pure Reason,*[1] notably in the first edition, that forcefully invite comparison with Berkeley's views; and there is an over-all orientation in Kant's critical position that is also reminiscent of Berkeley. As to the former, it suffices to compare Kant's conception of "appearances" (as opposed to things-in-themselves)[2] with Berkeley's quite similar conception. (PHK §§ 87 *et al.*) As to the over-all orientation, it is but necessary to point out that Kant "found it necessary to deny knowledge [of ultimate things] in order to make room for faith" (*Critique* 29), and that Berkeley was strongly motivated by religious considerations. (PHK §§ 92 *et al.*)

It is a fact, nevertheless, that Kant was completely out of sympathy with

[1] All page references will be made to the translation by Norman Kemp Smith (New York: 1929).

[2] *Critique,* pp. 24, 82 ff., *et al.*

Berkeley;[3] that he saw in Berkeley's idealism the prototype of a philosophical position which had to be repudiated. One cannot help but feel, however, that Kant radically misunderstood Berkeley. The two references to him in the *Critique of Pure Reason* prove it. Says Kant: "We cannot blame the good Berkeley for degrading bodies to mere illusion" (89); and, referring to "the dogmatic idealism of Berkeley," Kant adds: "He [Berkeley] regards the things in space as merely imaginary entities." (244)

In the *Prolegomena,* furthermore, Kant speaks of "the mystical and visionary idealism of Berkeley, against which and other similar phantasms our Critique contains the proper antidote."[4] And he adds: "The dictum of all genuine idealists from the Eleatic school to Bishop Berkeley, is contained in the formula: 'All cognition through the senses and experience is nothing but sheer illusion, and only in the ideas of the pure understanding and reason there is truth.'" (151) On page 153, we once more have a reference to "the dogmatic Idealism of Berkeley." And, Kant says, "the dogmatic idealist [is] one who denies the existence of matter," basing his view on "the supposed contradictions in the possibility of there being such a thing as matter at all." (*Critique* 350)

It would be interesting at this point to trace Kant's own arguments that culminate in his assertion that the "external things . . . are in all their configurations and alterations nothing but mere appearances" (*ibid.,* 347), and to compare them with Berkeley's arguments. I am sure that we should soon discover that Kant could have made good use of the latter. Such a comparison, however, is not our concern at this time. What interests me is the fact that Kant did not make use of Berkeley's arguments, and that he completely misunderstood Berkeley's position.

In his introduction to the 1878 edition of Kant's *Prolegomena,* Benno Erdmann points out that it is clear from what Kant says concerning Berkeley that he did not know his philosophy at first hand. (lxxvi). I agree. But now the question is: Just what did Kant know of Berkeley's philosophy? And how did he come to know this?

It is reasonably certain that Kant did not know English and that, therefore, he had to depend on translations. It is also a fact that the first of Berkeley's essays appeared in German in 1781—the same year as the first *Critique;* and that Berkeley's *Principles of Human Knowledge* was not translated into German until 1869. Hume, of course, was available in translation prior to 1769, when Kant became acquainted with his writings.

But we know also that Beattie's *Essay on the Nature and Immutability of Truth in Opposition to Sophistry and Scepticism* (first edition 1770) was available in translation in 1772, and that, shortly thereafter, a copy of the

[3] Janitsch, Julius, *Kants Urteile über Berkeley* (Strassburg: 1879), 1: "Berkeley hatte unter Kants weitgehender Abneigung ganz besonders zu leiden."

[4] *Prolegomena to Any Future Metaphysics* (tr. Paul Carus, La Salle: 1902), 49.

book was actually in the library of the University of Königsberg.[5] We know, furthermore, that Kant must have read Beattie.[6] His references to him can leave no doubt about this. Thus, Kant says that "it is positively painful to see how utterly . . . Beattie missed the point of [Hume's] problem." (*Prolegomena* 5) And: "I should think that Hume might fairly have laid as much claim to common sense as Beattie, and in addition to a critical reason (such as the latter did not possess), which keeps common sense in check." (*ibid.* 6) The question now is, What impression of Berkeley's philosophy would Kant get from reading Beattie?

To begin with, Beattie's own philosophical position was that of "common sense realism." "To believe our senses," he assures us, "is . . . according to the law of our nature; and we are prompted to this belief, not by reason, but by instinct, or common sense."[7] Beattie, moreover, regarded it as his mission to combat skepticism. "Scepticism," he explicitly stated, "is now the profession of every fashionable inquirer into human nature." (6) This skepticism is dangerous, "not because it is ingenious, but because it is subtle and obscure." (7–8) Beattie's own "prejudices are all in favor of truth and virtue," for "in them is laid the foundation of human happiness, and . . . on them depends the very existence of human society, and of human creatures." (6–7) That a thinker so committed should completely misunderstand the arguments and intentions of Berkeley's philosophy can come as no surprise. It would be strange were it otherwise.

A good many of Beattie's "arguments" against Berkeley are subtle—and, at times, not so subtle—*ad hominem* indictments. Thus, having stated that Locke "was one of the most amiable, and most illustrious men, that ever our nation produced," Beattie continues: "Dr. Berkeley was equally amiable in his life, and equally a friend to truth and virtue. In elegance of composition he was perhaps superior. I admire his virtues: I can never sufficiently applaud his zeal in the cause of religion: but some of his reasonings on the subject of human nature I cannot admit, without renouncing my claim to rationality." (9) Again: "I shall be told, that Berkeley was a good man [compare Kant's reference to "the good Berkeley"], and that his principles did him no hurt. I shall allow it; he was indeed a most excellent person. . . . But does it appear, that he ever acted according to his principles, or that he thoroughly understood them?" (299) And again: "Notwithstanding our reverence for the character of Berkeley, [we must] be permitted to affirm . . . that his

[5] Janitsch, *op. cit.*, 35–38. The Königsberg copy was last reported as being in the library of Strassburg.

[6] James Beattie (1735–1803), poet and essayist, was appointed professor of moral philosophy and logic in the Marischal College and University of Aberdeen in 1760.

[7] *Essay, on the Nature and Immutability of Truth in Opposition to Sophistry and Scepticism,* p. 62. All references are to the first edition of the *Essay* because it was the translation of this edition that Kant knew. However, I have also consulted the "corrected and enlarged" edition of 1771.

doctrine is subversive of man's most important interests, as a moral, intelligent, and percipient being." (301) "Berkeley's book, though written with a good design, did more harm than good, by recommending and exemplifying a method of argumentation subversive of all knowledge, and leading directly to universal scepticism." (415)

When we now turn to Beattie's arguments against Berkeley's position, we encounter again his contention that "our author's doctrine is contrary to common belief, and leads to universal scepticism." (298–299) Elaborating this contention, Beattie argues thus: "Common Sense tells me, that the ground on which I stand is hard, material, and solid, and has a real, separate, independent existence. Berkeley and Hume tell me, that . . . the ground under my feet is really an idea in my mind; that its very essence consists in being perceived; and that the same instant it ceases to be perceived, it must also cease to exist: in a word, that *to be,* and *to be perceived,* when predicated of the ground, the sun, the starry heavens or any other corporeal object, signify precisely the same thing." (49–50). That this interpretation of Berkeley is a distortion of Berkeley's real position is evident without further argument, for it neglects completely the good Bishop's faith in God's sustaining presence. But that the subjectivism here ascribed to Berkeley—and in other passages too numerous to quote—could lead Kant to believe that Berkeley "degraded bodies to mere illusion" and to "merely imaginary entities" is not difficult to see.

To back up his own interpretation of Berkeley's philosophy, Beattie now contends that "Berkeley's pretended demonstration of the non-existence of matter, at which common sense stood aghast for many years, hath no better foundation, than the ambiguous use of a word. . . . No man of common sense ever did or could believe, that the horse he saw coming toward him at full gallop, was an idea in his mind, and nothing else." (155) Berkeley's doctrine, thus, "attacks the most incontestable dictates of common sense; and professeth to demonstrate, that the clearest, most decisive, and most general, principles of conviction, are certainly fallacious." (248)

It is Beattie's conviction that "all our knowledge of external and material things" depends upon "the evidence of the external senses."[8] If Berkeley now argues that my "sensation of hardness" is "not hardness itself, nor anything like hardness"; that "it is nothing more than a sensation or feeling in my mind," then Beattie maintains "with as much assurance" that "the external thing exists, and is hard"; that, "by experience," I know that "the sensation" is but "the sign of my touching a hard body." (*ibid.*) That so dogmatic an assertion is no adequate answer to Berkeley's detailed arguments goes without saying.

In Section 8 of the same chapter, Beattie augments his argument by maintaining that "if men ought to believe the contrary of what their senses de-

[8] *Ibid.*, Part I, Chap. II, Sect. 2.

clare to be true, the evidence of all history, of all testimony, and indeed of all external perception, is no longer any evidence of the reality of the facts warranted by it; but becomes, on the contrary, an irrefragable proof that those facts did never happen." In view of such a conclusion, Beattie holds that Berkeley neither believed nor understood his own doctrine.

Admitting that he had read Berkeley's *Principles of Human Knowledge* and *The Dialogues between Hylas and Philonous* (278), Beattie at once staunchly maintains that his own "belief is now precisely the same as before." "Till the frame of my nature be unhinged, and a new set of faculties given me, I cannot believe this strange doctrine, because it is perfectly incredible." (279) A mere beginner in elementary logic should be able to point out that fallacy! But Beattie continues: "Where is the harm in my believing, that if I were to fall down yonder precipice, and break my neck, I should be no more a man of this world? My neck, Sir, may be an idea to you, but to me it is a reality, and a very important one too." (*ibid.*) No one, Beattie points out later, has ever broken his neck by falling over a precipice that is merely an idea in his own mind. And yet, if Berkeley's "doctrine" were true, so Beattie argues, it should make a "total change in the circumstances of men . . . by removing body out of the universe." The difference cannot be "merely verbal." (288–289) But no such change in human affairs is observable, Beattie continues. Berkeley's doctrine, therefore, cannot be true.

Two more "arguments" complete Beattie's case against Berkeley. The first may be called an argument from consensus. As Beattie puts it: "I have known many who could not answer Berkeley's arguments; I never knew one who believed his doctrine. I have mentioned it to some who were unacquainted with philosophy, and therefore could not be supposed to have any bias in favour of either system; they all treated it as most contemptible jargon, and what no man in his senses ever did or could believe." (292)

That much of the response which Beattie obtained by discussing Berkeley's position was colored, if not elicited, by his own misinterpretation of Berkeley can be taken for granted; and that, under such condition, consensus is an even flimsier argument than usual is obvious.

The last argument Beattie states thus: "When I lay systems and syllogisms aside, when I enter on any part of the business of life, or when I refer the matter to the unbiased decision of my own mind, I plainly see, that I had no distinct meaning to my words when I said, that the material world hath no existence but in the mind that perceives it." (293)

In this case it would have been incumbent upon Beattie to clarify his ideas and to try to understand in what particular sense Berkeley used his terms—especially the term "matter." His repudiation of Berkeley's philosophy would then not have been so dogmatic and ill-conceived.

In conclusion, let me quote two more passages from Beattie's work: "That I may have misunderstood the author's doctrine, is not only possible, but highly probable; nay, I have reason to think, that it was not perfectly understood even by himself." (297–298) And: "Perhaps they [men] do not foresee the consequences of their doctrines. Berkeley most certainly did not. . . . He erred . . . but his intensions were irreproachable." (499)

A Berkeley Parallel

When Berkeley's *Essay Towards a New Theory of Vision* and his *Treatise Concerning the Principles of Human Knowledge* were first published in Dublin (in 1709 and 1710, respectively), they attracted very little attention. There was no review of books or any other written response for some years. In London in particular—as was the fate of practically all books published in Dublin at that time—Berkeley's writings remained essentially unknown. In fact, it was not until 1734 when, following the success of *Alciphron* (1732), the *Principles* were reprinted, that Berkeley's philosophy attracted wide attention. It is, therefore, not surprising that Arthur Collier, "Rector of Langford Magna, near Sarum," knew nothing about Berkeley when, in 1713, he published in London a slender volume entitled *Clavis Universalis:* or, *A New Inquiry after Truth, Being a Demonstration of the Non-Existence, or Impossibility, of an External World.* In this book, Collier argues for a philosophical point of view that in many respects is strikingly similar to Berkeley's position. In what follows, I shall attempt to point up, albeit but briefly, some at least of the similarities and differences in the two positions, hoping that, in doing so, I may contribute to a better understanding of both views.

In the course of his discussions, Collier refers freely, not only to Descartes and Malebranche, but to such obscure philosophers as Baronius, Norris (*Theory of the Ideal World*), and Christopher Scheibler. Malebranche's *Inquiry Into Truth* was available to him in Taylor's translation, second edition; and to this book, in particular, he reacted. I am convinced, however, that during the "ten years of deliberation" prior to the publication of *Clavis Universalis* Collier did not know Berkeley's philosophy; that his own theory, therefore, was original with him; and that it reflects, if anything, a general philosophical climate of the times. After all, Berkeley himself, aged twenty-five, but reacted to Newton, Locke, Descartes, and Malebranche. Newton, it may be remembered, had called space the "sensorium of God" (*Optics* III, Query 28); and Malebranche had spoken of "seeing all things in God" (*Inquiry* III, ii, 6).

It may be well, to begin with, to recall briefly some of the key ideas of Berkeley's philosophy as developed in the *Principles of Human Knowledge.* Thus, we must keep in mind that whenever Berkeley speaks of "idea" he means "sensory object," and that, therefore, when he says that we know nothing but "ideas," he is really saying that we know a visible and tangible world as disclosed to us through our senses; that the corporeal world is exactly what it is experienced to be, but that it has no meaning or existence out of all relation to sensing. "Matter," on the other hand—if by "matter" we mean a reality beyond or behind the sensory objects—is inaccessible to perceiving mind and is, in fact, unthinkable. Berkeley's arguments are, thus, directed essentially against Locke's conception of an "unknowable somewhat" which, presumably, underlies all corporeal qualities in the manner of Kant's thing-in-itself.

Specifically, Berkeley assures us that, as far as the things of this world are concerned, they are but "ideas." "Their *esse* is *percipi.*" It is not possible for them to have any existence "out of the minds or thinking things which perceive them." (PHK § 3) Still, they are *"real things"* and "do really exist." (PHK §§ 33, 90) They "may be termed *external,* with regard to their origin, in that they are not generated from within, by the mind itself" (PHK § 90), but are "imprinted on the senses by the Author of Nature." (PHK § 33) They are "in the mind only as they are perceived by it, that is, not by way of *mode* or *attribute,* but only by way of idea." (PHK § 49) They "may likewise be said to be without the mind . . . namely when they exist in some other mind" (PHK § 90). Berkeley's assertion, therefore, that "bodies" "have no existence without the mind" does not mean that they depend on "this or that particular mind," but on "all minds whatsoever" (PHK § 48); in other words, that even to speak of them is possible only in relation to some mind.

What Berkeley means to deny is the existence of "matter" unrelated to mind. As he sees it, "the very notion of what is called *matter* or *corporeal substance* involves a contradiction." (PHK §§ 9, 24) Moreover, "for bodies to exist without the mind . . . is to suppose . . . that God has created innumerable beings that are entirely useless, and serve to no manner of purpose." (PHK § 19) On the other hand, the "consistent uniform working," observed by us in the world around us, "displays the goodness and wisdom of that governing spirit whose will constitutes the Laws of Nature." (PHK § 32) "The *uniformity,*" we are told, "is in the production of natural effects." (PHK § 62) And yet—and this is important—"the connexion of ideas does not imply the relation of *cause* and *effect,* but only of a mark or sign with the thing signified." (PHK § 65) The Creator alone it is "who *upholding all things by the Word of his power,* maintains that intercourse between spirits whereby they are able to perceive the existence of each other." (PHK § 147)

Let it be noted, finally, that Berkeley's *Principles,* as published, is only Part I of a projected work. Part II, unfortunately "lost," was to have dealt with the problem of mind. Collier's work is incomplete in the very same sense, although we have no evidence that his original project included more than is now in print. However, if Berkeley had published Part II of the *Principles,* or if Collier had carried his work to a similar conclusion, it would have been interesting to see how Hume might have met their arguments.

But let us now turn to Collier's book. The question with which Collier is concerned is, "whether there be any such Thing as An *External* World." And he intends to "demonstrate" the negative. (p. 2)

By "world" Collier means "whatsoever is usually understood by the Terms,

Body, Extension, Space, Matter, Quantity, etc." (2) The crucial term, however, is the term "external." By this our author means "the same as is usually understood by the Words, *Absolute, Self-existent, Independent,* etc."; and he denies such attributes of "all Matter, Body, Extension, etc." (2) Positively stated, Collier means to defend the thesis that "all Matter, Body, Extension, etc. exists *in, or in Dependance* [*sic*] *on Mind, Thought,* or *Perception,* and that it is not *capable* of an Existence, which is not thus Dependant." (3)

The basic premise for Collier's argument is that "*whatsoever is seen,* Is." (5) It follows at once that the "visible world" is not a creation of our imagination but actually does exist; that it is "there" as we see it. What Collier denies is that this "visible world" is an "absolute" or "self-existent" world—a world which, in his sense of the term, is "*External.*" (6) To be sure, "the World which *John* sees is External to Peter, and the World which *Peter* sees is External to John" (8)—a striking parallel to Berkeley's argument! In fact, Collier continues, "there is a *Universe,* or *Material* World of Being, which is at least, numerically different from every material World perceived by meer Creatures." (9). This is the world "*by* which the Great God gives Sensations to all thinking Creatures." (10) But it is not absolute or self-existent, and, thus, is not an independent world.

Collier's arguments in support of his position are essentially of two types. One group is designed to show that "the *Visible* World, *as Visible* [that is, "every material Object which *is,* or *has been,* or *can* be seen"—that is: perceived] is not External" (11–12); the other is intended to demonstrate that "an External World is a Being utterly impossible." (11)

As far as the first line of reasoning is concerned, Collier specifically admits that his own arguments follow those of Descartes, Malebranche, and Norris. (20) The crux of the matter is that "the *Seeming* Externity of a Visible Object, is no Argument of its *Real Externity*" (14, 27); that the inference from "visible Externity" to "Real Externity" is logically unacceptable. (29) The argument had a semblance of validity as long as the "effluvium" theory of vision was acceptable as true. But in the light of Newton's new theory of vision (39), the argument obviously begs the question. The role which "the new theory of vision" thus plays in Collier's argument must be especially noted!

Summing up the conclusion of the First Part of his book, Collier says: "*External Matter* is, at least to us, *Invisible;* and consequently . . . *Visible* or *Seen* Matter is not *External;* which is all that I am here concerned for, leaving others to explain . . . what they mean when they affirm, that External Matter is Visible to *God* and Angels." (45)

In the Second Part of his book, Collier attempts to show "that there is no External World, and, That an External World is a Being Utterly Impossible." (59) The arguments in support of this position rest, in part, upon the previously established conclusion that "an External World is a Being utterly

Unknown." (60) One of these arguments simply is that an unknown world "is of no Use at all, and consequently [I] affirm that there is no such World." (65) We may smile at the naiveté of the argument, but we must remember that Berkeley also employed it!

Beginning on page 68, Collier next tries to show that all arguments designed to support the conception of an "External World" are self-contradictory. Thus, he shows that an "External World" would have to be finite and infinite (73), and "Finitely and Infinitely Divisible." (74) In it, motion must be both, possible and impossible. (91) And a world "whose Existence is encumbered with the forementioned Contradictions" cannot exist. (79) "It is absolutely Impossible there should be any such Thing." (80)

However, the nonexistence of the "External World" does not undermine the existence of our "visible World." "A Visible World, or Visible Matter, consider'd as *not External,* Exists plainly as Visible, and consequently, *as such,* is extended, *as such* is Divisible." (79)

To argue, as Descartes did, that God is good and will therefore not deceive us about the existence of an external world, is to miss the point—so Collier holds; for "it is according to the Will of God, that the Visible World should carry in it every character of being External, except the Truth of Fact, which is absolutely impossible." (95) "Things," Collier concedes, "Subsist altogether by a Relation to the Intellect, or in Dependance [*sic*] on the Will of God"; but such is not the case with an "External Piece of Matter" (98) which, by definition, has "an absolute kind of Existence." (99) Being absolute, the "External Piece of Matter" cannot possibly be a "Creature" depending on the "Will of God." (101 f.) Indeed, "an External World," so conceived, would be "God himself, and not a Creature of God" (105); and such a thought Collier finds not even worthy of consideration. "All the Choice we are left to is to acknowledge *God* or an *External* World; which, I think, is a Choice we need not long be deliberating upon. I conclude therefore, that if God is, there is no External World." (105) "The Thing that is not to be doubted," however, "is the *Existence* of Bodies, the *Existence* of a Natural World, which is *supposed* to be the Object of Sense. . . . I have . . . contended on all Occasions that nothing is or can be more evident than the *Existence* of *Bodies,* or of a *Sensible* World.—Not the *Existence,* but the *Extra-existence* of the Sensible World, is the Point I have been arguing against." (126) "Not a Natural, *supposed* to be *Sensible,* World, but an *External* World, *as such,* is impossible." (126)

I have quoted so extensively from Collier's book for two reasons. First, the work may not be generally available;[9] and, second, one does not get the full flavor of the author's argumentation without recourse to extensive parts of

[9] The 1713 edition is available in the Hoose Library, School of Philosophy, University of Southern California. An Open Court edition by Ethel Bowman, published in 1909, appears to be out of print.

the text. It is, I believe, evident from what I have presented, that striking similarities between the views of Collier and Berkeley do exist; but there is no evidence of dependence. Moreover, the differences are also apparent—especially as far as they pertain to the conception and interpretation of the "Sensible" or "Natural" world, its existence, and its relation to God. I leave it to others to trace these similarities and differences in greater detail than I have done here—if they desire to do so. As indicated in the title of the present chapter: I have provided some "notes" to an interpretation of Berkeley.

A Select Bibliography*

T. E. JESSOP

I. Berkeley's Own Publications

Collected Works

1898, 3 Vols., ed. George Sampson (London)
1901, 4 Vols., ed. A. C. Fraser (Oxford)
1948–1957, 9 Vols., ed. A. A. Luce and T. E. Jessop (Edinburgh) (Includes all of Berkeley's known letters.)

Philosophical

A Treatise Concerning the Principles of Human Knowledge: Part I, 1710
Revised edition with *Three Dialogues,* 1734
Recent editions:
1935, ed. P. Wheelwright (New York)
1937, ed. T. E. Jessop (London). (The only reprint of the 1710 text, with variants of 1734.)
1957, ed. C. M. Turbayne (New York)
1962, with *Three Dialogues,* ed. G. J. Warnock (London), also 1963 (Cleveland)

The two extant notebooks (to which Fraser gave the name *Commonplace Book*) in which Berkeley recorded his thoughts while preparing the *Principles* and *Essay on Vision,* were re-transcribed and re-edited by A. A. Luce with

* [A complete *Bibliography of George Berkeley,* to date, prepared by Professor Jessop, is to be published in The Hague by M. Nijhoff in 1966. It is a revision of his earlier bibliography (Oxford: 1934) and incorporates much new material including Turbayne and Ware's "A Bibliography of George Berkeley, 1933–1962," *Jour. Phil.,* 60(1963), 93–112.–Ed.]

relevant scholarship and remarkable insight, radically antiquating previous editions, in *Philosophical Commentaries* (Luce's new name for the notes) (Edinburgh; 1944), which shows Berkeley's many erasures, corrections, and additions. In Vol. I of *Works* (Edinburgh: 1948) Luce printed simply Berkeley's finally corrected text and abbreviated his annotations.

Three Dialogues Between Hylas and Philonous, 1713
Second edition, 1725, unrevised.
Revised edition with the *Principles,* 1734.
Recent editions:
1954, ed. C. M. Turbayne (New York).
1962, ed. G. J. Warnock (see under *Principles*).

De Motu; sive, de motu principio & natura, et de causa communicationis motuum, 1721
Reprinted, unrevised, in Berkeley's *A Miscellany,* 1752.
No separate edition after 1721. There are English translations by Wright in *Works of Berkeley,* 1843 (reprinted in Sampson's edition of *Works,* 1898); by A. A. Luce in Vol. 4 of *Works,* 1951; and by T. E. Jessop, of main passages, in *Berkeley: Select Philosophical Writings* (Edinburgh: 1952).

Alciphron: or, the Minute Philosopher. Containing an apology for the Christian religion against those who are called free-thinkers, 1732
Second edition, revised, 1732.
Third edition, further revised, 1752.
There has been no separate edition since 1803 (New Haven).

The Analyst; or a discourse addressed to an infidel mathematician, 1734
Not reprinted by Berkeley. Only separate reprint in 1754, unrevised.
In the ensuing controversy Berkeley intervened in 1735 with two pamphlets, *A Defence of Free-thinking in Mathematics* and *Reasons for not Replying to Mr. Walton's Full Answer.*

Siris: A Chain of Philosophical Reflexions and Inquiries Concerning the Virtues of Tar-water, and Divers other Subjects, 1744
Six further editions the same year, and one in 1747.
Final text is in "Second edition improved and corrected by the author. By G.L.B.O.C." (George, Lord Bishop of Cloyne), 1744.
No separate edition after 1747.

Social, Political, Economic

Passive Obedience, 1712
Advice to the Tories who have taken the oaths, 1715
Essay Towards Preventing the Ruin of Gt. Britain, 1721
The Querist, 1735–1737
Letter on the Project of a National Bank, 1737
Discourse Addressed to Magistrates, 1738
Three Letters on the Militia, 1745–1746
A Word to the Wise, 1749
Maxims Concerning Patriotism, 1750

Miscellaneous

Essays in *The Guardian,* 1713
Letter on the eruptions from Mount Vesuvio, 1717
Proposal for the better supplying of churches in our foreign plantations, 1724
A sermon preached before the Society for the Propagation of the Gospel in Foreign Parts, 1732
Letter to his clergy, 1745
Letter to the Roman Catholic clergy of his diocese, 1745
Letter on the petrifactions of Lough Neagh in Ireland, 1746
Observations concerning earthquakes, 1750
Verses on America, 1752

Berkeley's *A Miscellany* (1752) consists of reprints of five of the above, four under the preceding heading, the *De Motu,* and a new short piece on tar-water.

On Tar-water

Siris (see under Philosophical): nine pieces, 1744–1747, and one in 1752.

II. Some Writings on Berkeley

Papers in the various fields are compendiously collected in the following, devoted to the celebration of the bicentenary of Berkeley's death:

Hermathena, Trinity College, Dublin, No. 82, 1953.
British Journal for the Philosophy of Science, Edinburgh, Vol. 4, No. 13, 1953.
Revue philosophique, Paris, Vol. 143, April–June, 1953.
Revue international de philosophie, Brussels, Vol. 7, Nos. 23–24, 1953.
George Berkeley (Lectures before the Philosophical Union of the University of California), ed. S. Pepper, K. Aschenbrenner, and B. Mates. *University of California Publications in Philosophy,* Vol. 29, March 1957.

Biographical

Brayton, Alice, *George Berkeley in Apulia.* Boston: 1946.
Brayton, Alice, *George Berkeley in Newport.* Boston: 1954.
Luce, A. A., *The Life of George Berkeley.* Edinburgh: 1949. Being based on prolonged further research, supersedes the biographies of Fraser (1871) and Hone & Rossi (1931).
Rand, Benjamin, *Berkeley's American Sojourn.* Cambridge: 1932.

Literature

Davie, Donald A., "Berkeley's Style in *Siris,*" *Cambridge Review,* 4(1951), 427–433.
Davie, Donald A., "Irony and Conciseness in Berkeley and Swift," *Dublin Magazine,* 27(1952), 20–29.

Davie, Donald A., "Berkeley and 'Philosophic Words,'" *Studies* (Dublin), 44(1955), 319–324.

Dobrée, Bonamy, "Berkeley as a Man of Letters," *Hermathena,* #82(1953), 49–75.

Moulton, C. W., "Berkeley" in *Library of Literary Criticism,* Vol. 3, New York: 1902. (Reprinted 1910 and 1935.)

Oertel, Hans J., *George Berkeley und die englische Literatur,* Halle: 1934 (*Studien zur engl. Philologie,* Heft 80).

Papajewski, H., "Swift and Berkeley," *Anglia: Zeitschr. für engl. Philologie* (Tübingen), 77(1959), 29–53.

Rauter, H., "The Veil of Words: Sprachauffassung und Dialogform bei George Berkeley," *ibid.,* 79(1962), 378–404.

Economics

Hutchison, T. W., "Berkeley's Place in the Economic Thought of the Eighteenth Century," *Brit. J. Phil. Sci.,* 4(1953), 52–77.

Johnston, J., "Berkeley and the Abortive Bank Project of 1721," *Hermathena,* #29(1939), 110–119.

Johnston, J., "A Synopsis of Berkeley's Monetary Philosophy," *ibid.,* #55(1940), 73–86.

Johnston, J., "Locke, Berkeley and Hume as Monetary Theorists," *ibid.,* #56(1940), 77–83.

Johnston, J., "Bishop Berkeley and Kindred Monetary Thinkers," *ibid.,* #59(1942), 30–43.

Johnston, J., "Berkeley's Influence as an Economist," *ibid.,* #82(1953), 76–89.

Raffel, Fr. A., *Ist Berkeley ein Freihändler?,* Kiel: 1904.

Ward, I. D. S., "George Berkeley: Precursor of Keynes, or Moral Economist on Underdevelopment," *J. Political Economy,* 67(1959), 31–40. (Criticism by T. W. Hutchison and reply, *ibid.,* 68(1960), 302–310.

Theory of Vision

Armstrong, D. M., *Berkeley's Theory of Vision: A Critical Examination of Bishop Berkeley's Essay towards a New Theory of Vision,* Melbourne: 1960. (A philosophical treatment.)

Brett, G. S., Section on Berkeley in *History of Psychology,* Vol. 2, London: 1921, 264–270.

Carter, W. B., "Some Problems of the Relation between Berkeley's *New Theory of Vision* and his *Principles,*" *Ratio,* 3(1961), 174–192.

Chance, B., "George Berkeley and 'An Essay on Vision,'" *Archives of Ophthalmology,* 29(1943), 605–614.

McFee, D., *Berkeleys neue Theorie des Sehens und ihre Weiterentwicklung in der englischen Assoziations-Schule und in der modernen empiristischen Schule in Deutschland,* Zurich: 1895.

Murray, M., "An Introduction to Berkeley's Theory of Vision," *Brit. J. of Ophthalmology,* 28(1944), 600–611.

Pirenne, M. M., "Psychological Mechanisms in the Perception of Distance by Sight and Berkeley's Theory of Vision," *Brit. J. Phil. Sci.,* 4(1953), 13–21.

Titely, G. W. I., "Berkeley and Helmholtz Theories of Space Perception," *Optometric Weekly* (Chicago), 46(1955), 1823–1826; 1849–1852.

Turbayne, C. M., "Berkeley and Molyneux on Retinal Images," *J. Hist. Ideas,* 16(1955), 339–355.

Philosophy of Mathematics

Boyer, Carl B. *The Concepts of the Calculus: A Critical and Historical Discussion of the Derivative and the Integral,* New York: 1939. (Berkeley is treated *passim* in chapter 6. This book re-issued under title: *The History of the Calculus and its Conceptual Development* in 1949; also New York: 1959.)

Cajori, Florian, *History of the Conceptions of Limits and Fluxions in Great Britain from Newton to Woodhouse,* Chicago: 1919. (Chapter 3 is on Berkeley.)

Devaux, P., "Berkeley et les mathématiques," *Revue internat. de Phil.,* 7(1953), Nos. 23–24, 101–133.

Leroy, André L., "Valeur exemplaire des erreurs mathématiques de Berkeley," *Revue de Synthèse* (Paris), 77(1956), 155–169.

Meyer, E., *Humes und Berkeleys Philosophie der Mathematik, vergleichend und kritisch dargestellt,* Halle: 1894.

Stammler, G., *Berkeleys Philosophie der Mathematik,* Berlin: 1921. (*Kant-Studien,* Suppl. 55.)

Whitrow, G. J., "Berkeley's Critique of the Newtonian Analysis of Motion," *Hermathena,* #82(1953), 90–112.

Wisdom, J. O., "The Analyst Controversy: Berkeley's Influence on the Development of Mathematics," *ibid.,* #29(1939), 3–29.

Wisdom, J. O., "The Compensation of Errors in the Method of Fluxions," *ibid.,* #57(1941), 49–81.

Wisdom, J. O., "The Analyst Controversy: Berkeley as a Mathematician," *ibid.,* #59(1942), 111–128.

Epistemology and Metaphysics

1. *Notable monographs:*

Amante, Lina, *Il problema degli spiriti finiti in Berkeley,* Rome, 1932.

Ardley, G. W. R., *Berkeley's Philosophy of Nature,* Auckland: 1962 (Univ. of Auckland, Bulletin 63).

Baladi, N., *La pensée religieuse de Berkeley et l'unité de sa philosophie,* Cairo: Institut français d'archéologie orientale, 1945.

Bracken, H. M., *The Early Reception of Berkeley's Immaterialism,* The Hague: 1959 (revised 1965). (Notices of Berkeley from 1711, Continental and English, hitherto overlooked.)

Cassirer, Erich, *Berkeleys System: Ein Beitrag zur Geschichte und Systematik des Idealismus,* Giessen: 1906.

Del Boca, S., *L'unità del pensiero di Giorgio Berkeley,* Florence: 1937.

Fraser, A. C., *Berkeley,* London: 1881 (reprinted 1884, 1901, and in Philadelphia, 1894).

Gueroult, M., *Berkeley: Quatre études sur la perception et sur Dieu,* Paris: 1956.

Hedenius, I., *Sensationalism and Theology in Berkeley's Philosophy,* Uppsala: 1936.

Hicks, G. Dawes, *Berkeley,* London: 1932.

Johnston, G. A., *The Development of Berkeley's Philosophy,* London: 1923.

Joussain, A., *Exposé critique de la philosophie de Berkeley,* Paris: 1920.

Kaveeshwar, G. W., *The Metaphysics of Berkeley Critically Examined in the Light of Modern Philosophy,* Khandwa, India: 1933.

Leroy, André L., *George Berkeley,* Paris: 1959.

Levi, A., *La Filosofia di Giorgio Berkeley,* Turin: 1922 (reprinted Milan: 1947).

Loewy, Th., *Der Idealismus Berkeleys in den Grundlagen untersucht,* Vienna: 1891. *Sitzungsberichte der kaiserl Akad. der Wissenschaften, Wien, philos.-hist. Klasse,* Vol. 1, pp. 1–142.

Luce, A. A., *Berkeley and Malebranche: A Study in the Origins of Berkeley's Thought,* Oxford: 1934.

Luce, A. A., *Berkeley's Immaterialism,* Edinburgh: 1945.

Luce, A. A., *The Dialectic of Immaterialism: An Account of the Making of Berkeley's Principles,* London: 1963. (A detailed study of the stages of Berkeley's thought in his notebooks.)

Metz, Rudolf, *George Berkeley, Leben und Lehre,* Stuttgart: 1925. (The most comprehensive account in German of Berkeley's writings.)

Olgiati, F., *L'idealismo di Giorgi Berkeley ed il suo Significato Storico,* Milan: 1926. (The author was a leading Neo-Thomist.)

Penjon, A., *Étude sur la Vie et les Oeuvres Philosophiques de Berkeley,* Paris: 1879.

Rossi, M. M., *Saggio su Berkeley,* Bari: 1955. (A contemptuous estimate of Berkeley.)

Rotta, P., *La Dottrina Gnoseologico-ontologica di G. Berkeley,* Bologna: 1922 (reprinted, Brescia: 1943).

Sillem, E. A., *George Berkeley and the Proofs of the Existence of God,* London: 1957.

Warnock, G. J., *Berkeley,* London: 1953. (Written from the standpoint of the Linguistic Analysis school.)

Wild, John, *George Berkeley,* Cambridge, Mass.: 1936 (reprinted, 1962). (Especially useful on the sources of *Siris.*)

2. *Some articles and chapters:*

Aaron, R. I., "Locke's Theory of Universals," *Proc. Brit. Acad.,* 33(1933), 173–202.

Aschenbrenner, K., "Bishop Berkeley on Existence in the Mind," in *George Berkeley* (ed. Pepper, Aschenbrenner, and Mates) *Univ. of Calif. Publ. in Phil.,* 29(1957), 37–64.

Baker, J. T., "Historical and Critical Examination of English Space and Time Theories from Henry More to Bishop Berkeley," Dissertation, Bronxville, N.Y.: 1930.

Baumann, J., *Die Lehren von Raum, Zeit und Mathematik in der neueren Philosophie,* Berlin: 1869 (Vol. 2, 348–480 on Berkeley).

Bracken, H. M., "Berkeley's Realisms," *Phil. Quart.,* (St. Andrews), 8(1958), 3–15. (A clear treatment of the question whether Berkeley's "ideas" are to be read as sensa or as physical things.)

Broad, C. D., "Berkeley's Argument about Material Substance," *Proc. Brit. Acad.,* 28(1942), 119–138.

Carlini, A., *La Filosofia di Giovanni Locke,* Florence: 1921. (Treatment of Berkeley in Vol. 2, Pt. 4, Chap. 1.)

Cassirer, Ernst, *Das Erkenntnisproblem in der Philosophie . . . der neueren Zeit.* Berlin: 1906 (third ed., 1922). (Chapter Two of Bk. 6, Vol. 2, is on Berkeley).

Cathcart, H. R., "Berkeley's Philosophy through Soviet Eyes," *Hermathena,* #98(1964), 33–42.

Cummins, P., "Perceptual Relativity and Ideas in the Mind," *Phil. & Phen. Res.,* 24(1963), 202–214. (Berkeley seen in the context of Bayle instead of Locke.)

Day, J. P. de, "George Berkeley, 1685–1753," *Rev. Meta.,* 6(1952–1953), 81–113; 265–286; 447–469; 583–596.

Devaux P., "La Place de Berkeley dans la Philosophie Moderne," *Theoria* (Lund), 20(1954), 1–22. (Bicentenary lecture given in Brussels in 1953.)

Gentile, G., *Teoria Generale dello Spirito come Atto Puro,* Pisa: 1916 (reprinted at Bari). (Chapter One is chiefly on Berkeley.)

Gossmann, L., "Berkeley, Hume and Maupertuis," *French Studies* (Oxford), 14(1960), 304–324.

Grossmann, R., "Digby and Berkeley on Notions," *Theoria* (Lund), 26(1960), 17–30.

Hoernlé, R. F. A., *Idealism,* London: 1924. (Chapter Two is on Berkeley. Reprinted, New York: 1927, under title *Idealism as a Philosophy,* with different pagination.)

Joseph, H. W. B., "A Comparison of Kant's Idealism with that of Berkeley," *Proc. Brit. Acad.,* 15(1929) (reprinted in his *Essays in Ancient and Modern Philosophy,* Oxford: 1935).

Lehec, C., "Trente années d'études berkeleyennes," *Rev. phil. France étrang.,* 143 (April–June 1953), 244–265.

Lyon, G., *L'idéalisme en Angleterre au 18e Siècle,* Paris: 1879. (Chapter Eight [294–370] is on Berkeley and Chapter Nine on the American Samuel Johnson.)

March, W. W. S., "Analogy, Aquinas and Bishop Berkeley," *Theology* (London), 44(1942), 321–329.

Meinong, A., "Hume-Studien I," *Sitzungsberichte der kaiserl. Akad., Wien, philos.-hist. Klasse,* Vienna, 87(1877), 185–217. (On Berkeley's denial of abstract ideas. [Reprinted in his *Gesammelte Abhandlungen, Vol. 1,* Leipzig: 1914].)

Papini, G., "George Berkeley," *Il Rinnovamento* (Milan), fasc. 2(1908), 235–261. (Reprinted in 1912 in his "24 *cervelli*"; "Four and Twenty Minds," London: 1923.)

Popkin, R. H., "Berkeley and Pyrrhonism," *Rev. Meta.*, 5(1951), 223–246. (On a neglected aspect of the historical scene.)

Prior, A. N., "Berkeley in Logical Form," *Theoria* (Lund), 21(1955), 117–122.

Renouvier, C., *Histoire et Solution des Problèmes Métaphysiques*, Paris: 1901. (Chapters 30 f. are on Berkeley.)

Ritchie, A. D., "George Berkeley's *Siris:* The Philosophy of the Great Chain of Being and the Alchemist Theory," *Proc. Brit. Acad.*, 40(1954), 41–55.

Turbayne, C. M., "Kant's Refutation of Dogmatic Idealism," *Phil. Quart.* (St. Andrews), 5(1955), 225–244.

Turbayne, C. M., "Berkeley's Two Concepts of Mind," *Phil. & Phen. Res.*, 20(1959), 85–92; 22(1962), 577–580.

Ueberweg, F., "Ist Berkeleys Lehre Wissenschaftlich Unwiderlegbar?" *Zeitschrift für Phil. und phil. Kritik*, 55(1869), 63–84. (This evoked articles from several hands: 56(1870), 250–265; 57(1871), 120–174; 58(1872), 166–180; 59(1873), 144–146 and 149–152; and in *Phil. Monatshefte*, 5(1870), 142–185 and 416–435; 7(1872), 383–392.)

White, A. R., "The Ambiguity of Berkeley's 'Without the mind,'" *Hermathena*, #83(1954), 55–65.

Wiener, P., "Did Hume Read Berkeley?" *J. Phil.*, 56(1959), 533–535. (The subject was continued by R. H. Popkin, *ibid.*, 535–545; E. Mossner, *ibid.*, 992–993; A. Flew, *ibid.*, 58(1961), 50–51; reply by Wiener, *ibid.*, 58 (1961), 207–209; 327–328; and an affirmative answer established by Popkin "So Hume Did Read Berkeley," *ibid.*, 61(1964), 773–778.

Index of References

Index of References

Index of Names

Index of Names

N

P

R

S

T

U

V

W

Index of Subjects

Index of Subjects

M

N

O

P

Q

R

S

T

V